CONCEPTUAL
BLOCKBUSTING

ALSO BY JAMES L. ADAMS:

Good Products, Bad Products:
Essential Elements to Achieving Superior Quality

Flying Buttresses, Entropy, and O-Rings:
The World of an Engineer

The Care and Feeding of Ideas:
A Guide to Encouraging Creativity (out of print)

The Building of an Engineer:
Making, Teaching, and Thinking

CONCEPTUAL BLOCKBUSTING

A Guide to Better Ideas

FIFTH EDITION

JAMES L. ADAMS

BASIC BOOKS
New York

Basic Books
Hachette Book Group
1290 Avenue of the Americas, New York, NY 10104
www.basicbooks.com

Printed in the United States of America
Originally published in 1986 by Addison-Wesley Publishing Company
Trade Paperback, Fifth Edition: September 2019

Published by Basic Books, an imprint of Perseus Books, LLC, a subsidiary of Hachette Book Group, Inc. The Basic Books name and logo is a trademark of the Hachette Book Group.

The publisher is not responsible for websites (or their content) that are not owned by the publisher.

All art is courtesy of the author.

List, page 180: Osborn, Alex F. (1963) *Applied Imagination*. Reprinted with permission from the copyright holder, The Creative Education Foundation, 1050 Union Road, Buffalo, NY 14224.

List, pages 182–183: Reprinted by permission of Princeton University Press from *How to Solve It: A New Aspect of Mathematical Method*, 2nd ed., by G. Pólya. Copyright 1945, Princeton University Press, © 1957 by G. Polya.

Print book interior design by Jeff Williams.

Library of Congress Cataloging-in-Publication Data

Names: Adams, James L., author.

Title: Conceptual blockbusting : a guide to better ideas / James L. Adams.

Description: Fifth edition. | New York : Basic Books, [2019] | Includes bibliographical references and index.

Identifiers: LCCN 2019003750| ISBN 9781541674042 (paperback) | ISBN 9781541674059 (ebook)

Subjects: LCSH: Problem solving. | Creative thinking. | Concepts.

Classification: LCC BF449 .A25 2019 | DDC 153.4/3—dc23

LC record available at https://lccn.loc.gov/2019003750

ISBNs: 978-1-5416-7404-2 (paperback), 978-1-5416-7405-9 (ebook)

LSC-C

10 9 8 7 6 5 4 3 2

Contents

Introduction

THIS IS A BOOK ABOUT COMMON MENTAL (AND SOMETIMES physical) blocks that inhibit creativity. When the first edition of the book was published in 1974, I was a professor in the School of Engineering at the university, had worked as an engineer and consultant, and was teaching courses and giving talks intended to help people experiment with and improve their creative potential. At the time, there was not nearly as much interest in the topic as there is today—fewer books, many fewer computers, not nearly as much research on the brain and nervous system, and less fervor surrounding innovation and start-up companies. By 2001, the book was into its fourth edition. Yet a new and revised edition became necessary given how many things have changed since 2001 in helping us understand and better utilize the creative potential that we all have.

The human brain and nervous system are wonderful—so wonderful that we are a long way from fully understanding them. In fact, I sometimes agree with those who think that it will take something more powerful than a human brain to understand human brains. But other times I am less pessimistic, such as now, due to the increasing interest in cognition in many disciplines and the use of the resulting knowledge. We are rapidly learning more about the brain and nervous system. We have powerful ways to "watch" the brain at work, such as fMRI, EEG, CAT, and PET scans, which are capable of tracing blood flow and electrical activity in the functioning brain. We can now measure with precision how injury, aging, disease, drugs, and other phenomena influence brain function. We can consult brain autopsies and the findings of those who experiment on lab animals that have brains and nervous systems. We also are learning more through the study of DNA and genomes. And finally, there is great fascination with the similarities and differences between human brains and computers. There is unprecedented activity and investment in better understanding these, as neuroscientists explore computers' ability to do "brain-like" things, while computer people seek to re-create human thinking through artificial intelligence, machine learning, neural nets, and the like.

The better we understand the brain and nervous system, the better we can understand conceptual blocks, which have both good and bad features. They are part of the brain's mechanisms to keep its load under control, but they inhibit creativity.

As I look around at what people are doing in industry, the arts, medicine, and life in general at Stanford and in Silicon Valley (where I live), and indeed in many parts of the world, I can see why it is sometimes called the cognitive age: it is an age of cognitive science, cognitive psychology, cognitive psychiatry, cognitive behavioral therapy, and much else. And one of the greatest contributions of this work now occurring is that it demolishes a lot of our beliefs about thinking that are simply not true. For instance, our brain is not as logical as we might think. Although a marvel, it is not infinite, and therefore seeks ways to simplify its job. As an example, there is a theory in psychology that is enjoying great popularity called confirmation bias. It says that you are more likely to seek out evidence confirming your preexisting beliefs, and if you encounter evidence contradicting them, you will discount the evidence. If the evidence is really strong, it will reinforce your belief. That is called the backward effect. For example, a strong media attack on a political candidate could actually strengthen the resolve of his or her followers. These two responses to input simplify the job of the brain by reinforcing what you already think, right or wrong, thereby relieving your brain from the difficult task of changing your beliefs. But maybe creativity needs you to change your beliefs.

You will find as you read that I am somewhat of a pragmatist as far as creativity and change are concerned, perhaps because of my age and experience. I certainly believe that people should be aware of the creative process and how it can be affected, both positively and negatively. I have devoted much of my life to this, as a teacher, a practicing engineer, and a consultant. I am an exponent of increasing creativity. But I also think that people should think about the bad effects of the resulting change. Creativity and change are central to the immense improvements in the human condition, but they also cause problems, currently ranging from a decrease in privacy for individuals—which we trade for the latest, perhaps unnecessary, software—to snarls of traffic, the existence of nuclear weapons, and the rapid increase in global warming. Hopefully, these too will be put under control by creativity.

Certainly ideas are central to creativity and change. But to be interesting, creativity needs to amount to more than an imaginative, even brilliant, idea. It has to have a tangible output that should make someone, if not the world, better off.

The original idea is, as the mathematicians say, necessary but not sufficient. Creativity is required all the way through the process of producing things that are worthwhile. Your original idea will be improved as you work. Ideas will be needed to reduce whatever it is to a form that is producible and to sell it, support it, and, more and more these days, get rid of it. Occasionally there are ideas so brilliant, simple, and needed that, as they say, the idea sells itself, but not often.

Let me now make a few comments about the structure of this book. Much of the book is an updated version of the last edition, taking into account new insights into the brain and nervous system, other research that has been done on creativity and change, and things I have come to believe based on my own experience. I am not going deeply into cognitive science—since it is not my field—but I cannot help but love research shedding light on such things as our ability to not believe things that have been repeatedly proven and to act in ways that conflict with existing disciplines. So you will see a bit of it, especially in chapters one and ten. I firmly believe that the more we understand conceptual blocks, their purpose, and their nature, the better we can get around, over, or through them.

The first chapter will discuss the brain and the nervous system a bit, and generally talk about conceptual blocks. We all have them, but they vary in quantity and intensity from individual to individual. Most of us are not aware of the extent of our conceptual blocks. Awareness of them can not only allow us to better know our strengths and weaknesses, but lead to the motivation and the knowledge necessary to modify or avoid such blocks.

Chapters two through five will discuss some common conceptual blocks—perceptual, emotional, cultural, environmental, intellectual, and expressive—giving examples and exploring their causes. The blocks are closely related, as you will see when you begin to consider them. The particular scheme used to categorize them is for convenience only, and is not meant to be the ultimate morphology of conceptual blocks.

Chapters six and seven are concerned with techniques that allow one to overcome (or sidestep) these blocks. Chapter eight examines a few conceptual blocks that limit group creativity.

Chapter nine does the same at the organizational level. Chapter ten goes a bit deeper into cognitive science and the development of creativity in children, and is a brief look into my present interest in creativity in very large populations (nations, religions, etc.). As the number of people involved increases, change and creativity become more difficult because of the increased resistance to change and the political force of different power groups. Perhaps this can be seen in world politics at the time of this writing.

The final section of the book, the reader's guide, contains information for those interested in pursuing this subject in greater depth. In the recommended reading, I suggest books rather than academic journal papers. Most of the books reference academic papers and other resources, should you desire to dig even deeper. There is interesting work in academic papers, but I find much of it difficult to apply. A great deal of material exists on creativity, innovation, problem-solving, general thinking, and conceptualization in these recommended books, and most of it is accessible without a specialist's vocabulary. Much of the material in the reader's guide has appeared since the last edition of the book. I recommend it as a not only fascinating but also unique experience, in that you are simultaneously able to acquire knowledge and improve your idea-having and problem-solving capability.

Have fun.

CHAPTER 1

The Hardworking Brain and Nervous Systems

A Few Details

WE HOMO SAPIENS ARE CREATIVE. WE HAVE HAD TO BE, TO come this far with our puny teeth, lack of claws, and relative inability to move quickly. Over the many years of our existence, we have used this creativity to improve our lives. We are not alone among animals in our ability to be creative. I am always dazzled by the ability of rats to build a unique and comfortable home in back of my car engine using nothing but sticks, insulation from the wires, and a bit of stuffing from the seats. I am particularly annoyed by their love of insulation, because the car will not run with short circuits in the harness and I then have to give a considerable amount of money to the Acura dealer. Nevertheless, I am impressed, since the rat has a two-gram mind compared to my 1,400-gram one. But humans' creativity equipment far outshines that of other living beings. Rats can live in New York City, but they could not have built it.

We are very creative, but we are also capable of being even more so. There is a series of common blocks that keep us from getting there. This book is about those blocks, and what can be done to diminish them.

Before I begin, I should address what are called mind-body and mind-brain problems. These are questions about the primacy of the metaphysical mind versus the physical body that have engaged philosophers and thinkers for hundreds of years. An early theory, dating back to René Descartes, is that the mind is completely separate from the body but can influence it. Most people now at least give the brain prime billing, but many feel that the mind extends beyond the brain into matters of faith, feeling, soul, and, in some cases, use of computers. If you would like a new way to argue with friends, assuming they are willing, put "mind-body" or "mind-brain problem" into your browser and discuss what you find with them. I am not going there in this book.

I believe the brain that lives happily inside our skull, along with its associated nerves in the central nervous system, is in charge. Of course, this equipment would be of little value, and short-lived indeed, without our bodies. Since they are nicely interconnected, and dependent on each other, for this book I will consider them a tightly integrated system, with the most important subsystem being the brain and nervous system. Maybe we are the ship and the brain is the captain. If I were to say, "You should take an inventory of your conceptual blocks" (which I won't), I am obviously thinking your brain should do that. We won't quibble about who "you" is.

If you are not familiar with the brain and nervous system, perhaps a few additional comments are in order here. I don't intend to go into great detail, because if you are familiar with brains and how they work, it would bore you, but if you are unfamiliar with them, a conceptual block would click into action and prevent you from engaging with the book. After all, one of my goals in this book is to encourage you to be more conscious of what's going on in your brain when you are being creative.

Becoming more creative requires conscious learning. Learning is done through repetition, utilization, information, and desire.

If you have never seen a human brain (presumably dead), you should try to. Brains look like what they are—three and a half pounds of meat—and the parts are not different colors like in the books. But the brain is not just ordinary meat, because it contains around eighty-five billion neurons (the gray matter), each with up to ten thousand dendritic spines that carry signals to be processed. Each neuron is also equipped with an axon or two that will split into many branches, conveying the result of the neuron's deliberation to other neurons, muscle cells, organs, or to itself if feedback is required. These are linked together in an amazingly complicated tangle called a neural network. That term, "network," is heard more often in relation to computers. But though networks of computers can do a number of things better than us, they lack the flexibility of the human version. As one of my friends says, computers can't even fall in love.

Between neurons there are gaps called synapses. Signals are amplified and modified by releasing chemicals called neurotransmitters that travel across such synapses. The journeys of the signals through the brain and nervous system are extremely intricate, some requiring the conversion of an analog signal from a nerve sensor to an electrical signal, then to a chemical one, and then back to an electrical one. Some signals travel the length of axons that are up to three feet long, and the signals are affected by the hormones that interact with the brain. The brain also contains white matter, or glial cells, that form structures for the neurons and act as an insulator to increase the speed of signals through the axons and dendrites.

There are microscopic photographs of the human brain on the internet that can give a better feeling for its complex structure than the simple images of brain regions and nerve endings one is used to seeing. As each neuron in the brain can connect to up to ten thousand other neurons, you can have on the order of a quadrillion synapses in your body and brain (a number you cannot possibly have a feeling for, unless you are a computer addict).

All this should make it possible for the brain to accomplish a phenomenal amount, and it does, operating with amazing reliability 24/7 from your birth until your death. Even though much of your cortex shuts down when you sleep, your neurons continue to be active, as your senses must continue to work so you can hear the baby cry or smell smoke even in a deep sleep.

Our brains begin forming about three weeks after conception, and at birth we are equipped with more than the number of neurons we will eventually need. However, they are not hooked up the way they will be eventually. In the first years of our lives, connections are made between the neurons via the dendrites and axons. These connections are made partly according to information we inherit through our genomes and partly from what we learn from parents, other adults, and siblings, as well as, eventually, schools, experiences, and peers. This process is not complete until we reach our midtwenties, and during this relatively long period of time, the "wiring" changes and connections that are no longer needed go away. The wiring continues to change all of our lives—getting rid of old connections and building new ones—making the brain one of our more flexible parts. And that allows us to keep learning, changing our conceptual blocks. Over my life I have been privileged to see this happen in students, professors, engineers, managers, friends, children, and even myself.

If you would like more details on brains, minds, nerves, and such things, I will discuss them more in chapter ten and supply the names of a couple of good books in the reader's guide that will tell you perhaps more than you want to know. But I'll leave it there for now, first, because the biology is not primarily what this book is about and, second, although I am fascinated by the brain and nervous system, I am not an expert in them (although I do have experts looking over my shoulder).

We will touch on the brain and nervous system throughout this book, but their complexity and electrochemical-mechanical nature offers us a good place to start as we learn to be more creative.

THE BRAIN AND CREATIVITY

What we call "thinking" usually includes activities like solving problems, storing and using information, and communicating. Yet the brain also controls hormones and feelings, responds to emergencies, and manages your social, economic, and spiritual life. It is also the source of your consciousness and the self, concepts that show up in many cognitive-science theories. Although our knowledge of consciousness is incomplete, those tasks alone must take a good bit of our brain's ability. And if you add acting as the librarian for your memory and keeping the body operating so that it can, among other things, protect you from harm, produce the energy you need, keep your heart beating, and provide the activities necessary to keep you healthy and happy, the brain has an impressive number of tasks to do.

When I was a kid, my father would occasionally say things like, "Quit playing with your dog and use some of the 90 percent of your brain that is loafing to count the number of boxes on that truck." This stems from an ancient rumor that we only use 5 or 10 or maybe 20 percent of our brain. I now believe the opposite is true—that the brain is fully loaded and is necessarily very efficient.

Although marvelous, the brain is finite in its capacity and takes time to do its job. The speed of a signal in some axons can reach 120 meters per second, but this is slow compared to the 200 million meters per second that a signal can travel along a standard glass fiber. Your brain also doesn't contain all the world's knowledge in its memory. What it does hold is a function of your genome, the people you associate with, the schools you have gone to, the books you have read, the TV you have watched, and a great many other factors that are unique to you.

In order to keep up with its routine workload, the brain copes by prioritizing, coding, ignoring, and forgetting much of its input, as well as minimizing when possible. It must be efficient. But creativity is not routine. So what brain in its right mind (how do you like that—I used both words!) would be creative? Better to offer the first idea it has. And that is what often happens. As a result, the brain is often called lazy—an unfair slur.

Quick response is often appreciated by people because they find it easier to make choices and solve problems by instinct rather than by thinking. But, as we will see, increasing creativity often requires generating more ideas and even making multiple prototypes to test their value. So it is not surprising that brains wouldn't always seek the complications involved in creativity, if present practice will suffice. Can you feel the topic of conceptual blocks coming on?

Let me give you an example of an attempt to change this behavior from my personal experience. As you may know, universities frequently host conversations on how to decrease what is sometimes called the "two cultures" problem. This is named after a famous Rede Lecture once delivered by C. P. Snow, and it refers to the classic intellectual separation of "techies" (mathematicians, scientists, engineers) and "fuzzies" (humanists and social scientists). Although this gap is slowly decreasing, it is still common and comes with a personal and social cost (see chapters five and six).

At one point, since I personally try to straddle both cultures, I was a member of a Sloan Foundation attempt to try to blur the division. One of the sponsored efforts was a yearlong course sequence taught at Stanford by a mathematician (Bob Osserman), a physicist (Sandy Fetter), and an engineer (me). It was designed for students who did not plan to major in math, science, or engineering. In fact, we were aiming for students who outright thought they disliked these areas of study. The three of us were in our prime: articulate, entertaining, tenured, and good-looking. We were also friends, and we were committed to the task of helping the students in our class change their rather negative attitudes toward what was then dismissed as techie material. Maybe we would even get some of them to love it. We worked very hard, limited the class size, used material that was relatively advanced for undergraduates but of current interest and importance, and included all sorts of good things like discussions, guest lecturers, and projects. We had some success: most of the students hated the material less but weren't to the point of loving it. Amazingly, a few even changed their major from fuzzy to techie, but we noticed no stampedes. We loved teaching the course, and considered it a victory, but we were overloaded with other classes and jobs at the university, and it took a large amount of work and time on the part of both us and the students. We taught the course for five years but failed to secure other professors to take our place. They were bright enough to realize that it was easier to teach in their specialty than play crusader.

I was not surprised, since I have spent my life as a techie with many fuzzy friends and colleagues. My wife was educated as and is every inch a historian. Am I comfortable in her area of expertise? Much more than I used to be. After all, I continually fight my own blocks. I even went to art school for a year to break down a few of them. It worked—now I appreciate medieval triptychs and impressionist and expressionist paintings. But my wife doesn't seem to want to study engineering for a year. My experience at Stanford reaffirmed that the division between fuzzies and techies can be attacked, but that it is difficult at the college level. It's much better to try to address the problem earlier in life, as early as the first grade, as is now being attempted by others.

The two-culture problem is a good example of a conceptual block. You don't need math, science, or engineering to get through life, nor even to get through a formal course of study in the humanities and social sciences, but they are very useful in solving many problems—as well as magnificently beautiful topics in which to wallow. If I were to teach the course again, I would spend much more time on making the students more conscious of why they are uncomfortable with one of the cultures but comfortable with the other. I would, among other things, assign them this book.

THINKING

Now let's focus on the activity of the brain called thinking. It is certainly a most important function. But is it automatic? Is it learned consciously? Should we learn all we can about thinking and then practice and monitor our result?

The time-honored method of improving one's skill is to be continually conscious of one's performance and seek to improve it, usually according to an ideal or standard of what is desirable. The serious golfer studies and practices, comparing his or her performance against an ideal, reading books and newspaper columns on golf form, and watching other more sophisticated golfers as they play. In fact, I began previous editions of this book with an antique drawing of Arnold Palmer (among the greatest golfers of his time), demonstrating how to move the left foot on a swing in order to help golfers improve their performance. Should the thinker act like this? Should we compare our thinking with that done by more sophisticated thinkers? I believe that the answer is yes: we should do all of the above if we want to increase our creativity.

The world abounds with material on how to play sports, cook, grow plants, build houses, fix plumbing, develop magnificent abs, and use Photoshop. How often do you see a similar treatment of thinking? All of us are thinkers. However, most of us are surprisingly unconscious of the process of our own thinking. When we speak of improving the mind, we are usually referring to the acquisition of knowledge, or to the type of thoughts one should have, and not to the actual functioning of the mind. We spend little time monitoring our own thinking and comparing it with a more sophisticated ideal.

A lot of attention has been drawn to a professor named K. Anders Ericsson at Florida State University, who for some time has been studying how many hours it takes to reach excellence. The answer depends on many factors. He initially found that outstanding musicians have put five thousand to ten thousand hours into acquiring the necessary knowledge, skill, and appreciation. Since then, he has found this to be true for many activities, although in a recent interview, he revealed that he was miffed because Malcolm Gladwell had oversimplified his work in his book *Outliers*. He explained that ten thousand hours isn't a magic number; the time is variable among people, and some never reach excellence at all. For all our education and training as thinkers, we acquire knowledge, perhaps skill, and maybe appreciation, but we could go much further if we just spent more time thinking about the process of thinking.

There are reasons this does not happen, of course. The proper "form" for thinking is much more difficult to observe than, say, golfing form. Thinking is also a much more complex function than golf. If you were to tease out the analogy, how could you select the "thinker of the decade"? How could you extract a simple element—like the role of the left foot in golf—from the complex process of thinking? Yet, despite these problems, effort spent in monitoring the thinking process and attempting to improve it is a good investment for the problem solver.

We know a lot more about thinking, creativity, and problem-solving than we did when the first edition of this book appeared in 1974. Tremendous amounts of literature and software have appeared to tackle problem-solving and creativity. A large number of consultants and experts on creativity and innovation occupy podiums and operate retreat centers across the land. The cognitive sciences have unlocked some of the secrets of information processing and electrochemistry in the brain and nervous system. But despite what we may have learned from the cognitive revolution, most of us continue to think in traditional and habitual ways.

I was very pleased to see the publication of *Thinking, Fast and Slow* by Daniel Kahneman, who won the Nobel Prize in economics in 2002. I have never met him personally, but I did know his close friend and collaborator Amos Tversky, who was a professor at Stanford until his death in 1996. Had Tversky not died, he would have shared the Nobel Prize, because he and Kahneman were intellectually inseparable and worked together for many years. If you would like a broad view of them and some of the things they accomplished, you should read *The Undoing Project* by Michael Lewis. In brief, through clever tests, the application of their backgrounds in decision theory and psychology, and the use of statistics, the two of them proved that our reasoning is imperfect, that we make errors in judgment, and that small differences in how information is presented can have a substantial effect on our reactions. You will be much happier if the surgeon tells you that there is a 95 percent survival rate than if she tells you that 5 percent of the patients who went through the procedure died. What is really interesting is that people act like they don't believe it, as illustrated by an example from Tversky's work.

I first met Tversky when I joined the Stanford faculty. He was a professor who was already well known and controversial because he was attacking such things as logic and reasoning in an institution that worshipped them. I was tempted to offer myself to him as a follower. He was working at the time on what was later to be called the "hot hand" theory. By studying the meticulous information that two basketball teams, a professional one and a top college team, kept for a year, he concluded that there is no such a thing as a hot hand—a superstition held by basketball coaches and most others that if a player sinks an unusual number of baskets in a game, especially consecutively, he is having a hot hand and should receive the ball more often. Tversky found out that these streaks are simply statistical probability. The same effect can be seen in many areas of life, such as in casinos. People tend to bet on the person who is on a winning streak, or a losing streak, even though the probability of a toss of the dice coming up in a certain way remains the same for each one. The old question asked to students in beginning statistics courses is, "If a flipped penny came up tails three times in a row, what would you think the odds are for a fourth flip coming up tails?" People will usually guess very high or very low. Of course, as you know, the odds are the same each time: exactly 50 percent if it is a fair coin. Tversky proved that there was no such a thing as a hot hand, and yet people often reacted with complete outrage, if they didn't ignore his conclusion completely.

In *Thinking, Fast and Slow,* Kahneman describes two types of thinking, which the brain uses depending on the problem it is facing. Two psychologists, Keith Stanovich and Richard West, named them System 1 and System 2. As Kahneman describes, System 1 operates automatically and quickly, with little or no effort and no sense of voluntary control. System 2 allocates attention to effortful mental activities, including complex computations. Kahneman states that the operations of System 2 are often associated with the subjective experience of agency, choice, and concentration. To that list, I would like to add creativity.

In the previous edition of this book, I talked about conscious, unconscious, and habitual thinking and problem-solving, for which I occasionally took a bit of heat. I also referred to automatic thinking, which annoyed my cognitive science friends because it implied that thinking could not be understood. But being an engineer, I didn't know any better. Now that I am older and better read, I will use System 1 and System 2, rather than conscious and unconscious, since they are apparently the prevailing terms and the well-deserved sales of Kahneman's book have made a lot of people aware of them. But I will cling to use of the word "habitual," since it describes what I am talking about: noncreative thinking.

We use System 1 to drive our car if there is little traffic, to wave to a friend, to read a billboard, to order a meal at McDonald's, or to decide rapidly whether we like someone we have just met. In a way, it is the source of our instincts. System 2 turns on if we are figuring out our income tax, preparing for a party, or deciding whether our company should merge with another one. We also use it if we are trying to be more creative.

A couple of exercises will help demonstrate my point. However, before I give them to you, let me diverge a moment and make a more general comment. This book contains occasional examples and exercises. The contents of the book will be much more meaningful and much more likely to influence your thinking if you work through the exercises and problems and then analyze your thinking approach. You can do this either alone or with other people. I have found that most of the exercises are usually more entertaining and more successful if several people are involved. It is always of interest to see the variation in thinking among a number of people. Try the exercises on your friends and associates at whatever occasion may seem appropriate, whether they are reading the book or not. In any case, try to work on them yourself. You will need only paper and pencil, if that. It is surprisingly easy to read material about thinking, accept it intellectually, and yet not have one's own thinking processes affected. It's a little bit like reading a book about jogging: it won't do you nearly as much good unless you run a little. And if you really want to get into thinking, design some brand new exercises, like the ones in the book, and try them on your friends.

In my creativity work, I have always used puzzles to illuminate conceptual blocks. People tend not to like them, because they make people feel dumb as they realize the block. I confess that I hate puzzles too, when someone lays one on me. But they give one an excellent chance to analyze one's thinking. And I suspect that they annoy the brain enough to help train it to be more suspicious about these blocks. That is a good thing.

The following puzzle, which originates with Karl Duncker, is taken from *The Act of Creation,* a classic book on creativity by Arthur Koestler. Work on it awhile. When you get the answer or get tired of thinking about it, proceed. Or if you cheat and don't work on it, show it to a friend and watch them think.

Puzzle: One morning, exactly at sunrise, a Buddhist monk began to climb a tall mountain. A narrow path, no more than a foot or two wide, spiraled around the mountain to a glittering temple at the summit. The monk ascended at varying rates of speed, stopping many times along the way to rest and eat dried fruit he carried with him. He reached the temple shortly before sunset. After several days of fasting and meditation he began his journey back along the same path, starting at sunrise and again walking at variable speeds with many pauses along the way. His average speed descending was, of course, greater than his average climbing speed. Prove that there is a spot along the path that the monk will occupy on both trips at precisely the same time of day.

Did you solve the puzzle? More importantly, for our purposes, can you remember what thinking processes you used in working on the puzzle? Instinct? Did you verbalize? Did you use imagery? Mathematics? Did you consciously try different strategies or modes of attack on the problem?

It is probable that you tried several methods of working the problem, but that your mind automatically switched from one to the other. You were probably not particularly aware of what mental processes you were employing as you thought about the problem. You were playing a game (like tennis) without being very aware of what you were doing or of the techniques by which you could improve your game (like getting your racket back faster). Your brain probably wanted to use System 1 thinking so you could quickly solve the problem and get on to other things.

The problem is given in words, which probably encouraged your brain to start working with an internal discussion (brains often talk to themselves—very noticeable when you try to go to sleep or when you wake up at 2 a.m.). But an internal discussion may simply make you vacillate between the conclusion that there is such a spot and there is not such a spot. But suppose your brain had visualized: shown itself a video of two monks, one at the bottom of the path and one at the top as the sun is rising. Let the bottom monk duplicate the upward journey as the upper monk duplicates the downward journey. It should be apparent that at some time and at some point on the path they will collide.

If you happened to choose visual imagery as the method of thinking to apply to this problem, you probably solved it. (A slightly more abstract approach is to imagine a plot on a graph of each monk's position as a function of time. The two lines will necessarily cross at a common position and time.) If you chose verbalization, you might not have solved the problem. In fact, even after knowing the visual solution, if you revert to a verbal approach, the problem becomes confusing again. If you attempted an abstract mathematical approach that did not involve graphing, you probably also failed to solve the problem and expended much more effort than was necessary. If you were tricked into either of these ways of thinking, you ran up against a conceptual block, which could have been avoided by thinking a bit about how you should approach the problem. Now show or tell the puzzle to your friends. You are likely get some who think there is no such spot, so let them argue and feel superior.

As another example, determine how you would complete the sequence below:

$$\frac{A \qquad EF}{BCD \qquad G}$$

In other words, how would you place the remaining letters of the alphabet above and below the line to make some kind of sense to you?

Unless you were suspicious that you were being tricked or that there was a "correct" answer, you probably reached a conclusion in a relatively short time. If you think about it, the task you performed was quite impressive. You needed to have knowledge (of alphabets and words), strategies (of patterns and general problem-solving), and the ability to make some decisions. Yet you may have reached an answer in a few seconds. The mind is wonderful at handling uncertainty, forming patterns, and reaching decisions. You also probably arrived at a solution that satisfied you and then turned your attention away from the problem and back toward the text. This particular behavior was named "satisficing" by Herbert Simon, an economist and student of decision-making, in one of his early works, and it is quite common. (Did you really brood about the suitability of your answer?) The mind generally does not compulsively continue to unearth additional options. It sacrifices concepts in order to reach a speedy decision. Simon characterized a satisficer as one who stopped looking through a haystack when he found a needle. An optimizer, on the other hand, would take the whole haystack apart looking for all possible needles in order to be able to pick the sharpest one. Obviously life does not allow us time to completely disassemble all of the haystacks we encounter. However—and this is pertinent to problem-solving—our natural behavior may often lead us to the less-than-sharpest needle.

I have used the ABC problem with many individuals and groups. They usually reach an answer in a short time and then sit back and look pleased. But, to their surprise, there are many answers. Some of those answers are summarized on the next page.

A. Group size

1. $\dfrac{\text{A} \quad\quad \text{EF} \quad \text{HIJ}}{\text{BCD} \quad\quad \text{G} \quad\quad \text{KL}}$ $\dfrac{1 \quad 2 \quad 3}{3 \quad 1 \quad 2}$ etc.

2. $\dfrac{\text{A} \quad\quad \text{EF} \quad \text{KLM}}{\text{BCD} \quad \text{GHIJ}}$ $\dfrac{1 \quad 2 \quad 3}{3 \quad 4}$ etc.

3. Random, all on top, all on bottom, or otherwise get it over with.

B. Letter shapes

1. Letters with curved lines below; letters without curved lines above.
2. Letters with crossbars above; letters without crossbars below.
3. Letters below can be formed without lifting pencil from paper; letters above cannot.

C. Sound

1. Top letters are soft; bottom letters are hard.
2. Top letters would take the article "an"; bottom letters would take the article "a."
3. Top letters begin with vowel sound.

D. Miscellaneous

1. $\dfrac{\text{A} \quad\quad \text{EF} \quad\quad \text{IJK}}{\text{BCD} \quad \text{GH}}$ (Top groups begin with vowels.)
2. Move BCDG up and put all on top (or move AEF down and put all on bottom).
3. Letters correspond to musical notes (people have sung it to me).
4. Bottom letters seem warmer (more friendly).
5. Top letters are easier to type.
6. Top letters are initials of Western industrialized countries (America, England, France); bottom letters are initials of nonindustrialized countries.
7. Top letters are all in "elephant" (wrong, but wonderful).

What are your reactions to these? Are any of them amusing? Annoying? Wrong? Can you guess why you react the way you do? The answer probably has to do with the fact that you did not think of them. If you satisficed, are you now less satisfied? It is often the case that we become less satisfied with our original answer if the problem seems to be turning into a contest. Satisficing seems to depend somewhat on the rules of the game, and a little conscious thinking can change these rules.

Finally, how did you arrive at the answer(s) you chose? Think about it a while. How much of the process was conscious? You probably remember some conscious thinking that occurred. How much was not conscious? You probably did not consciously pick the problem-solving strategy you used. Did the answer merely occur to you? If so, your mind relied upon its familiar mix of conscious and unconscious activity and satisfaction with System 1 thinking.

This is why I often say that problem-solving is quite habitual. We are all programmed in our thinking to a remarkable degree. If we are optimists, we suspect that habit must be beneficial in life. Not only is it beneficial, it is absolutely necessary to life as we know it. If we consider physical habits, our conscious abilities are simply not rapid enough to control our bodies as we play tennis or a piano concerto, or even as we walk, eat, or tie our shoes. It is fortunate for us that our brains have a subsystem called the cerebellum, which learns complex combinations of movements and plays them back when needed. These habits, or System 1 thinking, do not require much from our consciousness, and they allow us to live our complex physical lives.

Similarly, System 1 thinking allows us to solve intellectual problems much more rapidly than we could if we had to rely completely upon consciousness. We look at twelve times twelve and 144 appears. We scan printed material and hear it being spoken. We look at a balance sheet and have a sense of the health of the company. We appraise a structure and know that it is a good design. We take one look at a patient and know she is not well. These things we do because we have constructions of knowledge and mental processes that are available for our use when we need them. These constructions also minimize our intellectual risk, since they have usually been tested and found to be successful in the past. In addition, they give us precision as we perform repetitive tasks. Habit allows us to move rapidly, accurately, and safely. It would be impossible for us to complete our mental tasks without habit.

Habit also gives us stability. You would not think much of me if you met me each day and every time I was using a totally different set of problem-solving habits. I would be unpredictable and possibly considered insane. In a sense, a schizophrenic discomforts us by constantly changing problem-solving habits. Groups and large organizations also could not acquire their character and uniqueness without habits. Companies worry about their company culture, which depends on habits. Useful characteristics such as technical sophistication, marketing aggressiveness, and ability to weather economic downturns require habits. Finally, the mind depends heavily on structures, models, and stereotypes. These are part and parcel of habit. In a sense, we have a one-watt mind in a megawatt world. Without habit, we couldn't process the information we need in order to exist.

But although habitual thinking is good in many, if not most, situations, it is not good if one is trying to be creative. Creativity implies deviance from past procedure. Habits are consistent with it. Habits often destroy creative ideas before they see the light of day. Habits include conceptual blocks, which not only occur because of the mechanisms of our limited brains but also are imparted by socialization, education, and professional specialization. Creativity requires System 2 thinking and more work for your mind.

This book aims to make you more aware of what is going on in your mind and to give you a few techniques that may improve your capability to solve problems. We will be concentrating upon conceptualization, or the process by which one has ideas. This process is key in problem-solving, since the more creative concepts you have to choose from, the better. This is true at all stages of the problem-solving process, whether you are attempting to decide upon a broad direction or implement a detailed solution.

By concentrating on conceptualization, I am not attempting to downgrade the many other processes necessary in problem-solving, such as judgment, analysis, definition, and implementation. Neither am I trying to insult your intelligence by pointing out the obvious value of having a rich store of concepts to choose from. However, my work with students, professional people, and others over the years has convinced me that conceptualization does not always receive the attention it should in problem-solving. Conceptualization should be creative and should be treated as a major activity. Unfortunately, in actual problem-solving situations people often fall short of this goal.

As mentioned earlier, the natural response to a problem seems to be to try to get rid of it by finding an answer—often taking the first answer that occurs and pursuing it, because of one's reluctance to spend the time and mental effort needed to conjure up a richer storehouse of alternatives from which to choose. This hit-and-run approach to problem-solving begets all sorts of oddities—including, often, a chain of solutions causing problems requiring solutions, ad infinitum. In engineering one finds the Rube Goldberg effect, in which the problem is solved by an inelegant and complicated collection of partial solutions. I am sure that many of you are familiar with some example of this in the form of an appliance you have attempted to repair.

SOLUTIONS TO PROBLEMS THAT DON'T EXIST

In problem-solving, we also encounter solutions to problems that do not really exist. Remember the early (and unpopular) computer-generated voices in automobiles informing the operator of the state of the vehicle? And I assume at least some of you used to giggle at television spots of Andy Rooney pointing out useless features on appliances. I am presently looking at a kitchen blender whose buttons are marked mix, puree, grate, stir, liquefy, chop, blend, and whip. Care to put them in the proper order?

Since we will be talking about the problem of perception in the next chapter, I will offer up a story of a long-lasting lesson that I learned while working at the Jet Propulsion Laboratory long ago.

I was part of an extremely competent group of engineers involved in the development of the *Mariner 4,* which was the first spacecraft to fly by Mars. The *Mariner 4* was to be provided with electrical power by four solar panels, which were to be latched together during launch and then released and opened by spring-loaded actuators until they hit an energy-absorbing stop. Since there is no air in space to damp the opening of such panels and since they were covered with fragile and expensive solar cells, it was the custom to use a device to retard their opening.

Such devices had been used successfully on earlier *Ranger* lunar spacecraft. Ordinarily, the philosophy at the Jet Propulsion Laboratory was to use hardware that had proved successful on previous missions. But the lunar device was heavy and weight was extremely critical, because every scientist in the world seemed to have an instrument that simply had to be on the first Mars shot. Also, the *Ranger* device was not really proven for the trip of nine months that would be necessary to reach Mars.

Furthermore, since the *Ranger* device was full of oil, there was a risk of it leaking out and coating the spacecraft with a lethal layer of slime during the nine-month-long flight (temperature control in spacecraft depends on clean external surfaces). This was a high-priority problem for our group, so we jumped on it.

Our first attempt, which contained no oil, was extremely complex and no lighter than the retarders on the lunar spacecraft. Its complexity and the results from a large amount of testing resulted in its rejection on the grounds of inadequate reliability.

The second solution was a central retarder that would control the opening speed of all four panels. Although it was filled with oil, the oil could not leak and the device was lightweight. However, it also proved to be unreliable as originally developed. At this point, full panic occurred in the program. There was no longer time to try a third approach, since planetary spacecraft cannot be delayed (the planet becomes much more difficult to reach until the next favorable alignment of the solar system, which usually does not occur for several years). An extremely expensive, around-the-clock emergency effort was therefore launched to increase the reliability of the damper, along with a simultaneous program of testing in order to measure the adverse effects of various malfunctions that might occur in flight and damage the solar panels—and therefore deprive the spacecraft of power.

One of the malfunctions investigated was that in which the retarder failed completely. A test version of the spacecraft was put in the space-simulation chamber (a huge vacuum tank with cold walls and a simulated sun) with no retarder at all, just the simple energy absorbers at the end of the panels' travel. When the panels were released, the springs opened them at a frightening speed (no air damping) and the panels definitely rocked and rolled when they hit, but nothing broke. The retarder was not, in fact, necessary at all. It was possible to allow the panels to open freely and then catch them with the energy absorbers.

Mariner 4 went to Mars without panel retarders—the most elegant possible solution to the problem, and probably the least risky because there were fewer devices to fail.

The moral in the story is obvious. The apparent shortage of time in the development of this project, coupled with the natural desire of those involved to solve problems as quickly as possible, resulted in overlooking alternative concepts (such as no retardation) that could have prevented the wild-goose chase. The cost was a lot of anxiety, a lot of hours from talented people, and a lot of dollars. The cause was inadequate time spent thinking about the problem definition and a mind-set of relying on what had been done in the past.

CHAPTER 2

Perceptual Blocks

PERCEPTUAL BLOCKS ARE OBSTACLES THAT PREVENT THE problem solver from clearly perceiving either the problem itself or the information needed to solve the problem. Perhaps the best way of helping you overcome perceptual blocks is to talk about some common and specific ones.

DETECTING WHAT YOU EXPECT: STEREOTYPING

We are continually reminded of the existence of stereotyping. Members of ethnic minorities, women, homosexuals, the elderly, the disabled, and others have successfully taught us that social stereotypes are wrong. Yet no matter how much we prepare ourselves for the prevalence of stereotypes, their effects can still catch us by surprise.

I used to play around with facial hair, partly to experience the change in people's reactions. I had grown a short beard, but once I noticed that it was beginning to curl I decided to grow it longer, in particular until Christmas. I doubt Santa has to live with the reactions my beard caused. Most people, ranging from my mother to friends to strangers, didn't like it, though some actually did: while walking through San Francisco in older clothes, a nice lady actually tried to give me a dollar. I doubt

Santa has considered shaving off his beard, but the reactions were enough to make me do so.

Shave your head if you are a woman and you will experience a low level of the reaction the public has to cancer patients. My wife and I are often in the yard, so I have mounted large bells with ropes to pull, which then ring them on both porches. But people who visit us for the first time still knock on the doors, which of course we can't hear. Stereotyping and labeling are extremely prevalent and effective perceptual blocks. They limit most of us when it comes to matters of gender and race. The simple truth of the matter is, you are limited in your ability to be creative if you are controlled by preconceptions. Evidence that violates preconceptions is often ignored.

As another example of the power of stereotyping, I occasionally wear neckties. I do not like them, and at one time considered never wearing them again. However, I decided that this was a foolish battle, because the stereotyping associated with a necktie is so strong that I can accomplish certain professional things much more easily by wearing one, since people assume I am important. (This is true of the automobile industry and financial firms, but not especially true in Silicon Valley.) I also learned that unless I wear them once in a while, I forget how to tie my fancy full-Windsor knot.

Perceptual stereotyping is part of the explanation for the success of various types of optical trickery, such as optical illusions. Perceptual stereotyping is not all bad, since it helps us complete incomplete data. However, it can be a serious handicap to perceiving new combinations. Creativity has sometimes been called the combining of seemingly disparate parts into a functioning and useful whole. Stereotyped conceptions of the parts hinder their combination into a new whole, where the roles they play may be quite different.

Once a label (professor, housewife, chair, butterfly, automobile, laxative) has been applied, people are less likely to notice the actual qualities or attributes of what is being labeled. For instance, say I am trying to think of what to do with a warehouse full of chairs. If I can think of them only as chairs, I can probably only come up with such uses as sitting on them, standing on them, or hitting villains with them in B movies. But if I think of the attributes of the chairs (fabric, padding, wooden legs, screws, etc.), I can come up with many more uses. Maybe I should take the chairs apart, and sell the seats to people who attend football games, make purses from the leather back covering, sell the screws as surplus hardware, and sell the wood to home craftsmen. Stereotyping inhibits this type of thinking.

There are obvious reasons why we stereotype. It simplifies the brain's work, but memory is central to creativity and innovation. In complex projects, not only is a great deal of information pertinent to the project necessary, but bending it in new directions often results in fresh and profitable ideas. The process of storing and recalling information in memory is quite complex. Much of the information used in conceptualizing is first recorded in the memory and later recalled, rather than used immediately upon acquisition. Memory cannot retain all of the raw information that comes in through the senses. The brain therefore processes it by filtering out what is judged to be less useful, categorizing the rest to be as consistent as possible with information already stored in the memory, and then coding it. When the information is later recalled, it is in a simplified and regularized form—in a sense, a stereotype of the original.

At present, people talk about three types of memory function: sensory memory, short-term memory (STM, also known as working memory), and long-term memory (LTM). LTM is in turn divided into explicit (conscious, for example, the act of remembering the Gettysburg Address) and implicit (unconscious, how to ride your bicycle). Explicit memory is further divided into episodic (events that happened to you) and semantic (general knowledge of the world). Implicit memory is divided into procedural (motor activities) and priming (aid to recall). The structures handling this information are by no means located in a single area of the brain. Various types of information are held in locations where they are likely to be most valuable. Among other portions of the brain, the amygdala, the hippocampus, the cerebellum, and the prefrontal cortex are involved in memory.

Sensory memory holds the information from the senses (sight, sound, smell, texture, etc.). This input lasts from a fraction of a second (visual) to a few seconds (auditory), in which time decisions are made as to whether to keep it or let it go unrecorded. If the sensory information is to be recorded, it is sent along with accompanying emotions to the STM, which includes present information. The STM holds information for a longer time than sensory memory (several seconds), but can only hold a small amount of information—to be specific, seven plus or minus two pieces. This does not say much about the content of these pieces, but fortunately the brain is capable of packaging it in efficient ways, including by the way that it is coded and the context of what is going on in your life at the time. STM holds such things as the phone number you just got. (Allegedly, that is why phone numbers at one time consisted of seven digits.) If you don't either rapidly use the number or do something such as write it down, record it, or repeat it to yourself, it disappears.

Although STM is extremely important in carrying out our daily activities, we are particularly interested in LTM, which allows us to solve problems, gives us our sense of self, and enables us to communicate sensibly. Only a small portion of the information that enters our sensory register and filters through the STM ends up in the LTM. Attention provides the focusing mechanism of LTM. While performing the complex tasks of living (such as driving to work in the morning), LTM is attending to only a small fraction of the inputs from the senses. Most of these inputs merely cycle through STM.

It is the material already in LTM that determines attention, and the mind tends to reinforce what is already there. For instance, if you are an oenophile, you will record a great deal of new material you encounter on wine to add to your already considerable store of knowledge. Similarly, you will record very little information on a topic you dislike. If you hate math, you will record little new math-related information. This tendency should make you suspicious as to whether material you recall from your memory contains an honest representation of detail about subjects you aren't interested in. (It does not.) It should also make you suspect that stereotyping is particularly strong in areas that have been unimportant to you or unpleasant for you to think about. (It is.)

Information reaching LTM must be filed, and this process involves coding. Ideally, this coding will not only efficiently organize knowledge, but make it easier to decode it when needed. Context is also a component of memory. The following exercise illustrates this.

Exercise: Remember the following list. Read it and close the book. Then see if you can repeat it to yourself.

saw, when, panicked, Jim, ripped, haystack, the, relaxed, when, cloth, the, but, he

I assume not only was this difficult (more than seven pieces), but also your brain resisted such an apparently useless exercise. However, I will now make these words into a relatively meaningless sentence and, although the sentence may seem both dumb and amusing, you will be able to remember it more easily.

> **Exercise:** Remember the following sentence. Read it and close the book. Then see if you can repeat it to yourself.

> Jim panicked when the cloth ripped, but relaxed when he saw the haystack.

You have now chunked the words, turning them from thirteen meaningless words into one nonsensical sentence. However, your brain, although more cooperative, is still not completely satisfied. It seeks meaning or consistency with some logical structure already within memory. I can give your brain this meaning through a simple phrase: parachute jumping. You have a structure for parachute jumping that will make the sentence above meaningful, and when you now return and read it again, you will be happy. Also you will be more easily able to remember the sentence over a long period. See if you can recall it when you awaken tomorrow morning.

In this exercise, the information you originally saw was of little use to you because it was out of context. Your brain does not like to transfer this type of information to LTM, because it seems random rather than important. However, once more information was attached, the clues from context you already possessed made it easy to solve the problems and transfer the information to your LTM.

Context is a key element in many memory techniques. One of the best known of these is the method of loci. In this technique, you first take a familiar walk and remember a number of scenes from the walk. To remember a number of items, superimpose a visual image of one item on each of the walk scenes.

Recall then requires only mentally retracing the walk. Try it. This technique is surprisingly effective, especially for people with good visual-imagery ability. It is rumored that Cicero used this method to remember his orations to the Roman senate. It is further rumored that the technique is the origin of the phrase, "In the first place . . . in the second place . . ." Probably not true, but it is such a good rumor that it should be. Magically enough, having memorized the walk, you can use it to better remember different lists of items with it.

We usually remember information in context, and that context goes into our memory along with the information. When we later recall the information for use in problem-solving, the residual information and feelings from the original context tend to accompany it. This can aid recall. I am a fan of Khan Academy, founded by Salman Khan to teach mathematics over the internet to a cousin. It offers free, short, easy-to-understand, and often amusing courses. Although originally meant for children, it now includes advanced placement (AP) class material for high school students, as well as general education material. One of my sons, who earned an MS degree in engineering and was one of the early employees of Tesla, defines Khan Academy as where you go to understand what your professor is trying to say. As I was looking through a series of short articles on human memory on its site, I was mightily amused by a piece of advice explaining the value of location and mood in recalling material from memory: if you acquire information in a particular place while drunk, you should return to that place and get drunk again to better recall it.

But this memory of context is not always useful. It limits your thinking. If your first introduction to organ music is at a funeral, it may be difficult later to think of using organ music in a joyful pageant. Organ music has been, in a sense, stereotyped. Suppose you are trying to think of an original theme for a restaurant. What comes to mind? Waiters? Candles? Wine? Napkins? Lots of forks? Other restaurants you've seen? Did you think of a snake? What about a tractor? A snake or tractor is unlikely, since they are not in your "restaurant" file, but kids like tractors and so do I—as do many people who grew up happy on a farm—and snakes definitely draw attention at zoos, so either might draw attention to your restaurant.

The structured information in your memory is so important to you that you may dismiss information that is inconsistent with what is already there. Psychologists write about an interesting internal state called cognitive dissonance that results from an inconsistency among a person's knowledge, feelings, beliefs, and behavior. The individual attempts to minimize this dissonance. One way to do this is to devalue information that does not fit one's stereotype. But a potential good characteristic of this structured memory is that when the information is coded and placed into memory, and then used and put back, it recodes and is changed depending on the context in which it is used. An example can be seen in the treatment of post-traumatic stress disorder (PTSD) in veterans. An early approach was to re-create the sound and turmoil of battle in a safe surrounding, and assume the people having PTSD would slowly understand that the battle environment was not as terrifying as they thought. A more modern approach is to place them in a very calm environment, and have them recall their experiences. The theory is that when they place those experiences back in memory, they will have been recoded in a safe context, with a resulting softening of trauma.

My father always drove a pickup and loved Chevrolets. He would spend what seemed to me to be long hours boasting about the superiority of the brand. But when I reached pickup age, I chose a Ford. My father was very disappointed in me and continued to try to convince me that Chevrolet was better —his stereotype—but I held firm, and we spent hours justifying our choices based on strong points (devaluing each other's, of course). But, after several Fords, I became disenchanted with what I perceived to be reliability problems and switched to Toyotas. Now I can waste endless amounts of your time explaining why they are superior. One's brain can't handle the idea that it bought a lesser pickup. As proof of this, some time ago, I read a study showing that people read the marketing literature after they buy the product, obviously to prove to themselves how brilliant they are. In retrospect, the pickups were all good, but I have repressed all of my father's arguments for Chevrolet, and mine for Ford, but of course remember those for Toyota, since I still have one.

With this in mind, let's look a bit further at labeling as applied to people. We all have stereotypes about people, and these often lead to social and interpersonal problems. I am a retired (so-called emeritus) professor. Most of you, having never met me, can conclude quite a bit about me from the label "professor" and your stereotyping ability. However, although some of the characteristics you attribute to me might be accurate, you would have trouble working or living with me with only that information, for I have my own particular group of characteristics. I am a grandfather, a good mechanic, machinist, cook, and carpenter, and married to a woman I love madly who is a retired educational consultant and wired to the world. I tend to be happier in rural environments than cities and like a great deal of contact with other people in my work but prefer a light social schedule. I have two outstanding knee implants, a messy office, white hair, and a 1909 brown shingle house. I am 6'1", 230 pounds (formerly 6'4" and 210, and I miss both of those), and have many hobbies, including restoring old heavy equipment, reading violent mystery books, acquiring mechanical antiques I don't need, and aimlessly driving through backcountry.

Although politically liberal and living in a politically correct area, I still drink Scotch, eat beef, and enjoy dirty jokes. Oh yes, I am also a professional engineer and a consultant. As I list these attributes, you should be able to move beyond your ideas of the stereotype to get a better feel for me as a person, and therefore be better able to interact with me. I have also enriched the stereotype you have of "professor" by adding information. Now you try it. In the following exercise, see how you label yourself and how people label you.

> **Exercise:** Find someone you like, but do not know too well (maybe someone you work with or a friend of your spouse). Each of you think of and tell the other a label (a few words) that describes yourself. Spend half a minute or so considering what the other person's label means to you. Then spend five minutes verbally exchanging additional characteristics. Alternate and keep moving. Do not succumb to the temptation to small talk (thereby being witty and engaging) to avoid trading information. Do not question the other person and do not try to steer the conversation. Just swap information.

Did you find this exercise a quick way to find out information about another person? Many people do. However, did you also find it difficult? Even after having lived a reasonably long and rich life, people generally run short on characteristics after a few minutes and spend more effort in thinking up their own attributes than in listening to those of the other person. They also generally experience an overwhelming desire for small talk. Did you?

In social and professional interactions we tend to stick to stereotypes and generalities, unless at some point it seems to our benefit to become specific about ourselves. The above exercise therefore invades our privacy, since it forces us to divulge information before we may be ready to do so. After this exercise is over, most participants agree that they know much more about the other person than they would have gleaned from the original label. They also gain a sense of the importance to themselves of their own stereotype, as well as a better feeling of how they cling to stereotypes to avoid taking social risk. The exercise also shows that we do not have a large store of characteristics about ourselves in our memory. If we did, the exercise would be much easier. We not only stereotype other people and things, but we also stereotype ourselves. Stereotyping is an obvious perceptual block, and a very important one to us.

DIFFICULTY IN ISOLATING THE PROBLEM

Many visual puzzles require the solver to detect meaning in the midst of apparent chaos. Problems we face may be similarly obscured by either inadequate clues or misleading information. Proper problem identification (sometimes called framing) is of extreme importance in problem-solving. If the problem is not correctly isolated, it will not be solved. Successful medical diagnosis depends on the ability to isolate the problem within the complexity of all of the real and imaginary information available to the physician. Successful coexistence between parents and teenage children requires the ability to isolate the real problems among the many apparent ones.

Is your problem really a bad tank of gas, or does your car need a timing belt or perhaps new distributor points? Or, is your problem a living situation that makes you overly dependent upon a car? Problem statements are often liberally laced with answers. The answers may be well-thought-out or poorly conceived. They may be right or wrong.

If you are working as a professional problem solver, you should continually be alert to properly perceive the problem.

The client, patient, or customer may not always see the problem clearly, and the problem solver is sometimes able to score heavily by simply curing the difficulties through a clearer perception of what the problem really is. In engineering, people occasionally become so involved in attempting to optimize a particular device that they lose sight of alternate ways to alleviate the difficulty. Much thinking went into the mechanical design of various prototype tomato pickers, for example, before someone decided that the real problem was not in optimizing these designs but rather in the susceptibility of the tomatoes to damage during picking. The answer to the problem was a new plant, with tougher-skinned, more accessible fruit.

People are also often swayed by their own competence. There is a famous statement, originally taken from Abraham Maslow's now-vintage book entitled *The Psychology of Science,* popularly phrased as something like, "If the only tool you have is a hammer, you tend to treat everything like a nail." It has often been the case when I have worked with design groups that people will assume their own discipline or specialty is the answer. Fortunately, I have not yet crossed a mechanical engineer proposing a mechanical television set, or an electrical engineer a digital shovel. But if you are an expert in a discipline, beware of being overly biased toward seeing the problem as best solved by your expertise.

Jerry Porras, who is an emeritus professor in the Stanford Graduate School of Business, wrote a book entitled *Stream Analysis,* where he claims that people, especially people in organizations, tend to work on getting rid of symptoms, rather than solving the real problems. I used to assign this book to my students and ask them to do an analysis of one of their own problems. After this exercise, they were forced to agree with the thesis in the book, but were sure that this could not possibly be the case in big-time corporations. Shortly after that, I had the good fortune to join Porras in a workshop for one of those very same big-time corporations, in which he went through the problem-analysis approach in his book. The results were overwhelming. We ended the exercise with some very bothered executives, who had been forced to realize that they were indeed ignoring the core problems. Not surprising, since core problems are more difficult to solve and their solution often creates greater controversy. This is perhaps not what we would like to think.

Early in my consulting career, I learned this lesson well. When I began consulting for companies about such things as creativity and innovation, my experience was heavily oriented toward aerospace and fairly exotic technology. But one client was a large company that was neither overwhelmingly creative nor innovative. After having been very successful for many years, the client was losing market share in what turned out was a nongrowing market. Having not done this type of consulting much, I requested that a few higher executives meet with me before we expanded the group and explain the problem in detail. Through the experience that followed, I learned that this was always a good idea.

A few days before the meeting was scheduled, I received a call asking to delay the meeting. Seemed reasonable to me, since the people who were to attend from the company were big wheels. But it happened a couple more times, and I of course began worrying that they didn't really want me to work with the larger group because of my relatively young age and questionable experience. Then they gave me a call, telling me that the smaller group had met without me several times because they couldn't agree on what their problems were, but that they had thought of some key issues and were working on them. So we never met—a bad outcome. However, they not only paid me but gave me a bonus because they felt their own meetings were so valuable. And they hired me again later—a good outcome after all.

Problems are, of course, often constrained by considerations other than mere removal of a difficulty, and the problem solver must be sensitive to this. Assume, for instance, that I am a consulting engineer retained to help in the design of an improved product by a company that is a leading manufacturer of mechanical equipment used to clear clogged drains and sewers. Assume further that I perceive the problem to be a general one of unclogging pipes (expanding the frame). This might lead me to a very elegant solution (a mixture of commonly available chemicals or bacteria) that would make obsolete the product line of the company and that would not take advantage of the company's field of competence. Although I could then proudly take my place among successful conceptualizers, my employer would probably not enjoy my solution. Properly isolating the problem is, of course, equally or more important if you are both problem definer and problem solver. Difficulty in isolating the problem is often due to the tendency to spend a minimum of effort on defining a problem in order to get to the important matter of solving it. Inadequately defining the problem is a tendency that is downright foolish on an important and extensive problem-solving task. A relatively short time spent carefully isolating and defining the problem can be extremely valuable, both in illuminating possible simple solutions and in ensuring that a great deal of effort is not spent only to find that the difficulties still exist—perhaps in even greater magnitude.

> **Exercise:** Think of a problem that is bothering you. State your problem in writing as concisely as you can. Can you think of alternative problem statements that might be causing the difficulties you are experiencing? If so, write them down and conjecture about the possible differences in solutions that occur to you.

TENDENCY TO DELIMIT
THE PROBLEM AREA POORLY

Just as it is sometimes difficult to isolate the problem properly, it is also difficult to avoid delimiting the problem too closely. In other words, one should not impose too many constraints upon it. The following puzzle is an example of the tendency to delimit too closely. Sam Loyd, who apparently included it his book *Cyclopedia of Puzzles* in 1914, is sometimes given credit for inventing it. But others argue that it is older than that. Suffice it to say that it has been around a long time, and you may feel smug because you know the answer, but that is System 1 thinking and you should read on.

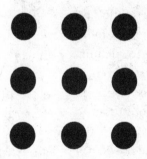

Puzzle: Draw no more than four straight lines (without lifting the pencil from the paper) which will cross through all nine dots

This puzzle is difficult to solve if the imaginary boundary enclosing the nine dots is not exceeded, as shown in one possible answer below.

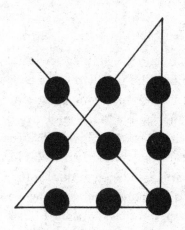

A surprising number of people will not exceed the imaginary boundary, for often this constraint is unconsciously in the mind of the problem solver, even though it is not in the definition of the problem at all. The overly strict limits are a block in the mind of the solver. The widespread nature of this block is what makes this puzzle classic.

Such blocks are subtle and pervasive. But let me talk more about this puzzle to demonstrate that awareness of blocks can and often does result in the ability and motivation to overcome them. I used to use this puzzle years ago when I first came to Stanford in order to demonstrate conceptual blocks. For a talk I once gave on the subject of problem-solving, an announcement was sent out with this puzzle on the cover. An anonymous party sent back this solution:

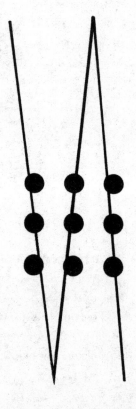

Ah ha, System 2 thinking. To add insult to this injury, one of my oldest friends later sent me a fiendish solution that allows all nine dots to be crossed off by one straight line, plus a little unblocked paper folding. Try this solution yourself—make a copy of the page (use thin paper) and start folding!

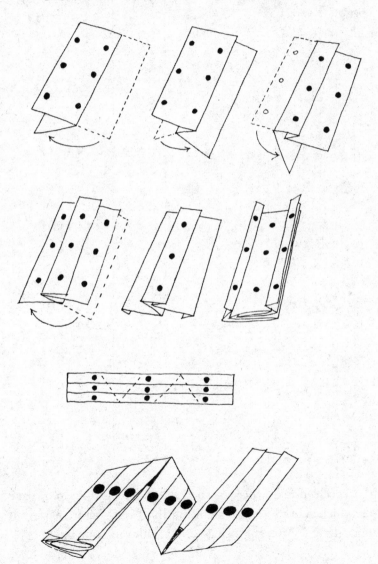

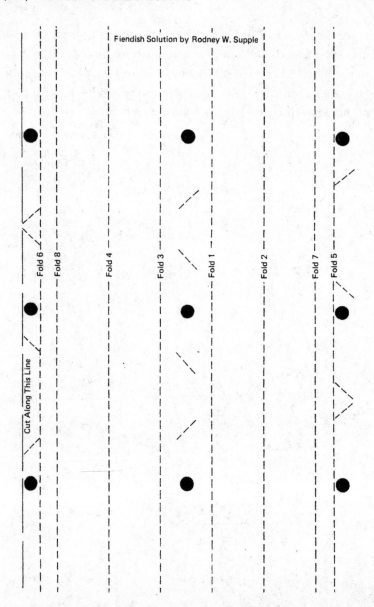

Fiendish Solution by Rodney W. Supple

Fold 6 — Fold 8 — Fold 4 — Fold 3 — Fold 1 — Fold 2 — Fold 7 — Fold 5

Cut Along This Line

I received many answers such as the one at the top of page 43, which merely requires cutting the puzzle apart, taping it together in a different format, and again using one line.

It is also possible to roll up the puzzle and draw a spiral through the dots, cut out the dots and shove the line through them, or otherwise violate the two-dimensional format.

Solutions continued to roll in.

1 Line 0 Folds

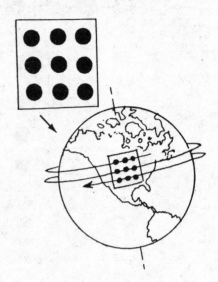

Lay the paper on the surface of the Earth. Circumnavigate the globe twice + a few inches, displacing a little each time so as to pass through the next row on each circuit as you "Go West, young man."

~ 2 Lines* 0 Folds

*Statistical

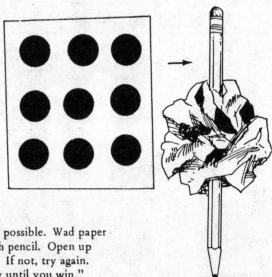

Draw dots as large as possible. Wad paper into a ball. Stab with pencil. Open up and see if you did it. If not, try again. "Nobody loses: Play until you win."

My all-time favorite is the letter that follows. By now I have received dozens of answers to this puzzle, all exceedingly clever and all depressing in that I had thought of none of them. Not only that, but the author of the letter, Becky Buechel, ended up in my classroom at one point—small world. I still receive solutions.

May 30, 1974
5 FDR Navosa
Roosevelt Rds. N.
Ceiba, P.R. 00635

Dear Prof. James L. Adams,
My dad and I were doing Puzzles from "Conceptual BLockbusting". We were mostly working on the dot ones, like ::: My dad said a man found a way to do it with one line. I tried and did it. Not with folding, But I used a fat line. I doesn't say you can't use a fat line. Like this

P.S.
acctually you need a very fat writing apparatice

Sincerely,
Becky Buechel
age: 10

Outbursts of creativity such as these are exciting. One of the messages of this book is that we place limits upon our own functioning (the fence around the dots) and that once we realize the existence of these limits we will be eager to escape and will no longer be as hampered by them. The nine-dot puzzle is certainly evidence of this phenomenon. Limits are negotiable.

Just as a solution is sensitive to the proper isolation of the problem, it is also sensitive to proper limitation and constraints.

The framing of a problem has great influence on its solution. In general, the more broadly the problem can be stated, the more room is available for conceptualization. A request for the design of a better door will probably result in a rectangular slab with hinges and a handle. Is this what is wanted, or is the problem really a better way to get through a wall? That would release one from the preconception of the rectangular slab that swings or slides. Students given this problem statement will come up with all manner of geometries for walls and openings, elastic diaphragms, mechanical shutters, curtains, and ingenious rotating and folding mechanisms. Is this what is wanted, or is the problem a better method of acoustical, visual, or environmental isolation? The solution of a laminar air curtain, as is used to keep heat in stores or out of freezers while permitting free passage, would not be likely to come from a harshly delivered "design a better door" problem statement.

If you hire an architect or a structural engineer or a lawyer, you are paying for expertise. It is therefore foolish to constrain a problem so closely ("Here is a floor plan and an elevation. Build it.") that you are not taking advantage of the professional's abilities. This principle applies equally if a single person is both stating the problem and solving it. A problem statement that is too limited inhibits creative ability.

It is, of course, possible to err in the opposite direction and not delimit the problem sufficiently. The resulting solution may be so general or basic as not to be useful. An automobile company looking for a better way to keep windshields clean cannot do much with a solution that does away with automobiles. The proper statement of a problem therefore becomes a critical art, since it enables the extraction of the maximum of creative thought from the solver while still delivering a useful answer. I would hazard a guess, however, that more problems are overly limited in statement than inadequately so. Because of that feeling and because this is a book on creativity, imposing too many constraints is expressly stated here to be verboten.

> **Exercise:** The next time you have a problem, solve it. Then, at your leisure, list at least three different possible delimitations of the problem and answers you might have come up with in each case.

For instance, suppose that you are a relatively new mother who took time off from your job to have your baby, and you are now torn between work and spending more time with your child.

Problem solutions are of course affected by pragmatic concerns, such as money and support from others, but let's assume that in this case money is not a problem and you have support from your spouse and friends. You might formulate your problem as "choosing between being a professional woman and a mother" and quit working outside the house in order to devote full time to your baby. (I am assuming that you would not give up your baby.) Alternately, you might see your problem as, "How can I continue to have the satisfaction of work and yet spend the time I want with my child?" This problem statement contains fewer limits and might lead to involving the father more in childcare or pursuing another career that allows you to work more flexible hours, work at home, work part time, etc.

You might phrase your problem as, "How can I ensure that my child will receive care that will best encourage its proper development?" This has even fewer limits and might cause you to work with other new mothers to set up an outstanding day care cooperative. You might decide that the problem is conflict between the natural role of mother and modern expectations that women should be respected professionals in the outside world. This might lead to conversations with other people in your situation, opinion makers, therapists, and educators. It might bring you to the conclusion that a major social problem exists and to you becoming a militant author and the organizer of a national effort devoted to helping women with new children escape this conflict.

As limits on the problem's definition are relaxed, one usually becomes involved in interdisciplinary considerations: economic, political, and ethical. If you see your problem as simply conforming with federal government smog regulations, your answer may be to put gadgets on existing engines. However, if you see your problem as minimizing air pollution, you may consider entirely new concepts in transportation and become involved in complex social as well as technical considerations.

INABILITY TO SEE THE PROBLEM FROM VARIOUS VIEWPOINTS

It is often difficult to see a problem from the viewpoint of all of the interests and parties involved. However, consideration of such viewpoints not only leads to a better solution to the problem, in that it pleases more interests and individuals, but it is also extremely helpful in conceptualizing. Certainly, in a problem between two people, the ability to see the problem from the other's point of view (empathy) is extremely important in keeping the tone of the debate within reasonable bounds of refinement. In many cases, no solution is possible until each person can gain a feeling for the viewpoint of the other. Most problem solutions affect people other than the solver, and their interests must be considered. The architect must view the design of his buildings from the perspectives of the clients, builders, suppliers, architectural critics, and others in the profession, as well as from his own. Designers of an automobile should worry about those who must manufacture, operate, and maintain their output. The property owner building a fence must consider the viewpoints not only of neighbors, the city council, visitors, the garbage man, and passing motorists who can no longer see around the corner, but also of nonhuman participants such as the lawn, which may die in the shade of the fence, and the neighborhood cats, who may sit on the fence to better communicate their wails of war and love.

> **Exercise:** Think of an interpersonal problem you presently have. Write a concise statement of the problem as seen by each party involved. If possible, show the statements to the corresponding parties and see if they agree with your interpretation of their perception of the problem.

In his book entitled *New Think,* Edward de Bono, a well-known thinker about creativity, talks about vertical and lateral thinking. Vertical thinking begins with a single concept and then proceeds with that concept until a solution is reached. Lateral thinking refers to thinking that generates alternative ways of seeing a problem before seeking a solution. At one point in his book, de Bono explains vertical and lateral thinking by referring to the digging of holes. He states:

> Logic is the tool that is used to dig holes deeper and bigger, to make them altogether better holes. But if the hole is in the wrong place, then no amount of improvement is going to put it in the right place. No matter how obvious this may seem to every digger, it is still easier to go on digging in the same place than to start all over again in a new place. Vertical thinking is digging the same hole deeper; lateral thinking is trying again elsewhere.

De Bono acknowledges the advantages in digging in the same hole, admitting that "a half-dug hole offers a direction in which to expend effort." He elaborates, "No one is paid to sit around being capable of achievement. As there is no way of assessing such capability it is necessary to pay and promote according to visible achievements. Far better to dig the wrong hole (even one that is recognized as being wrong) to an impressive depth than to sit around wondering where to start digging." However, de Bono makes the point that many holes are being dug to an impractical depth in the wrong place, and that breakthroughs usually result from someone abandoning a partly dug hole and beginning anew in a different place.

SATURATION

Saturation takes place with all sensory modes. If the mind recorded all inputs so that they were all consciously accessible, our conscious mind would be very full indeed. Many extremely familiar inputs are not recorded in a way that allows their simple recall.

> **Exercise:** Without looking at one, draw the push buttons on a landline phone, placing the letters, numbers, and symbols in the proper location. If you have forgotten landline phones, how about your smartphone?

Very few people can do this successfully, even though they use phones constantly. Maybe you never looked closely at the way the alphabet is delineated on the keypad. However, the mind does not hold onto the details on the buttons, since it does not have to. If they were not marked on the phone, the mind would store the information for easy recall.

As other examples of saturation, you might try to draw (without looking at it) the grill on your car, your lawn mower handle, or any other object that you see repeatedly, but whose visual details are unimportant to you. As with your phone, even though you might think that you know the details, you cannot produce them when desired. The trickiest aspect of saturation is that you think you have the data even though you are unable to recall it.

Visual saturation is a problem in art schools, because it is necessary to teach students to see things they are used to ignoring. For this reason, beginning art students are sometimes told (as I once was) to do things like bend over and look at the world upside down, since this new orientation makes visible details that are usually not noticed. Try it. Similarly, if you look away from a nice sunset you notice all manner of usually unnoticed visual activity in the easterly direction, such as colors on clouds, muted tones on buildings, and reflected lights on windows.

Another situation that requires attention to saturation in problem-solving occurs when data arrives only occasionally or in the presence of large amounts of distracting data. Radar inputs in the military or in air traffic control are examples of this, as are irregularities in the operation of an airplane or ground vehicle that appear after a long period of normal behavior. The life of a professional pilot, for instance, has occasionally been described as years of tedium interspersed with seconds of terror. When the information resulting in this terror becomes available, it is obviously extremely important that the pilot notice it as soon as possible. Fortunately for us passenger types, a great amount of effort on the part of humans—engineers, psychologists, and equipment designers—goes into ensuring that the tedium will be suitably interrupted.

FAILURE TO UTILIZE ALL SENSORY INPUTS

The senses are interconnected in a fairly direct manner. This will be discussed further in chapter six. Senses such as sight, hearing, taste, and smell are commonly linked. Taste is severely inhibited if smell is suppressed. Similarly, sight is augmented in a major way by sound (for example, in motion pictures).

Various sensory inputs, especially vision, are important to people who are extremely innovative. This is amply recorded in the literature. In a letter to Jacques Hadamard (published in *The Creative Process*), Albert Einstein said: "The words or the language, as they are written or spoken, do not seem to play any role in my mechanism of thought. The psychical entities that seem to serve as elements in thought are certain signs and more or less clear images that can be 'voluntarily' reproduced and combined. The above-mentioned elements are, in my case, of visual and some of muscular type. Conventional words or other signs have to be sought for laboriously only in a secondary stage, when the mentioned associative play is sufficiently established and can be reproduced at will."

Nikola Tesla, an extremely productive technological innovator (fluorescent lights, the AC generator, the Tesla coil), apparently had incredible visualization powers. As described by J. J. O'Neill in *Prodigal Genius: The Life of Nikola Tesla,* it was claimed that Tesla "could project before his eyes a picture complete in every detail, of every part of the machine. These pictures were more vivid than any blueprint." Further, Tesla claimed to be able to test his devices mentally by having them run in his imagination for weeks, after which time he would examine them thoroughly for signs of wear.

Problem solvers need all the help they can get. They should therefore be careful not to neglect any sensory inputs. An engineer working on an acoustics problem for a concert hall, for instance, should not get so carried away with theoretical analysis that she neglects to look at a wide variety of concert halls, listen to the quality of sound in each, and assure herself that she understands the different types of music to be played in the hall.

She must also be aware that her acoustical treatment, although successful to the ear, may overly offend the eye and, if her material choice is extreme enough, perhaps also the nose.

It is for this reason that designers sometimes will consciously deprive themselves temporarily of certain sensory inputs to make sure they have adequately recorded others. The designer of a patio cover intended to take the place of shade trees until they grow high enough in a new yard would be well advised not only to look at trees, but also to listen to them, feel them, smell them, climb them, and generally saturate himself with them for a good bit of time before starting the design. In a well-working marriage, one is sensitive not only to the appearance of one's partner, but also to the sound, smell, taste, and feel of him or her. Problems within the couple are best solved by utilizing inputs from all of these senses.

Convincing students that they should use all of the sensory inputs at their disposal was one of my most difficult challenges when I taught design at Stanford University. My students were highly verbal (they are admitted to school based on their writing skills, as well as academic record, tests, etc.) and were relatively less competent visually. They were not used to relying on taste, smell, or feel for problem-solving. Generally speaking, they were familiar with problems that can be solved (they thought) verbally or mathematically. They were not used to using sensory imagery in their thinking. This subject will be covered in more detail in chapter six, so we will dwell no more on it here. Suffice it to say that failure to utilize inputs from all the senses is a conceptual block that is quite common in problem-solving.

CHAPTER 3

Emotional Blocks

THIS CHAPTER WILL BEGIN WITH A GAME. IT REQUIRES A group of people, the larger the better, so try it at a party. It was, I think, invented by Bob McKim, an old colleague of mine who founded the product design program at Stanford University. This game is called Barnyard.

Exercise: Divide your group and assign them to be various animals as follows.

If their last names begin with:	they are:
A–E	sheep
F–K	pigs
L–R	cows
S–Z	turkeys

Now, tell each person to find a partner (preferably someone he or she does not know too well) and to look this partner in the eye. You will then count to three, at which time everyone is to make the sound of the animal as loudly as they possibly can, holding eye contact. See how loud a barnyard you can build.

The participants in this game will be able to experience a common emotional block to conceptualization—namely, that of feeling like an ass. If you did not play the game and want to experience the feeling, merely stand alone on any busy corner (or wherever you are right now) and loudly make the sound of one of the animals.

As we will see in the next chapter, conceptualization is risky and new ideas are hard to evaluate. The expression of a new idea, and especially the process of trying to convince someone else that it has value, sometimes makes you feel like an ass, since you are doing something that possibly exposes your imperfections. In order to avoid this feeling, people will often avoid conceptualization, or at least avoid publicizing the output.

THE MYSTERY OF EMOTION

Although emotions are central to problem-solving, indeed to being human, many of us seem to be a bit uncomfortable in dealing with them. This is partly due to the mysterious nature of their mechanisms. If we do not understand things that happen within our mind, we tend to ignore them. As an example, we are quite comfortable with certain aspects of vision. The eye is a convenient analog to a camera in that there is a lens, a diaphragm, and a layer of sensitive material (the retina) on which the image is captured. The optic nerve, which transmits this information to the brain, undoubtedly processing it a bit en route, is less well known. We sometimes think of it as something like a bundle of wires, but the processing of visual information in the brain is so far from our intuition that we prefer to avoid thinking about it at all. Researchers have discovered some correlation between particular neurons and components of images, but they do not yet have a model that allows us to comfortably deal with the process that converts the electrical signals from our eye to our visual reality. Therefore we avoid thinking about it, except through the equivalent of the homunculus, a little person sitting in the skull, watching a TV set displaying the image on the retina and deciding what to do with it. We ignore the mechanics and get on with our lives.

In the case of emotions, we don't even have the satisfaction of visualizing the homunculus and his TV. We smell the ocean and fill with joy. We awaken depressed. We are terrified of speaking in public. We hate our boss. What is going on? For those of us who like to understand process, it is much easier to think about the perceptual blocks in the last chapter than emotional ones.

Part of the problem has to do with the complexity of the mechanisms. At the time I wrote the last edition of this book, there was a very popular book entitled *Emotional Intelligence* by Daniel Goleman, once editor of *Psychology Today* and later the cognitive science editor for the *New York Times*. Summarizing research that attempts to explain various characteristics of emotion, the book pleads for more consideration of emotion as an important aspect of personal success. When Goleman lists the emotions, he comes up with the following: anger, sadness, fear, enjoyment, love, surprise, disgust, and shame. But he then lists synonyms for each. As an example, under anger we find fury, outrage, resentment, wrath, exasperation, indignation, vexation, acrimony, animosity, annoyance, irritability, hostility, pathological hatred, and violence.

My students repeatedly would come up with lists of emotions that differed from Goleman's and argue about the meanings of complementary descriptive words. Obviously, the complexity of emotions does not allow for a simple model—at least not one that can be made up of words in the English language. We can describe our sense of taste by saying it can distinguish sweet, sour, bitter, and salty. (Incidentally, that is all that taste can detect. The rest of the joy of food comes through smell, as well as appearance, texture, and memories of past experience with it.)

I would assign Goleman's book to my students because it described what researchers were discovering about the mechanics of emotion and why they play such a powerful role in problem-solving. When I went to school, we were taught that the cortex analyzes signals from the senses and triggers appropriate responses. For instance, we are awakened at night by a strange sound in the house and our cognitive machinery analyzes what it might be. If the conclusion is that it is a prowler in the house, we become frightened. But, now that we know more about the brain and nervous system, things appear much more complicated.

When we hear about the fight-or-flight response to danger, the reality is not simple. We are awakened by a strange sound in the house. A burglar? A disturbed intruder? Signals from the senses go both to the frontal lobe of the brain, where much of what we consider thinking takes place, and to the amygdala and hippocampus, two structures in the limbic system, located between the hindbrain (the swelling at the top of the spinal cord responsible for repetitive functions such as walking) and the frontal lobe. The limbic system is the home of many structures in the brain involved in the handling of emotion, and these two structures, the amygdala and hippocampus, have access to sensory signals that connote danger. We begin being frightened when the sensors deliver signals that the amygdala and hippocampus detect as possible danger, but before the cortex can analyze the data. Another structure in the limbic system, named the hypothalamus, starts the well-known fight-or-flight response, with heart rate and blood pressure increasing, circulation flowing toward large muscles and away from the gut, and breathing slowing. Still another structure, the cingulate cortex, tones the large muscles, freezes unrelated movements, and causes our face to assume a fearful expression. And the locus coreulus releases norepinephrine, focusing our attention and prioritizing our knowledge and memories. This is all automatic. Later, when the cortex reaches its conclusion, it may turn all of this off if the noise is simply the dog, who can't seem to learn that he can't open the refrigerator. Alternately, it may reinforce the response. Interestingly, emotions often lead, not follow, our System 2 thinking. This rapid response ability is clearly valuable to us as a species, because the sooner we take action, the better, even if the alarm is false.

In 1994, Robert Sapolsky, author of my present favorite book, *Behave*, wrote another very readable book entitled *Why Zebras Don't Get Ulcers*. It does a wonderful job of communicating cognitive science, particularly about the fight-or-flight response, to nonspecialists. The reason for the title is that zebras are wired differently than we are, at least when it comes to the flight instinct. If they sense a lion stalking them, or especially charging them, the flight system rapidly turns on and they are instantly running. But when they no longer sense the lion, they immediately return to grazing. We humans, instead, think and worry about our equivalent of lions before they appear and long after we realize they are no longer considering us for dinner. The book is mostly about the costs of this stress, which Sapolsky blames on our zebra wiring. (He does make it plain in the book that we now know that ulcers are a result of bacteria rather than stress, but it is a good title nonetheless.)

I couldn't help but think that a slow form of this fight-or-flight behavior might explain why we often form such a negative first impression of a person, even though subsequent experience slowly teaches us that we were wrong. It might be why emotions play a strong role in creativity and innovation. When one is working on complex problems, the action is slower than when one is awakened by an unknown sound. But while System 2 thinking is grinding away, the brain still produces feelings: sometimes of joy, but also of depression, fear, frustration, and other such mental states that can negatively impact our work, or even life. If we are afraid of the lion that is chasing us during a two-year project, we may become increasingly stressed and go for a traditional noncreative solution rather than exploring the possibilities for a radically improved one.

Unfortunately, scientific research, outside of what is being done by cognitive scientists, tends to avoid the topic of emotion because of its complexity. Rigorous research demands that experiments be repeatable and that the results be measurable. Academic psychology in the first half of the twentieth century was dominated by behaviorists like Ivan Pavlov and B. F. Skinner, who considered behavior to be a simple response to stimuli. They were not sure how to handle emotions. They did most of their experiments with animals such as rats, pigeons, cats, and dogs. If one runs a rat through a maze, does something to the rat, and then runs it through the maze again, one can quantitatively measure changes in its behavior and be somewhat confident in the ability to replicate the experiment. But how about using humans as experimental subjects? How do you keep your subjects from becoming annoyed with running the maze and going home? Imagine the loss in simplicity if one tries to do an experimental investigation of teenagers falling in love. Where is the repeatability? Where is the quantification? The cognitive psychologists who now dominate research have so far been hesitant to delve deeply into emotion, and this may be a reason why our models and our understanding of the mechanisms of emotion seem so inadequate.

On the other hand, I have been fascinated by the recent ascendency of what is called behavioral economics. In the early days of the field of economics, the responses of individual people to money was considered more significant than in recent years, where economic theory has become more like a physical science, in that it is based on data, statistical trends, and mathematical models. The behavioral economists have countered this trend. One of my favorite authors is Dan Ariely, a professor of psychology and behavioral science at Duke University, who has written books such as *Predictably Irrational, The Upside of Irrationality,* and *The Honest Truth about Dishonesty.* The books are based on the seemingly irrational thoughts and actions of people one would think to be highly rational, backed up by experiments involving large numbers of people.

Happily, behavioral economics has made it to the big time, resulting in Nobel Prizes in economics to Richard Thaler and Vernon Smith, as well as Kahneman, who we know about. Thaler is given credit for the concept of nudging (there is a book by him called *Nudge*), and Smith is an experimental economist who tests out how market theories work in practice. Although traditional economics still rules the show, it is being increasingly affected by the behavioral economists, because when people are involved in situations that cannot be perfectly modeled by mathematics and science and data is questionable, emotions become paramount.

Because of its fuzziness, psychological theory that deals more directly with emotion is often given the back seat by contemporary researchers. For instance, although they are alive and well in our culture and important viewpoints in therapy, the theories of Sigmund Freud, his followers, and humanistic psychologists such as Carl Rogers and Abraham Maslow are not presently given the same amount of attention as cognitive and behavioral psychology. We will not go far into the theories of such "ancients," but their conclusions are worth mentioning here, because they do give importance to feelings and because they are still prominent in many theories of creativity. Still, the pendulum has swung toward understanding human behavior as it exists, rather than as it should be, just as the treatment of worrisome behavior has swung toward drugs and away from talk therapy.

FREUD AND JUNG

Much of Freudian theory is based upon conflicts between the id (the instinctive animal part of ourselves), the ego (the socially aware and conscious aspect), and the superego (the moralistic portion that forbids and prohibits). The motivating force in the Freudian model is the id, which resides in the unconscious and is concerned with satisfying our needs. According to Freud, ideas originating in the unconscious must be subjected to the scrutiny of the ego, which may reject them because we cannot realistically carry them out, and the superego, which may reject them because we should not have let ourselves have such ideas in the first place. If these ideas are rejected, they will either be completely repressed or they will contribute to neurotic behavior because of unresolved conflict. If they are accepted, they will be admitted to the conscious mind. This acceptance may be accompanied by anxiety, since once the ego and superego identify with an idea, one can be hurt by its rejection. If the ego and superego are overly selective, relatively few creative ideas will reach the conscious mind. If they are not selective enough, a torrent of highly innovative but extremely impractical ideas will emerge.

Since Freud's death in 1939, his theory has been elaborated upon by his followers. A good example of this can be seen in a book by Lawrence S. Kubie (1896–1973), *Neurotic Distortion of the Creative Process,* in which he utilized the Freudian concept of the preconscious in his model of creative thinking. He relegated the subconscious portions of creative thought and problem-solving to this preconscious, reserving the unconscious for unsettled conflicts and repressed impulses. In this model, the preconscious mental processes are hindered both by the conscious and the unconscious processes. As Kubie states: "Preconscious processes are assailed from both sides. From one side they are nagged and prodded into rigid and distorted symbols by unconscious drives which are oriented away from reality and which consist of rigid compromise formations, lacking in fluid inventiveness. From the other side they are driven by literal conscious purpose, checked and corrected by conscious retrospective critique."

Like Freud, Kubie has a model of the mind in which creative thinking is inhibited by the conscious ego and superego and in which creativity occurs at least partly below the conscious level. However, neuroses play a much more villainous role in Kubie's model than in Freud's. Although they are not given much emphasis in today's thinking about creativity, neuroses still play a role in talk therapy and are sometimes discussed in the literature.

THE HUMANISTIC PSYCHOLOGISTS

Humanistic psychologists, who focus on the individual, agree that creativity is a response to basic inner needs, but they have a somewhat broader hierarchy of desires than the Freudians. They maintain that people create in order to grow and to fulfill themselves, as well as to solve conflicts and to answer the cravings of the id. They are more concerned with reaching upward and outward. Carl Rogers (1902–1987), in the article "Toward a Theory of Creativity" in *Creativity and Its Cultivation*, writes:

> The mainspring of creativity appears to be the same tendency which we discover so deeply as the curative force in psychotherapy—man's tendency to actualize himself, to become his potentialities. By this I mean the directional

trend which is evident in all organic and human life—the urge to expand, extend, develop, mature—the tendency to express and activate all the capacities of the organism, to the extent that such activation enhances the organism or the self. This tendency may become deeply buried under layer after layer of encrusted psychological defenses; it may be hidden behind elaborate facades which deny its existence; it is my belief, however, based on my experience, that it exists in every individual and awaits only the proper conditions to be released and expressed.

When I joined the Stanford faculty in 1966, Abraham Maslow, another humanistic psychologist, was very visible because of his development of the hierarchy of needs. He will be mentioned occasionally in the following pages, because his is a simple and believable theory that is still used in business schools and elsewhere to help understand people's motivations.

The humanistic psychologists feel that the creative person is emotionally healthy and sensitive to both the needs and the capabilities of the unconscious, and uses this to produce creative ideas. As in Freud's theory, the creative person possesses a strong ego and a realistic superego, which allow prolific conceptualizing and relative freedom from distracting neuroses.

From the theories of the Freudians and humanists, we can arrive at several interesting and believable conclusions:

1. Humans create for reasons of inner drive, whether it be for purposes of conflict resolution, self-fulfillment, or both. They can, of course, also create for other reasons, such as money.
2. At least part of creativity occurs in a part of the mind that is below the conscious level.

3. Although creativity and neuroses may stem from the same source, creativity tends to flow best in the absence of neuroses.
4. The conscious mind, or ego, is a control valve on creativity.
5. Creativity can provoke anxieties.

What can we conclude about creativity from other fields of psychology? Our handling of the perceptual blocks discussed in the previous chapter can benefit from the insights of the cognitive psychologists. Better understanding of the brain's function can result in an improved ability to use it in new ways. Behaviorists tell us about the effects of reward and punishment, and the social psychologists remind us of the powerful influence of friends, colleagues, and public opinion on our actions. We will be discussing such things more in chapters eight and nine. Neurophysiologists and pharmacologists are also learning about the importance of the physiological state of the brain and coming up with methods of altering brain behavior chemically (an approach to modifying creativity that is as yet highly controversial but not about to disappear).

Let us now turn to some specific examples of emotional blocks so that we can become clearer on their causes and characteristics. These blocks may interfere with our ability to explore and manipulate ideas and with our ability to conceptualize fluently and flexibly. They can also prevent us from communicating ideas to others in a manner that will gain them acceptance. A few of these blocks are:

1. Fear of making a mistake, failing, or taking a risk
2. Inability to tolerate ambiguity, an overriding desire for security and order, no appetite for chaos

3. Preference for judging ideas rather than generating them
4. Inability to relax, incubate, and sleep on it
5. Lack of challenge (problem fails to engage interest) or excessive zeal (over-motivation to succeed quickly)
6. Inability to distinguish reality from fantasy

FEAR OF TAKING A RISK

Fear of making a mistake, failing, or taking a risk is perhaps the most general and common emotional block. Most of us have grown up being rewarded when we produce the right answer and punished when we make a mistake. When we fail, we are made to realize that we have let others down. Similarly, we are taught to live safely (a bird in the hand is worth two in the bush, a penny saved is a penny earned) and avoid risk whenever possible. Obviously, when you produce and try to sell a creative idea, you are taking a risk: of making a mistake, failing, making an ass of yourself, losing money, hurting yourself, or whatever.

This type of fear is to a certain extent realistic. Something new is usually a threat to the status quo, and is therefore resisted with appropriate pressure upon its creator. The risks involved with innovation often can result in real hardship. Far be it from me to suggest that people should not be realistic in assessing the costs of creativity. For instance, I spend a great amount of time attempting to explain to students that the process of making money from a commercially practical idea seems to require at least eight years, quite a bit of physical and emotional degradation, and often the sacrifice of such things as marriages and food. However, as I also try to explain, the fears that inhibit conceptualization are often not based on a realistic assumption of the consequences. Certainly, a slightly far-out idea submitted as an answer to a class assignment is not going to result in loss of life, marriage, or net worth. The only possible difficulty would arise if I, the teacher, were annoyed with the answer, and I happen to like such responses from students. The fear involved here is a more generalized fear of taking a chance, and since undergraduates are still hooking up their prefrontal cortex—the last part of the brain to complete its connections, and which depends heavily on learning by experience—I think students should be experimenting more with their brains. They need to see what type of thinking is more rewarding to them, as well as what they are really good at.

One of the better ways of overcoming fear of failure is to realistically assess the possible negative consequences of an idea. As is sometimes asked, "What are your catastrophic expectations?" If you have an idea for a better bicycle lock and are considering quitting your job and founding a small business based on the lock and a not-yet-conceived product line to go with it, the risks are considerable, unless you happen to have large sums of money and important commercial contacts. If you invent a new method of flight (say, feather wings held together with wax), there may also be significant risks in perfecting the product. However, if you think of a new way to schedule your day, paint your bathroom, or relate to others in your dormitory, the risks are considerably less.

But there are real risks in creativity. Many—it seems like most—Stanford engineering students these days are thinking about starting a company. I think they are doing this because, judging from the successful examples, it seems like a quick and relatively easy path to success and wealth. But a look at the failures, estimated to be 70 to 90 percent of such ventures, reveals that a company's success depends on many factors, including whether they are venture-capital backed and if they are technology driven. In his book *Innovation and Entrepreneurship*, Peter Drucker explains why these failures are not considered more often. Entrepreneurs are, and must be, highly confident in their abilities and the value of their ideas. Because they are a sample of one, they believe statistics obviously do not apply to them—just like how I ignore the statistics that tell me about my life expectancy.

If students come to me with a great idea, I encourage them to show it to a lot of professionals with experience in starting companies, marketing, manufacturing, and everything else I can think of. If they want to drop out of school and start their company, I tell them that they should get their degree first, because if their idea is so terrific and unique, it will probably keep a couple of years while they develop it. But if they are not married and do not have young kids, if they have done the proper due diligence, and of course if I like their idea, I tell them to charge ahead. If they are forty, married with three kids who will probably go to college, successful and experienced in their job, and like their work, I tell them to think about it more. If they are sixty, I ask them whether they have enough money to support themselves and their dependents until they are one hundred.

Many people who teach or work in small or growing companies preach that failure is necessary for an entrepreneur. I have watched many people do this. One of them likes to put quotes on his e-mail messages; a recent one read: "Success is the ability to go from one failure to another with no loss of enthusiasm"— Sir Winston Churchill.

Many, if not most, of these people have either not gone all-in on start-ups (that is, they have operated from behind a paycheck, which is a clever way to begin if you can pull it off), have never failed, or have failed but then rebounded with a large success.

Often start-ups fall short of the goals of their founders. I was part of a start-up myself soon after I came to Stanford. One of my best friends from college was on the Stanford Medical School faculty when I arrived and was an immunologist who loved research. He had developed an accurate and low-cost method of diagnosing allergies from a blood sample, rather than from the standard expensive and somewhat painful scratch test. He wanted to start a company based on this, and since we knew each other well and I had management experience, he wanted me to quit the professor job I had just accepted and join him as president of his new company, so that he could be vice president of research and invent even more wonderful things.

I didn't feel good about quitting a job I had just accepted or being president of a company—a position I had no experience in, since my previous management roles had been in the air force and the Jet Propulsion Laboratory, which was funded by the government and run by Caltech. But I agreed to spend some time looking after the development of his test into a saleable product. So he quit his job, raised some money, and off we went, he temporarily as president, and I as vice president for product development—or whatever I wanted to call myself.

I will say here that the company is considered a success, since it was sold to a large corporation in Japan and we all made a little money from it (my friend made a lot, but he certainly earned it). But I did not like the experience. I didn't like the venture capitalist who was on our board alongside my friend and me. He so obviously wanted to fire my friend, since he viewed the company as something ripe for a quick sale that would benefit his investors, whereas my friend wanted to help all of the poor people in the world who had allergies. We also hired the wrong person for president and had to get rid of him. I was especially frustrated when we came up against the allergy-treatment community, which was making considerable money from scratch tests. Doctors resisted switching from the standard tests, which they were more familiar with and for which they charged hundreds of dollars. We figured that with some development and some help from medical professionals, my friend's test could be administered for tens of dollars. The venture capitalist on our board was obviously thinking of a cost much closer to that of the scratch test.

Also, our money was more limited than we thought—a new experience for me given my government-funded aerospace background. Looking back, we were terribly naive. But I felt fortunate that I had learned that I did not like the game of starting a company. From outside it looked glamorous, but from inside I learned, with minimal sacrifice, that it was not for me. I have come to believe that before one starts a startup, one should work in one.

If I am becoming a bit negative here, it is probably due to my overexposure to Silicon Valley, an area that has flourished economically because of start-ups and contains a large number of people who have become legends through their acquired wealth. But it has also acquired outrageous house prices and serious traffic, parking, and other transportation problems that have resulted in long commutes, boring architecture, and constant building. I have also talked to too many people whose start-ups have failed, or who have been successful only to find that their company owns them and they have altogether too little time to spend with their family and to enjoy other good things in life.

I have spent much of my life thinking about creativity and innovation. I believe in them, and that, in general, all of us would benefit from a bit more creativity. In my experience, people do not often realistically assess the probable consequences of a creative act. Either they blithely ignore any consequences, or their general fear of failure causes them to attach excessive importance to any mistake, no matter how minor it will appear in the eyes of future historians. Often the potential negative consequences of exposing a creative idea can be easily endured. If you have an idea that seems risky, it is well worth the time to do a brief study of the possible consequences. During the study, you should include catastrophic expectations by assuming everything goes badly, and then look at the result. By doing this, it will become apparent whether you want to take the risk or not.

> **Exercise:** Next time you are having difficulty deciding whether to push a creative idea, write a short (two pages) catastrophic expectations report. In it, detail as well as you can precisely what would happen to you if everything went wrong. By making such information explicit and facing it, you swap your fear of failure for analytical capability—a good trade.

NO APPETITE FOR CHAOS

The fear of making a mistake is, of course, rooted in insecurity, which most people suffer from to some extent. Such insecurities are also responsible for the next emotional block: the inability to tolerate ambiguity, overriding desire for order, and lack of appetite for chaos. Once again, some element of this block is rational. I am not suggesting that in order to be creative you should shun order and live in a totally chaotic situation. I am talking more of an excessive fondness for order in all things. The solution of a complex problem is a messy process. Rigorous and logical techniques are often necessary but not sufficient. You must usually wallow in misleading and ill-fitting data, hazy and difficult-to-test concepts, opinions, values, and other such untidy quantities. In a sense, problem-solving is bringing order to chaos. A desire for order is therefore necessary. However, the ability to tolerate chaos is a must.

We all know compulsive people, those who must have everything always in its place and who become quite upset if the order of their physical lives is violated. If this trait carries over into a person's mental process, she is severely impaired in her ability to work with certain types of problems. One reason for extreme ordering of the physical environment is efficiency. Another may be the aesthetic satisfaction of precise physical relationships. However, another reason is insecurity. If your underwear is precisely folded, you have control over your underwear and thus there is one less thing out of control and therefore threatening. I do not actually care how your underwear is stored. However, if your thoughts are precisely folded, you are probably a fairly limited problem solver. The process of bringing widely disparate thoughts together cannot work too well because your mind is not going to allow them to coexist long enough to combine.

JUDGING RATHER THAN GENERATING IDEAS

The next emotional block, the preference for judging ideas rather than generating them, is also the "safe" way to go. Judgment, criticism, tough-mindedness, and practicality are of course essential in problem-solving. No one wins if the process of developing a creative output results in junk. However, if applied too early or too indiscriminately in the problem-solving process, judgment is extremely detrimental to conceptualization.

In problem-solving, analysis, judgment, and synthesis are three distinct types of thinking. In analysis, there is usually a right answer. I am an engineer: if you pay me to tell you how large a beam is needed to hold up a patio roof, you rightly expect the answer. Fortunately, I know how to analyze such things mathematically and can give it to you, and hopefully I know enough about my analysis that I can also give you a reasonable safety factor. The next option, judgment, is generally used in a problem where there are several answers and one must be chosen. A court case is a good example: judgments about guilt or innocence are made by sensible people, but the situation is sufficiently complex that disagreements can occur. Synthesis is even more of a multi-answer situation. A design problem (for example, design a better way to store and serve ice cream at home) has an endless number of answers and there are few rigorous techniques to help in deciding between them.

If you analyze or judge too early in the problem-solving process, you will reject many ideas. This is detrimental for two reasons. First, newly formed ideas are fragile and imperfect—they need time to mature and acquire the detail needed to make them believable. Second, as I will discuss later, ideas often lead to other ideas. Many techniques of conceptualization, such as brainstorming, depend on maintaining far-out ideas long enough to let them mature and spawn other, more realistic ideas. It is sometimes difficult to hold onto such ideas because people generally do not want to be suspected of harboring impractical thoughts. However, in conceptualization one should not judge too quickly.

The judgment of ideas, unfortunately, is an extremely popular and rewarded pastime. One finds more newspaper space devoted to judgment (opinion columns, political analyses, editorials, etc.) than to the creation of ideas. In the university, much scholarship is devoted to judgment rather than creativity. One finds that people who heap negative criticism upon all ideas they encounter are often heralded for their practical sense and sophistication. Bad-mouthing everyone else's concepts is in fact a cheap way to attempt to demonstrate your own mental superiority.

If you are a professional idea person, your criticism tends to be somewhat more friendly. Professional designers are often much more receptive to the ideas of our students than non-design-oriented faculty members. Professional problem solvers have a working understanding of the difficulty in having ideas, and they have a respect for new concepts, even if they are flawed.

If you are a compulsive idea judger, you should realize that this is a habit that may exclude ideas from your own mind before they have had time to bear fruit. In judging, you are taking little risk (unless you are excluding ideas that could benefit you) and are perhaps feeding your ego with the thrill of being able to criticize the outputs of others, but you are also sacrificing some of your own creative potential.

INABILITY OR UNWILLINGNESS TO INCUBATE

Whether you believe that there is such a thing as unconscious thought or not, there is general agreement that answers to problems often suddenly appear in the mind, usually after thinking about the problem in some depth and often at strange times. One maddeningly familiar phenomenon to many people is a late answer to an important problem. You may work for days or weeks on a problem, complete it, and go on to other activities. Then, at some seemingly random point in time, a better answer appears. Since the original problem was probably completed in order to reach a deadline, this new answer often only serves to annoy you. It seems to result from an incubation process that was occurring in the mind. I have found in my own case that this process works and is reliable. I have the confidence to think hard about a problem (charging up my unconscious) and then forget about it for a period of time. When I begin work on it again, new answers are usually present.

Many symptoms of this incubation process are common. There is a widespread belief among students that they do their best work just before deadlines. If, in fact, they work on the material when they receive it long enough to store the data in their unconscious, then incubation can occur and a better solution may emerge at a later time. Incubation does often seem to produce the right answer at the appropriate time. Students often claim to have come up with a winning idea the morning that the project is due, after struggling futilely with the problem for days.

You should allow the mind to struggle with problems over time. Incubation is important in problem-solving, and it is poor planning not to allow adequate time for it. It is also important to be able to relax in the midst of problem-solving. Your overall compulsiveness is less fanatical when you are relaxed, and the brain is more likely to deal with seemingly silly combinations of thoughts. If you are never relaxed, your brain is usually on guard against nonserious activities, with resulting difficulties in the type of thinking necessary for fluent and flexible conceptualization.

LACK OF CHALLENGE VERSUS EXCESSIVE ZEAL

Lack of challenge and excessive zeal are opposite villains. You cannot do your best on a problem unless you are motivated. Professional problem solvers learn to be motivated somewhat by money and future work that may come their way if they succeed. To stay motivated, a challenge must be present for at least some of the time or the process ceases to be rewarding. On the other hand, excessive motivation to succeed, especially to succeed quickly, can inhibit the creative process. The tortoise-and-the-hare phenomenon is often apparent in problem-solving. The person who thinks up the simple elegant solution, although she may take longer to do so, often wins. As in the race, the tortoise depends upon an inconsistent performance from the rabbit. And if the rabbit spends so little time on conceptualization that he merely chooses the first answers that occur, such inconsistency is almost guaranteed.

REALITY AND FANTASY

The problems of lack of access to areas of imagination, lack of imaginative control, and inability to distinguish reality from fantasy will be discussed in more detail in chapter six. In brief, the imagination attempts to create objects and events. The creative person needs to be able to control his or her imagination and needs complete access to it. If all senses are not represented, the imagination cannot serve as well as it otherwise could. All the senses need to be used, not only to attack problems involving them but also to make imagery more powerful. If you think purely verbally, for instance, there will be little imagery available for solving problems concerning shapes and forms. If visual imagery is also present, the imagination will be much more useful, but still not as potent as if the other senses are also present. You can usually imagine a ballpark much more vividly if you are able to recall the smell of the grass, the taste of the peanuts and beer, the feel of the seats and the sunshine, and the sounds of the crowd.

The creative person must be able not only to vividly form complete images but also to manipulate them. Creativity requires the manipulation and recombination of experience. An imagination that cannot manipulate experience is limiting to the conceptualizer. You should be able to imagine a volcano being born in your ballpark, or an airplane landing in it, or the ballpark shrinking as the grass simultaneously turns purple, if you are to make maximum use of your imagination. Chapter six will contain some exercises to allow you to gauge your ability to control your imagination, as well as discussions on how to strengthen the mental muscle used in imagining.

The creative person needs the ability to fantasize freely and vividly, yet must be able to distinguish reality from fantasy. If fantasies become too realistic, they may be less controllable. When I first began teaching creativity courses, I drew from a 1955 book entitled *Put Your Mother on the Ceiling*, written by Richard de Mille. It was written for children but turned out to be a good resource for Stanford design students. The exercises required imagining all sorts of uncomfortable things—like inhaling fish, fire, dry leaves, and sand—and, of course, putting your mother on the ceiling. The object was to practice distinguishing reality from fantasy, a knack that is useful in creativity.

It would certainly be uncomfortable to inhale sand. Whether you can imagine the feeling of inhaling sand depends somewhat upon your ability to fantasize. No danger exists from imagining such an act, and any pain felt is imagined, not real. However, if your fantasies are confused with reality, it can be very difficult to fantasize such things. The imagination is extremely powerful because it can go beyond reality. But in order to do this, the imagination must be set free of the constraints placed upon real acts and events.

OF FLOW AND ANGST

Mihaly Csikszentmihalyi is distinguished professor of psychology and management at the Claremont Graduate University. He has interviewed a large number of creative people and concluded that when they are at their most creative, they are in a state he calls flow. He has written several books on this, notably one entitled *Flow*. He has found that, once in such a state, these people are completely consumed by their task. Time passes seemingly without notice and they are in a positive, perhaps even joyous mood. Most of us have experienced this, sometimes at work, sometimes at play, when the process of creating something new is so captivating that it pushes our fears, cares, and worries aside. This state of flow is certainly something to be sought, since it is not only a fulfilling experience but also consistent with the belief that negative emotions inhibit our creativity by influencing us toward the tried, true, and traditional. But we might ask about all of the famous creative people we hear about who have apparently lived fairly tortured lives.

Like most people, I have read the books and seen the movies about Vincent van Gogh, Wolfgang Amadeus Mozart, Oscar Wilde, Anne Sexton, and other highly creative people who apparently led traumatic and unhappy lives. But I do not personally know people in this category. This may be because I live a shallow life. It is also because I have not sought deeply disturbed people for friends, and because I have spent my professional life in organizations that, like most organizations, are not comfortable in including them. If the portrait of Mozart in the movie *Amadeus* was accurate, he would have had trouble as a professor of music at Stanford. Similarly, the commonly held impression of Van Gogh would have been a bit much for the art department.

I believe that people at the edge of the norm can be and have been highly creative. A recent study concluded that outstanding painters are in fact toward the ends of the distribution. Another study hypothesizes that those with bipolar disorder visualize in different ways than others. There are too many stories of eccentric-to-psychopathic geniuses to completely disbelieve them. However, my friends, colleagues, and past acquaintances include large numbers of people who are extremely successful in a wide variety of fields, including the arts, and who have won such things as Nobel, MacArthur, Pulitzer, and Fields prizes, Oscars, Tonys, presidential medals, and memberships and achievement awards from a bewildering number of learned, honorary, and professional societies.

Presumably, they are creative. They are, as one would expect, unusually bright, curious, motivated, and sometimes lucky. However, they are disturbingly normal and not unusually tortured. They tend to interrupt their flow to worry about their kids, try to outwit the raccoons destroying their lawn, watch television, and wonder what they are going to do next in life.

Because of the directions my life has taken, my personal involvement with creativity has been in activities that take years to come to fruition, rather than days or hours. Complex technical projects cannot be done in a week, and creativity is necessary the entire time. I have to teach a course a few times before I know how good and creative it is. Counting procrastination, it takes years for me to write a book. My friends with Nobel Prizes and equivalent have spent years in education and in the field. Such time periods require reasonably stable people. Not all of that time can be spent in flow. I was somewhat in flow the other day while working on this book, but my cursed computer crashed. I not only worked myself into a fit of fury trying to figure out what was ailing it, but got so steamed that I necessarily took the next day off to work on restoring an old Peterbilt truck. This instantly restored flow, even though not everyone would agree that it was highly creative.

During a creative activity, there are usually times of flow. How do we increase these times? Later in the book we will talk about motivation, but the short answer is that we are more likely to be creative and in a state of flow if we love the things we are doing. This is, of course, not an entirely useful answer. As an example, I am probably most in a state of flow (and perhaps most creative) when making things with my hands. Unfortunately, such activities do not seem to bring me other things I want in life. I also seem to be fascinated by organizational politics and drawn to tilting at windmills. I have therefore spent much time in jobs in which I have organizational responsibility—and which seem to involve hassle rather than flow. However, there are still times in such jobs when everything is going just right. The personal rewards in terms of pride in accomplishment, and excitement in continuing the chase, are great when one achieves flow.

CHAPTER 4

....

Cultural and Environmental Blocks

WE ARE MEMBERS OF MANY CULTURES. THERE ARE NOT ONLY national cultures, but cultures unique to regions, religious beliefs, age, ethnicity, values, and other characteristics. The trouble these groups have in understanding each other causes problems ranging from religious and racial wars to business failures to less-than-optimal vacation travel. Insensitivity to cultural factors inhibits creativity, while sensitivity can lead to success in solving problems. Some examples of cultural blocks within the United States are the following beliefs:

- Taboos must be observed
- Fantasy and reflection are a waste of time, lazy, or even crazy
- Playfulness is for children only
- Problem-solving is serious business and humor is out of place
- Reason, logic, numbers, utility, and practicality are good
- Feeling, intuition, qualitative judgments, and pleasure are bad

- Any problem can be solved by scientific thinking and lots of money
- Everyone should be like me
- Cyber is better
- Tradition is preferable to change
- Money is all-important
- Bigger is better

We also suffer from conceptual blocks due to the environment in which we solve problems, including the following:

- Distractions, such as phones and other easy intrusions
- A lack of cooperation and trust among colleagues
- Autocratic bosses who value only their own ideas and do not reward others (see chapters eight and nine)
- A lack of support to bring ideas into action (see chapters eight and nine)

CULTURAL BLOCKS

Let us discuss cultural blocks first. We will begin by working a problem that will make the message clearer.

Exercise: Assume that a steel pipe is imbedded in the concrete floor of a bare room as shown in the picture on the following page. The inside diameter is .06" larger than the diameter of a ping-pong ball (1.50") that is resting gently at the bottom of the pipe. You are one of a group of six people in the room, along with the following objects:

100' of clothesline
A carpenter's hammer
A chisel

A box of Wheaties
A file
A wire coat hanger
A monkey wrench
A light bulb

List as many ways as you can think of in five minutes to get the ball out of the pipe without damaging the ball, tube, or floor.

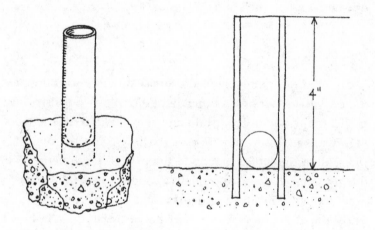

J. P. Guilford, who was a pioneer in the study of creativity, spoke a great deal about fluency and flexibility of thought. Fluency refers to the number of concepts one produces in a given length of time. If you are a fluent thinker, you have a long list of methods for retrieving the ball from the pipe. However, quantity is only part of the game. Flexibility refers to the diversity of the ideas generated. If you are a flexible thinker, you should have come up with a wide variety of methods. If you thought of filing the wire coat hanger in two, flattening the resulting ends, and making large tweezers to retrieve the ball, you came up with a solution to the problem, but a fairly common one. If you thought of smashing the handle of the hammer with the monkey wrench and using the resulting splinters to retrieve the ball, you were demonstrating a bit more flexibility of thought, since one does not usually think of using a tool as a source of splinters. If you managed to do something with the Wheaties, you are an even more flexible thinker.

Did you think of having your group urinate in the pipe? If you did not think of this, why not? The answer is probably a cultural block, in this case a taboo, since urinating in public is frowned upon in the United States.

Taboos

I have used this ping-pong ball exercise with many groups, and the response is not only a function of the culture but also of the particular people in the group and the ambiance of the meeting. A mixed group newly convened in elegant surroundings will seldom think of urinating in the pipe. Even if members in the group do come up with this as a solution, they will keep very quiet about it. A group of students or an all-male group of people who know each other and are drinking beer will probably have a more outspoken reaction. The importance of this answer is not that urinating in the pipe is necessarily the best of all solutions (although it is certainly a good one), but rather that cultural taboos can remove entire families of solutions from the ready grasp of the problem solver. Taboos therefore are conceptual blocks. This is not a tirade against taboos. Taboos usually are directed against acts that would cause displeasure to certain members of a society. They therefore can play a positive cultural role. However, it is the acts themselves that would offend. If imagined, rather than carried out, they are not harmful. Therefore, when working on problems within the privacy of your own mind, you do not have to be concerned with the violation of taboos.

If you want an example of the power of taboos, see if you can find a copy of a fascinating (and often out-of-print) book, produced in 1966 by the Cornell Department of Architecture and written by Alexander Kira, entitled *The Bathroom, Criteria for Design*. It is an analysis and critique of the Western bathroom, and it concludes that the bathroom is very poorly designed indeed—so poorly that the book is entertaining to read. It is not altogether surprising to read that bathtubs are extremely dangerous as well as uncomfortable and that toilets neither do a good job of catching male urine streams nor place one in a good configuration for elimination. But the extent of material in the book makes one wonder why we stick with our traditional models. The answer, of course, is that bathing and elimination are slightly taboo topics in our culture. We do them in private and don't want to talk about them much. Urinals are obviously effective, but we do not want to make such a visible revolution in our home bathrooms by swapping them in for toilets. Bidets are useful, but most American bathrooms do not contain them. This may be partly to save on floor space and plumbing, but I doubt this, because most French bathrooms do have a bidet, often with similar space and plumbing to ours. I think that it mostly reflects the reluctance of our society to admit to the need to apply water to genitalia.

Fantasy and Reflection Are a Waste of Time and Playfulness Is for Children Only

These two blocks are challenged by quite a bit of evidence that indicates that fantasy, reflection, and mental playfulness are essential to good conceptualization. They are properties that seem to exist in children and then unfortunately are to some extent socialized out of people in our culture. A four-year-old who amuses himself with an imaginary friend, with whom he shares his experiences and communicates, is cute. A thirty-year-old with a similar imaginary friend is something else. Daydreaming and woolgathering are often considered to be symptoms of an unproductive person. But opinion is changing on this. In fact, I recently read an article called "The Benefits of Mind-Wandering" in the *Wall Street Journal*. In it, scientist Robert Sapolsky points out that we spend up to half our time having thoughts unrelated to what we should be doing. But he argues that this might be valuable work for the brain, because, among other reasons, "truly creative solutions to tough problems are often found by following a wandering path."

Environmental and cultural blocks are somewhat interrelated. People can fantasize much more easily in a supportive environment. I used to frequently ask students to fantasize as part of a design task, and when assigned fantasy they did quite well. However, they tended to feel quite guilty if they spent their time fantasizing if it was not an assigned part of the problem, since it often seemed to be a diversion. Nevertheless, if you are attempting to solve a problem having to do with bickering children, is it not worth the time and effort to imagine a situation in which your children do not bicker and then examine the situation closely to see how it works? If you are designing a new recreational vehicle, should you not fantasize about what it would be like to use that vehicle?

Many psychologists have concluded that children are more creative than adults. One explanation for this is that the adult is so much more aware of practical constraints. Another explanation, which I believe, is that our culture trains mental playfulness, fantasy, and reflectiveness out of people by placing more stress on the value of channeled mental activities. We spend more time attempting to derive a better world directly from what we have than in imagining a better world and what it could be. Both are important.

Humor in Problem-Solving

Another cultural block is the idea that problem-solving is a serious business and humor is out of place. I mentioned Arthur Koestler before because he wrote about, among other topics, conceptualization. In an essay, "The Three Domains of Creativity," he identified these domains as artistic originality (which he called the "ah!" reaction), scientific discovery (the "aha!" reaction), and comic inspiration (the "ha ha!" reaction). He defined creative acts as the combination of previously unrelated structures in such a way that you get more out of the emergent whole than you have put in. He explained comic inspiration, for example, as stemming from "the interaction of two mutually exclusive associative contexts." As in artistic and scientific creativity, two ideas have to be brought together that are not ordinarily combined. This is one of the essentials of creative thinking. In the particular case of humor, according to Koestler, the interaction causes us "to perceive the situation in two self-consistent but habitually incompatible frames of reference." The joke teller typically starts a logical chain of events. The punch line then sharply cuts across the chain in a totally unexpected direction. The tension developed in the first line is therefore shown to be a put-on and, with its release, the audience laughs. Think of your favorite joke. Is Koestler's explanation of comic inspiration correct?

The critical point of interest here is that laughter may also greet an original idea. A concept may be so contrary to the logical progress of the problem, the precedent, or common intuition, that it may cause laughter. In fact, any answer to a problem releases tension. Your unbelievably insightful solution to a problem may therefore be greeted with giggles and hoots, not only from others but even from yourself.

Creative groups in which I have worked have been funny. So are creative people I know. Humor is present in all sorts of ways. It is important because not only is it inseparable from new and original solutions, but it decreases the perception of risk. The emotional blocks discussed in the previous chapter, such as fear of failure, are much less of a problem in a humorous atmosphere. Would you rather present a radical new idea to a group in good humor or one that is cold and completely analytical? I am not suggesting that creative activity is all fun, since it is fraught with frustration, detail work, and plain effort. However, humor is an essential ingredient of healthy conceptualization.

Reason and Intuition

The fifth and sixth cultural blocks on our list are the beliefs that reason, logic, numbers, utility, and practicality are good, but feeling, intuition, qualitative judgment, and pleasure are bad. Reason is good; but so, too, is intuition—especially if you are conceptualizing. This block against emotion and pleasure stems from our puritan heritage and our technology-based culture. It is extremely noticeable to me, since I work with large numbers of engineers and managers in situations where they must solve problems with a large amount of emotional content.

This block is particularly interesting because it has been affected by social changes that have occurred since I wrote the first edition of this book. Before the late 1960s, it was common to assign various mental activities and qualities by gender. It was thought that the female was sensitive, emotional, appreciative of the fine arts, and intuitive. The male was tough, physical, pragmatic, logical, and professionally productive. We now know that adhering to these constraints severely limited both sexes. Those interested in creativity knew it even then. Abraham Maslow described his findings about this block in his 1966 essay, "Emotional Blocks to Creativity."

One thing I haven't mentioned but have been interested in recently in my work with creative men (and uncreative men too) is the horrible fear of being called feminine or homosexual. If a man has been brought up in a tough environment, "feminine" can be applied to practically everything that's creative. Imagination, fantasy, color, poetry, music, tenderness, languishing, and romance are walled off as dangerous to the picture of his masculinity. Everything that's considered weak tends to be repressed in the typical masculine adult adjustment. But many of the things called weak are not weak at all.

The opposite of this block also existed, of course. Many women were culturally conditioned to be as uncomfortable about "masculine" traits (reason, logic, use of numbers, utility) as males were about "feminine" ones. But there was also a push against what was considered to be the unfeelingness of technology. In the early 1970s, when I wrote the first edition of this book, the United States was in a period in which the technological emphasis of our society was being blamed for many human difficulties. Those speaking out against this emphasis believed that feeling, intuition, and qualitative judgment were good and that reason, logic, numbers, utility, and practicality were not all that necessary.

In the 1970s, the period in the United States sometimes known as the sexual revolution (in reality, still ongoing to this day), gender roles generally were coming into question. At the time, intellectual stereotyping became much softer. Women were seeking and finding roles requiring toughness, quantitative thinking, and physical stamina, and men were accepting that they could win through increased sensitivity and reliance upon intuition. Since then, there has been continual experimentation and oscillation between traditional and modern roles. There is now some backlash against the tough woman and the sensitive man. Various influential individuals, groups, and religions are seeking to reestablish older relationships between the sexes, and there is much angst about resolving two-career families and child-rearing.

As far as creativity is concerned, the message is simple. Effective conceptualization requires the problem solver to be able to incorporate the use of reason and logic as well as intuition and feeling. The designer of physical things must be aesthetically sensitive if the quality of our world is going to improve, whether the designer happens to be male or female. Similarly, he or she must be able to view technology honestly and without disciplinary bias, whether from an art background or an engineering background. The business person must use intuition and the social scientist must use mathematics. The man must be sensitive and the woman strong, and vice versa.

Stuck on Left-Handed or Right-Handed Thinking

In reading the literature associated with conceptualization, one often encounters references to left- and right-handed thinking. This is discussed particularly well by Jerome Bruner in his book *On Knowing: Essays for the Left Hand*. The right hand has traditionally been linked to law, order, reason, logic, and mathematics, and the left with beauty, sensitivity, playfulness, feeling, openness, subjectivity, and imagery. The right hand has been symbolic of tools, disciplines, and achievement; the left with imagination, intuition, and subconscious thinking. In Bruner's words:

> The one the doer, the other the dreamer. The right is order and lawfulness, *le droit*. Its beauties are those of geometry and taut implication. Reaching for knowledge with the right hand is science. . . . Of the left hand we say that it is

awkward. . . . The French speak of the illegitimate descendant as being *à main gauche,* and though the heart is virtually at the center of the thoracic cavity, we listen for it on the left. Sentiment, intuition, bastardy. And should we say that reaching for knowledge with the left hand is art?

Oddly enough, this historical symbolic alignment of the two hands with two distinct types of thinking is somewhat consistent with some features of the brain. The left hemisphere of the brain, which controls the right hand, is strongly associated with speech and hearing and with analytical tasks such as solving an algebra problem. The right hemisphere, which controls the left hand, has particular strength in perception, synthesis of ideas, and aesthetic appreciation of art or music.

In the 1960s, a surgeon named Roger Sperry perfected a surgical procedure to decrease epileptic seizures in humans, following many experiments on animals. This procedure ultimately consisted of severing the corpus callosum, which is the largest structure connecting the right and left hemispheres of the brain. The procedure succeeded in eliminating the seizures, but also resulted in fascinating experiments showing that this procedure had essentially given the patient two brains, which operated in the above manner and sometimes did not communicate with each other. A well-known psychophysicist named Michael Gazzaniga, a student of Sperry's, has done a lot of additional work on this. For a while, this right-brain-left-brain theory was all the rage, as is common with simple explanations of brain functions, but it is no long taken that seriously by people who study the brain.

Still, it remains very much alive in folklore and arguments, and it is a handy way to describe two types of thinking that often seem estranged. C. P. Snow, in his Rede Lecture, "Two Cultures and the Scientific Revolution," spoke against the seemingly separate cultures of science and the humanities that often exist in universities. Fortunately, although there is some dominance of operation of the two halves of the brain, the overall wiring is very complex. If we were only operating on one side, we would not be maximizing our creative potential. The scientists who are responsible for breakthroughs in knowledge cannot operate entirely by extrapolating past work; they must utilize feelings also. Similarly, the humanists who disregard the logical are doomed to be ineffectual, even counterproductive, in influencing social actions.

An emphasis on either type of thinking to the disregard of the other is a cultural block. In the professional world, the focus is on right-handed thinking. It is easier to get money to support right-handed thinking than left-handed thinking. More parents want their children to be lawyers, doctors, or scientists than painters, poets, or musicians. Until the culture is willing to accept the equal importance of left- and right-handed thinking in both sexes, a large number of people will continue to suffer from this conceptual block.

Exercise: Put yourself into a left-handed thinking mode. Stay away from logic, order, mathematics, science. Think about your feelings, beauty, sadness, the inputs that are coming to your senses. You can probably do this better by placing yourself in a conducive environment, such as under a tree in the springtime or alone in your most comfortable chair. Then switch yourself into a right-handed mode by thinking of a detailed plan to make money out of one of your left-handed thoughts. Are you ambidextrous? Are you able to shift from one type of thinking to the other or, ideally, to do both at once? Or are you more comfortable with one type of thinking than the other?

The idea that any problem can be solved by scientific thinking and lots of money is of course a cultural one related to the emphasis on the importance of right-handed thinking. It is also interesting, because it exists partly as a result of a popular misconception about the scientific process. Science depends both on logical controlled progress (right-handed thinking) and breakthroughs, which are often necessarily a bit left-handed.

Primary and Secondary Creativity

Maslow, in his essay "Emotional Blocks to Creativity," discussed primary creativity, which he described as the "creativeness which comes out of the unconscious, and which is the source of new discovery (or real novelty) of ideas which depart from what exists at this point." This is the force behind the breakthroughs so necessary to science. He continues by speaking of what he calls secondary creativity, which he explains as follows: "I am used now to thinking of two kinds of science, and two kinds of technology. Science can be defined, if you want to, as a technique whereby uncreative people can create and discover, by working along with a lot of other people, by standing upon the shoulders of people who have come before them, by being cautious and careful, and so on. That I'll call secondary creativeness and secondary science."

It is easy to become confused as people talk about primary and secondary creativity, as well as right-handed and left-handed thinking. As Maslow states, both are necessary and both require high creativity. I don't use this separation, partly because I think it is impossible to separate creativity into two layers in such a reductive way. The present awesome progress in genetics and biochemistry, which includes a large amount of what Maslow would call secondary creativity, rests upon the discovery of RNA and DNA and their functions and structures, the product of primary creativity. Both are impressive. For years, I assigned James P. Watson's book *The Double Helix* to my classes, almost independently of what I was teaching. It is now an old book and carries some negative residue because a woman named Rosalind Franklin played a critical role in the project and yet was not included in the Nobel Prize. Even so, if you have not already read *The Double Helix,* forgive the sexism and do so. It is an intriguing book that talks about science in a way that is so contrary to many people's concept of the scientific method that it was very controversial when it first came out. It treats the discovery of the structure of DNA as a very human and very left-handed process. Watson and codiscoverer Francis Crick relied heavily on inspiration, iteration, and visualization. Even though they were superb biochemists, they had no precedent from which they could logically derive their structure and therefore relied heavily on left-handed thinking.

The US space effort during the 1960s, of which I was a tiny part, was extremely impressive and exemplified the power of science and technology. However, a great deal of secondary creativity and left-handed thinking was involved. Even such basic scientific decisions as whether to carry instruments to measure physical quantities or transport television cameras on the first lunar spacecraft were made in a left-handed way, since there was simply no way to make them with sheer logic. The design of the first spacecraft required a high degree of art—backed up, of course, by a great deal of analysis, detailed design, and sophisticated fabrication and development—because there was no precedent that the designers could logically draw upon.

Right-handed science and lots of money can only solve problems that are solely in the domain of understood phenomena. Problems with social and emotional content and high complexity, such as crime in cities, require everything from right-handed science to secondary creativity. We need breakthroughs *and* implementation.

Unfortunately, left-handed thinking and primary creativity are harder to explain and less predictable than right-handed thinking and secondary creativity. It is therefore more difficult to write proposals that will bring support for such activities. It is easier for me to secure funding to work on the application of some newly discovered scientific phenomena (even though the potential good of the application may be small, but publishable) than it is to find support for looking for a major breakthrough. In the first case, the funding agency and I can be quite confident of the detailed nature of the work that needs to be done, the approximate amount of money needed, the schedule, and the results. In the second, there is no such security. The funding agency must judge me on the basis of intangibles such as my previous performance, my motivations, and my knowledge. The second is more of a gamble than the first. Support for science, therefore, tends to be biased toward right-handed thinking, since most agencies handing out money must answer to someone and therefore tend to be somewhat conservative.

The vagueness of primary creativity and left-handed thinking, of course, also plagues those involved in the humanities and the social sciences. Many of the social sciences have sought to become more quantitative and rigorous in order to take better advantage of our cultural bias toward right-handed thinking. It is debatable whether this has been advantageous. Although an engineer, I am very sympathetic to the complaints of those in the humanities and social sciences as to the lack of monetary support they receive from our society. At one point in my education (after I had become an engineer), I was enrolled in art school. A painting teacher I knew would, from time to time, tell me that I had an excellent background for painting. His reasoning was economic. He believed that many painters were hampered in the beginning of their careers by the necessity of holding down low-paying and long-hour jobs in order to support their families. He figured that I should be able to support myself by doing engineering work part-time and would therefore have time and energy available to paint—a strange observation, but perhaps a true one. It is much easier for me to find support for my lifestyle than it is for friends of mine who want to write or paint as a primary occupation. The humanities and the social sciences are extremely vital in a mature society such as ours. Their importance is presently obscured by a massive cultural block.

Everybody Should Be Just Like Me

People have different viewpoints, value systems, and desires. They tend to reinforce this by associating with others with similar opinions. Humans are quite tribal in this way, and large collections of people, such as nations, consist of a large number of groups who disagree: liberals and conservatives, Catholics and Protestants, wealthy and poor, Bloods and Crips, Hatfields and McCoys. These interest groups tend to become more extreme in opposition to others over time. We therefore have the far right and the radical left, the fundamentalist Christians and those who believe that God is dead. There are even various groups that have become so radicalized that they adopt terrorist tactics.

The inability to see other people's viewpoints results not only in premature judgment but can result in instantaneous opposition. As an academic, I am classified as a liberal, and since I consult with technology-based businesses, often I am in discussion with people who are highly conservative in their views. Although I may be getting paranoid, I sometimes think people are hostile to my technical opinions simply because of their stereotyping about professors. On the other hand, I know that engineering professors often devalue opinions of people from industry who are dismissive of the academic life. Creativity can often result from the tension between the values and desires of different groups, but openness and acceptance are needed. To be convinced that all people who own guns are wrong, that abortion should be outlawed, that government should be abolished, or that the free market can solve all social problems pretty much guarantees that one will not contribute much creativity to problems having to do with gun deaths, unwanted pregnancies, national organization, or social welfare. To love information technology and to believe that eventually manual labor will be obsolete will not help one work with people who are not particularly interested in technology. To believe that one has the right answer to complicated problems that have previously been worked on by large numbers of bright and motivated people (health care, international relations, the economy, etc.) is a normal response, but restricts creativity by closing one off to the thinking of others. We will talk more about this in chapters nine and ten.

Bigger Is Better

Growth seems to be a natural tendency for Homo sapiens. When I first came to Stanford as a graduate student and lecturer, it was a different place: smaller, perhaps more fun, and in certain areas perhaps a better school. As an example, the Design Group in mechanical engineering, then called the Design Division, which was my initial academic home, consisted of two professors (John Arnold and Bob McKim), an administrative staff of one, and three graduate students to work hard as lecturers.

McKim and I were already hooked on trying to understand creativity. The graduate students Arnold brought with him were certainly familiar with it, and Arnold had a national reputation as a creativity expert. Arnold and us lecturers taught well over a reasonable teaching load, enjoyed playing tricks on each other and mixing with the students, and spent lots of time in Arnold's house listening to his sound system and drinking his wine (at least I did). Judging from grateful alumni who visit me, I think we had a very positive effect on our students.

By the time I returned as a professor, the Design Division had changed, but not that much: the faculty had grown a bit, and there were three administrators, more teaching assistants, and more graduate students, but it was in the same quarters and doing the same sort of things with a few more, larger classes.

But now, looking at the Design Group directory, it has thirty-three people listed as faculty and staff, twenty-six as administrative research technical staff, ten as postdoctoral scholars, and fourteen as visiting professors and scholars. There are thirteen laboratories or other subgroups. It has its own building with more space, but several of the laboratories are located in other buildings. It is a relative powerhouse if you include the Hasso Plattner Institute of Design, which prefers to be called the d. school and operates independently but is in a way an offspring of the group.

All of this is well and good, but the faculty as a whole does not seem to spend as much time taking turns teaching courses or sitting around talking and plotting new directions and schemes. Nor can students as easily find faculty members to drop in and talk to. The group is processing more students, doing more research, and is much more widely known, visited, and copied, but even though the staff has a two-hour meeting once a week, the group seems less cohesive. As an example, there seem to be fewer projects involving the people from the d.school, the center for design research, and those doing more traditional engineering work. And, although its many courses involve faculty from other departments and adjunct professors from outside Stanford, the Design Group does not have as strong a link with the art department as it once did—which, to me, is a loss if one is to use the word "design" in its name.

I will have a few more words to say about growth in chapters eight and nine, but suffice it to say now that, in the transformation of the Design Group at Stanford, one can see how a small collective with an interest in creativity can grow into something much larger, better funded, and more visible and influential. The trade-off is a loss in group cohesion and, from my viewpoint as a retired person, fun—a typical growth curve.

Cyber Is Better

Some people crave a world in which everyone is electronically interconnected, so that they can not only communicate but also have access to great amounts of information and computational ability. This is the so-called cyber world. Unfortunately, not everyone is going to want to be connected to everyone and spend their hours digesting and manipulating information. Many people who are in love with digital devices believe that this disinterest in their ideal reality is a temporary situation and eventually everyone will come to love the cyber world. This may be true as far as entertainment is concerned, but I think it is not universally accurate.

Twenty years ago at Stanford, one of our students, Adria Anuzis Brown, came to some interesting conclusions during her graduate research, which was a study of interaction between a US and a Japanese company cooperating on the development of a product. She looked at three aspects of communication, which she called personal (interacting in same location), cultural (commonalties of interest, background, and values), and cyber (interacting electronically). She found that the most successful professional interaction made use of all three. Electronic interaction alone was not as effective as when it was combined with the other two. In other words, the best creative work comes from people who are not only electronically interconnected but also share cultural values and interact personally in the same physical space. She should have received an award for prescience. Companies assuming that everyone will live in cyberspace will do fine as long as they are content with a customer base of like-minded people. If they want to go beyond that, they must become appreciative of the values of people like me, who have no interest at all in receiving more advertising messages or in carrying GPS receivers and cell phones while backpacking.

Tradition and Change

The final cultural block I will bring up here is the idea that tradition is preferable to change. In his book *Notes on the Synthesis of Form*, Christopher Alexander discussed two types of culture: the unselfconscious culture and the self-conscious culture. The unselfconscious culture is tradition oriented. Traditional form and ceremonies are perpetuated, and often taboos and legends work against change. The architect in such a culture would probably serve a long apprenticeship and learn how to make the traditional buildings (the long house, the temple, etc.). When he reached a stage where he was judged competent by his elders, he would presumably become a master and train other apprentices. The United States is hardly such a culture. Any young architect knows better than to study traditional building forms. Ours is a self-conscious culture. New religions, forms, social movements, and styles in dress, talk, entertainment, and living crop up continually. Age and experience are venerated only if relevant, and long apprenticeships are rapidly becoming extinct. A very high value seems to be placed on innovation.

Yet, strangely enough, many individuals in the United States value tradition more than they do change. This is probably good, since in my opinion our culture has little enough tradition. However, as far as good conceptualization is concerned, such an attitude can have negative effects. Motivation is essential to creativity. No matter how talented the problem solver, frustration and detail work are inescapable. Unless you truly want to solve a problem (for pleasure, money, prestige, comfort, or whatever) you probably will not do a very good job, unless you are convinced that change is needed in a particular area, you are not likely to hypothesize ways of accomplishing that change.

The problem arises when individuals become so universally in favor of tradition that they cannot see the need for and desirability of change in specific areas. The true conservative, I suppose, would fall in this category. Some environmentalists also lose their credibility by being totally against change in an area. If a person is truly grounded in the "good old days" and feels strongly that changes in the past twenty or thirty years have diminished rather than enhanced the quality of life, he is unlikely to be motivated to be a very good conceptualizer. He is blocked. The person who is in favor of change for change's sake may be a more dangerous animal to have around, yet, as far as conceptualization is concerned, he is probably in fairly good shape.

ENVIRONMENTAL BLOCKS

Non-Supportive Physical Environment

Let us now move on to environmental blocks. These are blocks that are imposed by our immediate social and physical environment. The most obvious blocks are the physical, as the physical surroundings of the problem solver influence his productivity.

I am sure that all of you are familiar with the effect of distractions. It is very difficult to work on complicated problems with continual interruptions from phones, computers, and friends dropping by. At times, even potential interruptions are a problem, since when you are in a frustrating phase of problem-solving, you are quite tempted to take advantage of such opportunities. Personally speaking, when involved in problem-solving I will sometimes go to heroic efforts to be distracted. Often I have to force myself out of bed at an inhuman hour in the morning to work on a problem, so that I am sure I can find no alternative activities available and no one to talk to. Even then, I often just sit, hoping that someone will walk by and distract me.

In fact, my wife loves it when I write books. Like many (most?) people who write, I love to have written books, but the process of writing them verges between taxing and torturous. The bad news is my increased grouchiness. The good news is that I escape by painting the house, sanding the floors, repairing the roof, improving the garden irrigation, and doing other worthwhile things that I ordinarily keep in my procrastination folder. I am not among the extreme, however. One of my professor friends, who had a very nice office at the university and a workspace in his home, was having little success in writing a book. He finally rented space in an office building in town, in which he put only material necessary to write his book—no phone, no extraneous books, no modem. He then paid the receptionist in the neighboring office to not only stop people who wanted to see him, but prevent him from leaving his office during the times he wanted to write. It worked!

The physical environment affects everyone. Yet, because of the individual habit patterns we all acquire, different individuals are affected differently. With regard to mental activity, some people work better in cold rooms, some in warm rooms, some in cold rooms with their feet wrapped in something warm.

Some people work better to music and some in silence; some around others and some in isolation; some in windowless rooms and some in rooms with windows. Some are impervious to their visual surroundings and others are very sensitive to them.

In his book, *The Art and Science of Creativity* (now out of print), George Kneller discussed the sometimes bizarre devices many writers and artists have adopted with respect to their working environment: "Schiller, for example, filled his desk with rotten apples; Proust worked in a cork-lined room; Mozart took exercise; Dr. Samuel Johnson surrounded himself with a purring cat, orange peel, and tea; Hart Crane played jazz loud on a Victrola." To these people, these steps were aids to the intense concentration required in creative thinking. As another example, an extreme case was Immanuel Kant, who would work in bed at certain times of the day with the blankets arranged around him in a way he had invented himself. "While writing *The Critique of Pure Reason* he would concentrate on a tower visible from his window. When some trees grew up to hide the tower, he became frustrated, and the authorities of Königsberg cut down the trees so that he could continue his work."

Some people may have a particular environment in which they are most effective at conceptual work of any kind. Therefore we sometimes find the all-purpose studio, in which a person may paint, write, sculpt, invent, and whatever else. Another person may have one environment in which he can best write, another in which he can best throw pots, and still a third in which he does woodworking. Even though such individual differences exist, we can still say that most individuals do conceptual work best in a particular type of environment.

These days, what with open offices, smartphones, and the internet, it is difficult to escape distractions. As will be discussed in chapter nine, a group is potentially more creative than an individual, so advantage should be taken of the potential of many brains. But there are also times when the individual needs to focus total attention for an extended period on a single problem. For many people like myself, it is often more enjoyable to chitchat with a friend than struggle with a difficult problem. I sometimes need a closed room to protect me from myself. But even knowing that, turning off my phone, ignoring my e-mail, and staying away from YouTube, someone, usually for good reasons, will interrupt me. To make matters worse, open offices seem to be a fad these days. I still have an office with a door, but if it were not for that, I would be forced to buy a remote cabin on a mountain top.

> **Exercise:** Take a piece of paper and list the characteristics of the most supportive possible environment you can think of for your own conceptual work (or different types of environments for different types of work). Do the environments in which you work resemble this? If not, why not? Assuming your hypothesized environment is practical for you (not the beaches of an as-yet-undiscovered South Pacific island), change your working environment to more closely resemble your hypothetical one. Does this make an appreciable difference on your conceptual productivity?

Non-Supportive Human Environment

Although environment usually has physical connotations, the most important environmental blocks are often not physical. If anything, they verge on the cultural and the emotional. As discussed in the last chapter, conceptualization involves a certain amount of emotional risk. Change is often threatening; therefore, so are new ideas. They can be quickly squelched, especially when newly born, imperfect, and not reduced to practice. The usual response of society, in fact, is to stifle such ideas. There are many ways to do this. One is to overanalyze them. Another is to laugh at them. Still another is to ignore them.

> **Exercise:** Think up a new idea, perhaps an invention that sounds reasonably plausible. Maybe an electric toilet brush, or a mail campaign to convince the post office to improve its service, or anything else. Then seriously propose this idea to friends and (if you are brave) others you meet from time to time. Note their reactions. Is anyone, other than your friends, enthusiastic? And are your friends really receptive, or are they merely being polite? This is a poor experiment, since some of your ideas may be brilliant and some terrible, and this conceivably could influence the response. However, I do not think that the difference in response will be that large. If you want to improve the experiment, try both a brilliant and a poor idea on the same people.

Most people are not happy with criticism and, to make matters worse, are somewhat unsure of the quality of their own ideas. They therefore require a supportive environment in which to work. One of our most serious problems with students in design classes is that they hesitate to expose ideas about which they are unsure, not only to the faculty but also to each other. Since many of their creative ideas naturally fall into this not-sure category, they hesitate to reveal them. We have to convert the class (usually a listening, competitive, no-risk situation) into a friendly, noncompetitive, interactive situation, in which people will take the risk of exposing their most impractical ideas to each other. Competition and lack of trust destroy such a supportive environment. No one likes to expose his magnificent concept if someone is going to steal it.

People tend to be critical of ideas that will lead to change. Non-supportive responses are especially harmful when they come from bosses, colleagues, or friends. In chapters eight and nine, I will discuss conceptualization in groups and organizations. However, a few comments are in order here. An atmosphere of honesty, trust, and support is absolutely necessary if most people are to make the best of their conceptual abilities.

There are certainly exceptions. Many of the outstanding inventors I have known have been quite confident of their abilities and less dependent on support from others. One of the best of these idea-havers worked with me at one time. Given a problem, he would instantly throw together a solution. These solutions were often so poorly thought-out that I would almost break out in a rash. He would then happily go to the next office and receive so much criticism on the idea that, had it been me, I would have been sent into a depression for several days. He would then incorporate the criticism into his idea and proceed to the next office. In this way, he would literally construct a solution step-by-step, usually an outstanding one. He was successful because of his ability to accept and incorporate criticism. However, people like this are rare.

Autocratic Bosses

Bosses with answers are a particular problem. Many productive problem solvers are strongheaded. They can carry a concept through to completion in spite of apathy or hostility from others and the difficulty of finding support for a new idea. If they happen to have good judgment, they are able to accomplish noticeable achievements in a company environment and are often promoted in management. One therefore often finds that many managers are successful idea-producers who are stubborn enough to push their concepts through to completion. They tend to continue in this mode when managing others. Although managers such as this can be effective problem solvers, they are essentially operating with their own conceptual ability and an in-house service organization—they are probably not going to make much use of the conceptual ability of their subordinates.

In order to maximize the creative output of a group, managers must be willing and able to encourage their subordinates to think conceptually and reward them when they succeed. They should, of course, conceptualize on their own. But they should do it somewhat in tandem with the other members of their group if they are attempting to use their employees to the fullest.

This is an obvious piece of advice that is ignored surprisingly often. Time and time again I have seen design groups operating mainly on the concepts of the group leader. Such a group admittedly can be successful if the leader is an outstanding conceptualizer and the members of the group are content to develop the leader's ideas. However, our concern is with environmental blocks, and such a working situation is hardly an environment conducive to conceptualization on the part of the group members.

Lack of Needed Resources

Lack of physical, economic, or organizational support to bring ideas into action is also another common problem. New ideas are typically hard to bring to fruition. A great amount of effort is involved in perfecting an idea and then selling it. Many conceptual breakthroughs in science, for instance, have taken years of work to validate to the point where they elicit interest from others in the scientific community. A completed novel is far removed from the original thought that inspired it. Even after the idea is fleshed out into a believable form, it must be sold to an often skeptical world. This may require money and time. For example, the small inventor is at a distinct disadvantage compared to the corporate inventor because of the fabrication needed, the test equipment desired, the legal and promotional expertise required, and the food and rent consumed while he or she is doing the inventing. Even the best of ideas is doomed if time and money are not available to push it forward.

Granted, the inventor is perhaps an extreme example. Nonetheless, even a concept for a new recipe is useless without the money to buy the ingredients and the time to cook it. A concept for a painting or a drawing is similarly futile without the supplies and the time. A concept of taking a vacation to improve a marriage requires economic and temporal support. All ideas require an environment that will produce the support necessary to bring them to fruition. This support may come from your friendly venture-capital firm, your bank, your spouse, your income surplus, or any other form of patronage. Lack of such patronage is a very effective environmental block.

THINKING THROUGH CULTURAL AND ENVIRONMENTAL BLOCKS

Projects that require thinking through cultural blocks are among the most popular with students, since the blocks are so difficult to overcome and yet so obvious once they have been identified. I often ask my students to design puzzles, games, or situations for each other that require breaking through a cultural block in order to reach a solution. One project that sticks in my mind required that a dollar bill be removed from beneath a precariously balanced object without tipping over the object. This was extremely easy to do if the bill was torn in half. However, for various cultural reasons (it's illegal to deface money, one doesn't usually tear up things of value), no one thought of this particular solution, with the result that no one could remove the dollar. Another project required that one playing card, out of a deck of fifty-two, be destroyed. Once again, no one thought of perpetrating such a crime; we are a society of cardplayers and most of us do not approve of incomplete decks of cards. Still a third I can remember was perhaps the most basic I have seen. The solution to the problem required that a number of objects be moved around a board in a prearranged sequence in order to reach the desired final configuration. It turned out to be impossible to follow the rules and solve the problem. The cultural block? Following rules! It was simple to attain the desired configuration if the rules were violated.

A less flippant situation occurs when students from more rigid and theory-oriented disciplines or cultures take courses in design. Expertise in design is somewhat different from expertise in, say, fluid mechanics. Design is a multi-answer situation and analysis is used to reach an end, not for its own sake. The teacher, although hopefully experienced in the design process and in command of the necessary techniques, is not the usual type of academic expert in that he or she does not have a monopoly on the right answers at the beginning of the course, and in fact may not even always come up with the best answer. Grading becomes much more subjective and the student must take more academic risk, since the evaluation standards are less orthodox. Students from a school system in which grading is extremely important, and in which the professor or teacher is an extreme authority figure, sometimes have difficulty adapting to design courses. They are often preoccupied with "What is the answer?" and "How do I ensure that I will get an A?"—as well they should, since their background has been exclusively oriented in such directions. The tragedy is that many students from countries that need capable designers and problem solvers suffer from such blocks, because academic risk-taking is somewhat of a taboo. Another culturally induced difference between students from less industrially developed countries, such as many in equatorial Africa, and those from the United States, Japan, China, Western

Europe, etc., is the difference in their knowledge of, and attitude toward, machines. Students from less industrially developed countries often have had less opportunity to be exposed to machinery and are therefore somewhat less experienced and more inhibited in working with it. But to the chagrin of the more industrially developed countries, the latter difference is fast disappearing, and the former is beginning to do so.

CHAPTER 5

Intellectual and Expressive Blocks

INTELLECTUAL BLOCKS RESULT IN AN INEFFICIENT CHOICE OF mental tactics or a shortage of intellectual ammunition. Expressive blocks inhibit your ability to communicate ideas—not only to others, but to yourself as well. Let us look at the following blocks:

1. Solving the problem using an incorrect language, for example, trying to solve a problem mathematically when it can more easily be accomplished visually
2. Inflexible or inadequate use of intellectual problem-solving strategies
3. Insufficient or incorrect information
4. Inadequate language skill to express and record ideas

A few examples should help us understand these blocks better. The monk puzzle described in the first chapter of this book is one in which choosing the correct language (visual) leads you rapidly toward a solution. Here is another language problem.

Exercise: Picture a large piece of paper, the thickness of this page. In your imagination, fold it once (now having two layers), fold it once more (now having four layers), and continue folding it over upon itself fifty times. How thick is the fifty-times-folded paper?

It is true that it is impossible to fold any piece of paper, no matter how big or how thick, fifty times. But for the sake of the problem, imagine that you can. When you either have the answer or have given up, continue.

Your first fold would result in a stack $2 \times$ the original thickness. Your second would give you a stack $2 \times 2 \times$ the original thickness. Your third: $2 \times 2 \times 2 \times$ the original thickness. Extending this, if you are somewhat of a mathematician, you should recognize that the answer to the problem is $2^{50} \times$ the original thickness (2^{50} happens to be about 1,100,000,000,000,000). If the paper is the thickness of typing paper, the answer is some 50,000,000 miles, or over half the distance from the earth to the sun.

If you tried to attack this particular problem with visual imagery (the clever way to handle the monk puzzle) you probably could not get an answer, since it is next to impossible to accurately visualize fifty folds. If you attacked it verbally, you probably also had trouble. If you are familiar with doubling problems, you knew that the answer was a surprisingly big number, but still could not place a value on it. The correct language in this problem was clearly mathematics.

CHOOSING YOUR PROBLEM-SOLVING LANGUAGE

How did you select the mental strategy you used to work on this problem? How did you decide to use visualization, mathematics, or whatever? If you were faked into visualization by our mention of the monk problem, you chose it consciously. If you are really getting the message of this book, you thought about various ways of working the problem and then picked one. However, many of you probably once again unconsciously selected a strategy and then switched from one strategy to the other. As I've said before, most people follow this habit pattern in problem-solving. Without conscious thought, a direction will occur in the mind. This direction may or may not be the right one. If it is a wrong one, another may or may not appear.

It is possible to aid strategy selection by consciously considering the various languages of thought you might use. For instance, you could have read the paper-folding problem and then said to yourself, "Let's see, this guy has been trying to sell me visual thinking. Can I solve it visually? I'll try a few folds." When that task becomes difficult, you would ask, "What else could I try? Verbalization? Probably not, since it is a physical problem asking for quantitative data. Hey, quantitative—how about mathematics?" At this point, you either solve it by inspection (you're a pro), write out equations and solve them (semipro), or ask someone you know who knows math (brilliant amateur).

Here is another puzzle. Before you try thinking of the answer, examine the problem and see which mental languages seem appropriate. Then attack the problem in the most appropriate language.

> **Exercise:** A man and a woman standing side by side begin walking so that their right feet hit the ground at the same time. The woman takes three steps for each two steps of the man. How many steps does the man take before their left feet simultaneously reach the ground?

This is a good problem to solve with visual thinking. A live experiment with another person, a drawing, or a musical rhythm analogy will all work well. A mathematical approach will work, although it is somewhat circuitous. Verbalization, once again, will not get you very far. What language did you pick? Did it work? Did you try alternate approaches? How did you know it was time to give up on one and try another? The answer is that their left feet never hit the ground simultaneously.

Choice of the proper problem-solving language is difficult not only because the choice is usually made unconsciously, but also because of the heavy emphasis on verbal thinking (with mathematical thinking a poor second) in our culture. The two problems you just worked were difficult because neither can be easily solved by the application of verbal thinking. Visualization, as expressed through the use of drawings, is almost always essential in designing physical things well. One reason for this is that verbal thinking, when applied to design, has the strange attribute of allowing you to think that you have an answer when in fact you do not. Verbal thinking among articulate people is fraught with glib generalities. And in design, it is not until one backs an idea up with the visual mode that one can see whether one is fooling oneself or not.

Now that you are sensitized to this situation, let me give you an exercise that will give you some insight to your own biases. It subjects you to three types of problem-solving: verbal-expressive, visual-design, and mathematical. As in past exercises, try to remain aware of how you respond to the three parts of the exercise both cognitively and emotionally.

Find a few friends to do this with. It will make the differences in specialization more apparent. The exercise takes about twenty minutes. If you have a representative group of friends, everyone will feel somewhat uncomfortable during at least one of the five-minute exercises. Some of you may not like any of them. All three of the activities require creativity, are of high status, and earn people fame and money. However, to the extent that you feel uncomfortable doing one of them, you probably avoid such activities and do not communicate too well with those who enjoy them. We tend to stay within our habits, with an accompanying loss of creativity.

Exercise

1. Spend five minutes writing a short and serious poem on love. Strive for beauty and expression. At the end of five minutes, read your poems to each other.
2. Spend five minutes designing (graphically—draw it on paper) a better desk lamp. Desk lamps usually have shortcomings, whether functional or aesthetic. Draw one that is both functionally successful and beautiful. At the end of the time, show your design to the others in the group and discuss it for a few minutes.
3. Spend five minutes working on the following problem: An ant is in a top corner of a square room that measures 24 ft on a side and is 8 ft high. He sees an edible crumb at the opposite bottom corner. The ant wants to walk to the crumb over the shortest possible path. How long is the path? After the five minutes are over, make sure that everyone in the group understands and agrees upon the answer.

Our reaction to intellectual problems does not necessarily reflect our present ability to solve them. We have all manner of outdated measures and anxieties that influence us. I often gave the poetry portion of the exercise to engineering and business students, professional engineers and managers, and business executives. The initial response typically ran the gamut from horror to an urgent need to leave the room. However, as the participants began working on their poems, they found that the process was less painful than they might have thought. They had long-dormant habits remaining from previous schooling with which to construct poetic forms. They also found that they had a lot to say about love, although it might not be information that is consistent with their usual communication habits. The pain returned, however, when they had to divulge their poems to others. After they had read their poems to each other, I usually found that if I asked those whose poems were terrible to raise their hands, all hands were raised. If I then asked the same of those who heard a poem that was surprisingly good, all hands were again raised. In other words, they all thought their own poems were terrible but that those written by the other people were pretty good.

I used to ask Diane Middlebrook, a published poet and then an English professor at Stanford, to help me do an advanced version of this exercise in executive programs, where the students tended to be managers in technology-based companies. She introduced the participants to poetry in a minicourse consisting of readings, outside writing, and about four hours of lecture. Middlebrook often began by reading the group a poem, and even the process of listening to poetry being read caused some of the students discomfort. Needless to say, their initial attempts at writing were painful. However, the beauty was there. Through a process of pleading, cajoling, explaining, praising, and criticizing, as well as the application of understanding and humor, Middlebrook coaxed the reluctant executives to write increasingly sophisticated verse. The poems on the next page are short examples written by some of the participants. The results of the minicourse were usually a few amateur poets and a great change in everyone's viewpoint toward their own poetic abilities.

Shapely brown bicycling legs
Flashing in the sun through Stanford arches
I am an old man

I comb my hairs with a ball point pen
aging ego
hostage to ratted locks

Fern Hill, you stir the little boy
Take me back
Leave me by the stream above the cliffs
Let me relive the year
The joy; my friends; my dog
. . . no chores!

economic elements of engineering arouse
    me, Anne
eleemosynary music modifies my
    arousal, Anne
elegant eulogies/expert algorithims/
    integrated implantation
    Anne, Anne, Anne

Cherub face glowing to the world,
inner thoughts not expressed.
A filling sponge, thirsty.

Cold night falls on deeps now
narrow path lit by full moon
Dog barks into silence

Paint the sky
Roll the meadow
Fathom the depths
Water under the bridge
No U turn!

Personal perks, privileges.
Mission seduced integrity.
Beguiled by a lofty
Self-esteem through arrogance
Clouded vision. Exquisite
Rationalization. A
Talent squandered, a life disrupted.
Power corrupts.

Invent bad verse—why?
To manifest our joy
before this episode ends

Poems by Students in a Stanford Engineering Executive Program.

Many people who feel terribly inadequate writing poetry are capable of constructing acceptable verse. They are merely suffering from a lack of confidence in their own ability and the remnants of the social climate that inhibited the writing of poetry in high school. Similarly, awkwardness with drawing may result from a confusion between the type of drawing that most people do and the drawing of professional artists. Discomfort with math may result from that long-ago day when a relative lack of speed in calculation (which does not have that much to do with mathematics) caused one to slide from one's rightful spot at the head of the third grade class.

I am sometimes amused at the creativity and energy people will expend in order to avoid a particular style of problem-solving with which they do not feel comfortable. A student submitted the short poem on love shown in the picture. Clever, but probably more taxing than writing an actual poem.

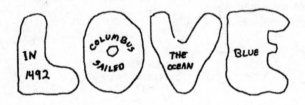

Another student submitted a paper in response to the desk-lamp assignment. It began, "Before you can appreciate my desk-lamp design, it is essential that you understand a few concepts from circuit design, solid state theory, and optics." It was obviously a high-tech desk lamp. This was followed by five pages of information about circuit design, solid state theory, and optical theory. Yet after all that, there was never a lamp design. After spending the allotted time telling me what he knew, the student conveniently avoided the process of visual imagery.

I clearly remember the response of an alumnus of Stanford who was working on the ant-in-the-room problem and covering a page with arithmetic. A simple way to solve it, assuming you remember the Pythagorean theorem you learned in school, is to flatten out the room as seen in the drawing. The answer is 40 ft, but you have to think of flattening the room. The block is obvious there: people don't flatten rooms.

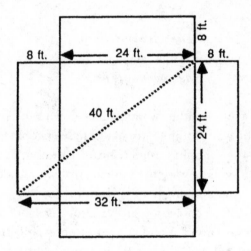

The Shortest Possible Path to the Crumb

Another problem I used with people who liked to calculate hypothesized two trains one mile apart on a single straight track, each traveling at ten miles per hour toward the other. A fly, which had been riding on the front of one, took off and flew toward the other at twenty miles per hour. Upon reaching the other (which was now less than one mile from the first train), the fly instantly turned and flew back to its original train, at which point it instantly turned again, and so on. The puzzle asks how far the fly flies before it is crushed in the train collision. This puzzle obviously has to do with mathematics. Many of the attempts would fall to trying to remember or write infinite series that would give the answer. It is merely necessary to realize that each train will travel one half-mile before they collide. Since the trains are traveling ten miles per hour, this will require 1/20th of an hour. The fly is traveling twenty miles per hour. In 1/20th of an hour the fly will fly one mile. However, one participant's answer was

Free capricious soaring fly,
why oh why
did you have to die?

Once again, a rather wonderful answer to the problem. In fact, just the type of thing I would like to see people do in classes and workshops emphasizing creativity. However, I suspect that the motivation here was not so much creativity as a desire not to spend the time thinking mathematically.

Our habitual choice of problem-solving languages (using the one we are good at and enjoy, not necessarily the one that can best solve the problem) can be consciously overcome, with a resulting increase in creative ability. The bad news is that overcoming habits is not easy. It requires, firstly, overcoming emotional signals and, secondly, becoming more of a novice than we are used to being. The process is well known. Think of changing a tennis swing. You first come to realize that your swing is not all you might wish. Either your opponents are destroying you, or after studious viewing of television you find that Roger Federer has a more effective serve than yours, or someone you respect comments on the deplorable state of your backhand. Usually the first step in modifying habits is an indication that present habits are not adequate.

The next part of habit modification involves conscious and usually analytical activity. You take lessons, read books, watch videotapes and other tennis players, and learn as much as you can about the form you would like as well as the one you presently possess. You then consciously build your new habit. Although it may feel extraordinarily awkward at first, it will presumably take you where you want to go. Finally, you practice your new habit until it becomes a natural and programmed act in its own right. This, of course, does not guarantee a lifetime of satisfaction and winning tennis games. It only means that you are set until the process begins again.

Naturally, such things as reward, punishment, and other types of motivational considerations are important in the process of habit modification. Also involved are time, energy, and perhaps money. However, for the purpose of this discussion, the main thing to note is the centrality of the conscious in modifying habits. Not only is it effective, it is the only thing we have to change our ways.

FLEXIBILITY IN YOUR USE OF STRATEGIES

David Straus and Michael Doyle, two people who had long been interested in problem-solving, founded the company Interaction Associates, which trained facilitators for problem-solving groups, offered educational programs, and conducted research in problem-solving. One of their techniques when working with groups was to keep track of the strategy or strategies being used at any time during a problem-solving session and to suggest changes or additions if the process appeared to be bogged down or overlooking possible approaches. In one of their publications, *Strategy Notebook*, they listed some sixty-six strategies, accompanying each with a description of the strategy, a list of its advantages and disadvantages, and a sample exercise. The strategy list is below.

Build up	Display	Simulate
Eliminate	Organize	Test
Work Forward	List	Play
Work Backward	Check	Manipulate
Associate	Diagram	Copy
Classify	Chart	Interpret
Generalize	Verbalize	Transform
Exemplify	Visualize	Translate
Compare	Memorize	Expand
Relate	Recall	Reduce
Commit	Record	Exaggerate
Defer	Retrieve	Understate
Leap In	Search	Adapt
Hold Back	Select	Substitute
Focus	Plan	Combine
Release	Predict	Separate
Force	Assume	Change
Relax	Question	Vary
Dream	Hypothesize	Cycle
Imagine	Guess	Repeat
Purge	Define	Systemize
Incubate	Symbolize	Randomize

Most people have no trouble understanding such problem-solving strategies, once definitions and examples are made available. In fact, most people have unconsciously used all of them or more at one time or another. However, since the mind is used to selecting strategies subconsciously, it takes awareness of them and conscious choice or an outside facilitator to make the best use of them on a specific problem. The *Introduction to Process Notebook,* also by Interaction Associates, summarized the situation as follows: "Just as we use physical tools for physical tasks, we employ conceptual tools for conceptual tasks. To familiarize yourself with a tool, you may experiment with it, test it in different situations, and evaluate its usefulness. The same method can be applied to conceptual tools. Our ability as thinkers is dependent on our range and skill with our own tools."

It is obvious that a compromise has to be reached in the conscious selection of thinking modes and problem-solving strategies. You should not devote 95 percent of your mental energy to the selection of strategies and thinking modes and reserve only 5 percent for the solving of the problem. Yet you should certainly spend some conscious effort thinking about strategies. First, by selecting strategies consciously you can often find approaches you would never have known about had you left the selection to your subconscious. Second, by becoming aware of various thinking strategies, what they can do, and how to use them, you can ensure that the mind has a larger selection when it selects subconsciously. You can essentially become your own facilitator.

THE COMPUTER

Interesting cases of intellectual inflexibility can be seen in the use of the computer. Society has accepted the computer, but a few individuals are still suspicious of it and reluctant to use it. It is a very powerful thinking tool. Not to take full advantage of it is a disadvantage. But some seem to almost worship it and have become completely chained to the intricacies of the internet and of new software and hardware products. Unless you work as a computer consultant, this is also a disadvantage. If you like gadgets and games, you can spend all of your time simply messing with computers rather than using them to solve problems. This may be fun, but one could hardly call it a meaningful contribution to the human condition.

Clifford Stoll, who has worked with computers since he built his first Altair kit in the 1970s, wrote an amusing book way back in 1995 entitled *Silicon Snake Oil*. At one point in the book, he complained about the large portion of his time that he spent trying to get his computer to do what he wanted it to do. In his mind, given all of the money and effort sunk into developing this technology, by now we shouldn't have to spend so much time fighting our systems. I agreed with him, as did most computer users I knew, even though at the time the book was thought to be almost heretical. Computers, after all, were supposed to increase the quality of life. He mentioned that when your computer crashed or gave you some strange error message, it not only took time to coax it back to happiness but also broke your train of thought. That situation has improved in the years since. But the improvement has been offset by increased complexity: attempts to force the user to upgrade, thereby losing valuable acquired skills; to buy things the user does not want; and to go off toward beguiling games, videos, apps, messages, porn, sporting events, and other diversions, as well as near-mandatory security programs and endless passwords. I still think that I spend too much time trying to get my computer to do what I want. After all, it is but a tool.

Computers affected my professional life early. When I worked there in the 1960s, the Jet Propulsion Laboratory was using large (in those days) computer-based structural analysis programs, and relatively primitive computers were included in spacecraft to do onboard guidance, control, and scientific data reduction. I dutifully bought a RadioShack TRS-80 and later an

Apple I, and tried to apply them to my life. I now rely upon a great deal of digital computer and communication equipment, which allows me to be much more effective than I used to be, but I am not a computer expert and do not want to become one. To me, the problem is one of balance. How do you make the best use of the digital revolution? Computers can be a great aid to creativity, but perhaps the greatest inhibition to personal creativity is lack of time, and if computers soak up too much time, they can inhibit creativity.

IMPORTANCE OF CORRECT INFORMATION

During the solution of a problem, correct and adequate information is, of course, extremely important. An intellectual block that may prevent the problem solver from acquiring well-balanced and pertinent information can be disastrous. Mechanical engineers with a block against electrical engineering may design mechanical television sets, or electrical engineers with a block against mechanical engineering may create complex electrical power control systems, where simple mechanical ones would be cheaper and more reliable. People who consistently resist utilizing mathematics limit their problem-solving abilities by being blocked from useful quantitative data, just as people who are blocked against considering aesthetic, emotional, and qualitative inputs are hindered in their decision-making. Engineers who are uncomfortable with aesthetics can make outstandingly inhumane and ugly devices that may, as a side issue, not even sell well. Environmentalists who ignore the use of quantitative facts and statistics cannot be very productive in designing effective solutions to environmental problems.

There is, however, disagreement as to whether information is universally valuable at all phases of problem-solving. One school of thought maintains that one of the worst enemies of innovation is the large impact of existing solutions on conceptual thinking. This is the school that says, "It is difficult to think of alternate methods of felling small trees if you have spent a lot of time swinging an axe." I know one extremely inventive engineer who finds it very important to operate with a clean mind—he avoids learning anything about previous solutions to his problems. However, I know another equally productive engineer who spends a great deal of effort learning everything she can about every previous development that seems even slightly related to her problem (a "dirty" mind?). It is true that if you do not know about axes, your solution to felling small trees may be reinventing the axe. You are also denied the use of the axe as a source of additional concepts.

In my opinion, the optimal situation in problem-solving is to be able to use a clean-minded approach to a problem, even though your mind is stuffed with information. I am, of course, biased by my own preferences. As I previously admitted, I grunt my way through problems instead of solving them in an effortless flash of insight. The more information I have about the problem and previous attempts to solve it, the better I do. However, it is sometimes necessary in the problem-solving process to hold this information at arm's length. Certainly, for instance, a massive amount of information is necessary when working with high technology, complex business situations, or interpersonal interactions. However, this abundant information can often prevent you from seeing very elegant solutions. Information makes you an expert, but William J. J. Gordon, the author of a book entitled *Synectics: The Development of Creative Capacity*, said this about expertise: "The specialized semantics of established knowledge constitutes conventions which make reality abstract and secondhand. Learned conventions can be windowless fortresses which exclude viewing the world in new ways."

I believe that it is possible to be an expert and still view the world in new ways. One does not need someone who grew up alone on a desert island to invent a better can opener. One can use people who not only are quite knowledgeable about electrical, mechanical, physical, chemical, and whatever other phenomena, but who also have been closely associated with presently existing can openers. It is only necessary that these people be able to view the world in new ways in spite of all of their prior knowledge. If they can do this, they should do better than someone from a desert island.

EXPRESSIVE BLOCKS

Turning now to expressive blocks, let us begin by doing another simple exercise.

> **Exercise:** This will require you to find (or make) a simple object whose shape cannot be described by a common name. It could be a block with a corner cut off and a groove along one face, a part from a machine, or any other object with a simple yet irregular three-dimensional shape. Do not use a pencil, a pair of scissors, a tonic water bottle, or other object that is so utilitarian and well known that its shape is familiar to everyone. Find several people, place the object you have chosen in a large paper bag, and have one of the people place his hand in the bag without looking at the object. He is to describe the object to the other people, who are to draw it.

This exercise is surprisingly difficult. The lack of feedback in the communication loop is of course a contributor to this. Some feedback can be obtained by allowing those drawing the object to ask questions of the describer, although the exercise is most impressive when questions are not allowed. The exercise is also difficult because it is not easy to identify shapes by feel. However, the chief difficulty is probably that of describing a physical object verbally. If your volunteers are mathematically oriented and communicate in terms of x, y, and z coordinates or other geometrical surface description techniques, they will do better at this task. However, if the common verbal approach is used (for example, "The bottom is a rectangular place with the corner cut off, and then there is a short side going up from the cut-off corner.") the task is abysmally difficult. Another reason for the difficulty is the rather low level of drawing talent developed in most people. Even if the shape could be perfectly described verbally, most people do not have the skill to capture it on paper.

I usually do this exercise with a large group so that I can compare drawings after it is over. Try it at a party. The presence of the audience adds some interesting emotional blocks. The person describing the object will do better if she spends some time feeling the object before describing it. However, it is difficult to spend this time in front of an impatient crowd, and the person usually will plunge right into describing. The description will then proceed at a rapid rate, even though the audience may be picking up no information of use, as the describer usually feels somewhat embarrassed standing in front of a group with her hand in a bag doing what, to her, may seem a trivial task. Since she will think she has a good idea of the shape of the object, she will find it difficult to believe that the audience does not. She may become impatient. She will undoubtedly demonstrate a form of incubation by thinking of a better way to have done the task after the exercise is over.

This exercise demonstrates both the use of inadequate language skills to express an idea and the imprecision in our verbal expression. It is an extremely common block that one finds often, for instance, in the engineering profession. Many students and engineers are not fond of drawing, partly because they may find it difficult and partly because in some fields drafting has somehow been given a lower status than, say, analysis. Therefore there are continual attempts to communicate geometrical ideas verbally. Often the degree of difficulty induced by this expressive block is not even appreciated, since the describer knows exactly what he is trying to describe, and the person to whom he is describing often naturally assumes that she understands exactly what he means. Another problem that demonstrates this block of imprecise verbal expression, if you have access to a dozen or so people or so, is the following.

> **Exercise:** Give a person a drawing of a simple object. It should be an abstract object so a name does not describe its shape. Ask him to look at it awhile and then describe it verbally to another person. The second person should then describe it verbally to a third person, and so on. This should be done in a manner so that the others in the group cannot overhear the descriptions. When the description of the object has been passed through ten people or so, have one last person draw the object. Comparison of the final drawing with the original drawing should prove fascinating.

I often use this game in classes. The figure on the next page shows a simple object; it is an engineering drawing, but the people playing the game were students in an engineering class. The next image shows some of the results. There was obviously some error along the way.

One of the difficult things in both of these exercises is that communication is one-way. This type of communication is amazingly weak unless the receiver has the same information

130

Engineering Drawing

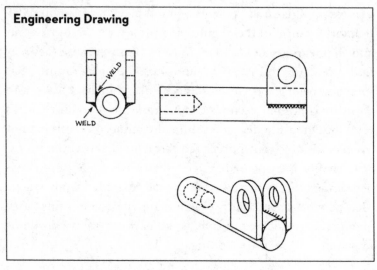

Student Results

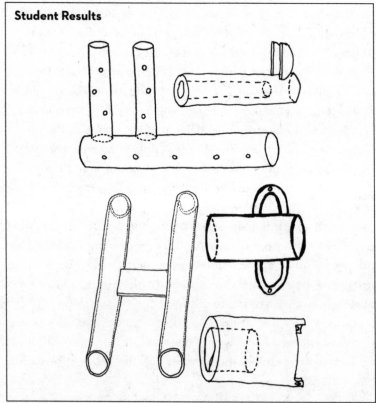

in mind as the sender, which is unlikely in situations involving creativity. If two-way communication is allowed in the exercises (receivers can ask questions) the process is much more accurate but agonizingly slow.

Are there other reasons why communication may be difficult in situations involving creativity? Sure, they are easy to find: the frustration of trying to present concepts in a foreign language, the frustration of the writer when his computer is broken, the frustration of the executive whose administrative assistant is sick, the frustration of the technically trained person trying to explain quantitative concepts to someone who hates mathematics.

In situations involving creativity, we often benefit by combining disciplines in new ways. Communication across disciplines is unusually difficult because our minds are not particularly eager to learn new jargon and techniques, or to admit that we need to do so. We are afraid that our need to learn new information will be mistakenly interpreted as a sign of ignorance. One of the great challenges in teaching is that one cannot rely upon students to ask questions when they do not understand things. It is quite easy to lose an entire class (usually if one student does not understand, the others don't either) with no indication. One of the common explanations for this reluctance to ask questions is that it admits ignorance.

I used to be called a systems engineer—a person working on a complex product to make sure all of the pieces fit together physically and functionally. When I was in the US Air Force, the military had just discovered the "systems" concept. No longer would there be an airplane, ammunition, starting carts, and a plug for the pitot tube. Now there would be a weapons system. People began to talk in terms of the systems concept, systems management, systems approach, and, of course, systems engineering. Companies such as Ramo-Wooldridge (the RW of TRW) leaped to prominence because of their systems design and management ability. This approach instantly infiltrated the aerospace industry, so that by the time I joined the Jet Propulsion Laboratory in 1959 it was known that a systems approach was necessary to design something as complex as a spacecraft. There was some dissension from certain senior people, who considered systems engineering to be just plain old good engineering, but we youngsters embraced it with enthusiasm. When I joined the faculty at Stanford, I taught systems engineering and spent a large portion of the summers in a NASA-sponsored program, which attempted to give engineering professors a better feel for systems engineering.

What is systems engineering? Just plain old good engineering. However, it has evolved its own philosophies and exists as a field because of the difficulty of communicating across different jargons, perceptions of importance, and perspectives in different technical fields. The communication engineers see nothing wrong with leaving an extra three-decibel margin in their system, even though some poor mechanical engineer may end up trying to design an antenna with twice the area as a result.

Interdisciplinary communication is not restricted to technology companies. Any organization has difficulties with communication between the various specialized groups within it, and any family has difficulty with communication between members in different roles. The traditional housewife (should any still exist) has as much difficulty communicating with the traditional husband (none still exist), because of the differences in their experiences, perceived priorities, and responsibilities.

The message here is a simple but important one. In situations involving change and creativity, communication cannot be taken for granted. Efforts must be made to ensure that communication is two-way and that adequate time and effort are taken to convey the information. It is also worthwhile to be suspicious of difficulties resulting from changes in the disciplinary mix.

Finally, priorities and values will perhaps need changing, and intensive communication is sometimes necessary to achieve this. In particular, a great amount of communication is required to convince people who have played a particular role for a long period of time to change their role. In such cases, expressive blocks can be crippling.

CHAPTER 6

Alternate Thinking Languages

In chapter five, I discussed conceptual blocks from the improper choice of a problem-solving language. In this chapter, I would like to elaborate on this point. The well-armed problem solver is fluent in many mental languages and is able to use them interchangeably to record information, communicate with the unconscious, and consciously manipulate. Some of these moves are more natural to us than others. They are often even more powerful when used in combination with each other than when used alone.

I will discuss some of these thinking modes or languages and put in a plug for some that I do not think receive their fair share of emphasis. To introduce this discussion, let me give you the following exercise.

Exercise: Imagine that you just gave a ride to a hitchhiker who turned out to be an eccentric wealthy builder. As a token of his gratitude, he offers to build an addition to your house according to your specifications, asking only that the total budget not exceed $100,000. Conceptualize the addition you would ask him to build for you. As you work on this problem, try to observe what is going on in your mind (concerning the addition, not the probability of the situation occurring).

Once again, you should have become aware of the difficulty in observing your thinking process as it swings back and forth between the conscious and the unconscious. However, were you roughly aware of what languages you employed? Did you think verbally? Quantitatively? Pictorially? Did you imagine smells? Sounds? Tactile sensations? Muscle sensations? Did you tend to work mostly in one language?

If you are typical of most people, you will most easily recall the thinking you did that was in a verbal mode. Verbal thinking is the most prestigious (and perhaps most common) mental language in our culture.

Many psychologists and general semanticists feel that verbal languages are the basis of thinking. For instance, L. S. Vygotsky in *Thought and Language* says, "Thought is born through words." Edward Sapir in *Language* says that "language and our thought grooves are inextricably interwoven, and are, in a sense, one and the same." Our educational systems reinforce this bias. As Rudolf Arnheim writes in his essay "Visual Thinking" in *Education of Vision:* "In our schools, reading, writing, and arithmetic are practiced as skills that detach the child from sensory (as opposed to verbal or mathematical) experience. . . . Only in kindergarten and first grade is education based on the cooperation of all the essential powers of the mind. Thereafter this natural and sensible procedure is dismissed as an obstacle to training in the proper kind of abstraction." In our culture, we find much emphasis on reading speed and comprehension, on IQ tests that rely heavily on verbal ability, and on the use of verbal aptitude scores as an extremely important indicator of intelligence relating to academic and professional potential.

Being a verbal person, I would be one of the last to impugn the sagacity of those who would sanctify the word. It is certainly true that many problems can be well solved verbally. Such solutions can then be easily communicated through well-established verbal channels. However, as we saw in our monk puzzle and our paper-folding problem, there are also problems that can be solved verbally only with great difficulty.

We now live with all kinds of quantities that are so large that we have no feeling for what they really amount to. We are surrounded by billionaires and discuss national debts and expenses in the trillions and even quadrillions. Many of us are uncomfortable with so-called scientific notation. I just read an estimate that there are 10^{24} stars in the observable universe. That is one followed by twenty-four zeroes, or one septillion, if you would prefer. How do you grasp a quantity like that?

As a more down-to-earth example, earlier in the book I stated that you have approximately one hundred billion neurons in your brain and nervous system. How big of a number is that? One common trick for getting a feel for this sort of number's size is to figure out how long it would take you to count to one hundred billion out loud. That is easier than picturing one hundred billion of anything. Let's assume that you had a counter that would allow you to count one neuron every second. That would mean that you could count on the order of thirty thousand neurons in an eight-hour day, or on the order of ten million a year. There you go. You could count all of your neurons in about one thousand years, working every day for eight hours. If you did count out loud, took breaks, and included time for losing track of where you were, eating, using the bathroom, and so on, probably five thousand years.

Clearly, if you attempt to predict the behavior of objects in space, components of complicated machines or structures, or populations and resources, you must include mathematics among your thinking modes. If you cook from recipes, balance your bank account, or use the directions on your lawn fertilizer, you must also use mathematics. If you do not use mathematics as a thinking mode, you are handicapped in working with problems that demand quantification.

Statistics is another area that is very important, but one in which many of us seem to be weak. I am always amused to see that people are more afraid of flying than driving, even though over thirty thousand people a year are killed in car accidents in the United States and very few planes crash, although I admit that the media makes much more of a plane crash than an automobile accident. As mentioned earlier, two Nobel Prize winners, Daniel Kahneman and Richard Thaler, have made much of the difference in people's reaction to odds stated in different ways. And there is always the question—"What are the odds of a fair coin coming up heads after doing so on the previous three tosses?"—that never fails to stump the average person.

Although mathematical aptitude and performance are highly respected in certain circles in our society, verbal aptitude and performance are more generally admired. In fact, in some circles, mathematical illiteracy seems to be a desirable characteristic. Some (usually older) people seem to feel the cultural need to reject mathematics and boast about their ineptness with quantitative matters. Some eschew mathematics as though it were automatic and without soul, a misconception, of course, since pure mathematicians are motivated and guided by a highly developed sense of aesthetics. Still, mathematicians are heavily stereotyped in the United States, and mathematical fluency is much less important than verbal glibness in the majority of high-reward positions in this country. For instance, if I were to run for the office of president of the United States (assuming that this is a high-reward position), I would probably not challenge my opponent to a mathematical problem-solving contest on national TV. In fact, if anything, I would probably conceal my mathematical ability in order not to lose the votes of all those who had rejected math as disagreeable in their childhood.

If more people would utilize mathematics in problem-solving (even at a low level of competence), the overall quality of solutions would benefit. Mathematical and verbal thinking together allow much more powerful attacks on problems than verbal thinking alone. I will not further elaborate on the usefulness of mathematical thinking, since it is generally accepted. I discussed verbal and mathematical thinking rather to demonstrate that two thinking languages make one a more potent and sophisticated problem solver, and that some languages are in higher repute and more frequently relied upon than others.

Discomfort with mathematics also probably results in discomfort with technology and the natural and social sciences, since they are heavy users of mathematics. The scientific and technological illiteracy that the media is so fond of writing about can result. This is sometimes blamed for everything from economic ills to loss of intellectual pleasure. It can certainly result in a loss of creativity. Science and technology are integral to our way of thinking, our industrial success, our health, and the quality of our lives. To avoid them professionally is difficult and may hamper one's effectiveness. To avoid them because of negative emotional reactions is a loss and a reason for a bit of self-analysis and perhaps study.

Let me now discuss some other languages that are extremely valuable in conceptualization. These are the languages of the senses: sight, sound, taste, smell, and touch.

VISUAL THINKING

A particularly important mode of thinking, which I have referred to several times before and which is presently receiving increased attention academically, is visual thinking. Visualization is an important thinking mode that is especially useful in solving problems where shapes, forms, or patterns are concerned. In his book *Visual Thinking*, Rudolf Arnheim explains: "Visual thinking is constantly used by everybody. It directs figures on a chess-board and designs global politics on the geographical map. Two dexterous moving men steering a piano along a winding staircase think visually in an intricate sequence of lifting, shifting, and turning." All of us are used to using visual imagery in some situations. For instance, visual imagery is extremely common in dreams. We use it if someone asks us a question about the appearance of a person or a place. But it is also used in conceptualization, at times when you would not obviously expect its use.

In *The Act of Creation*, Arthur Koestler quotes Friedrich August Kekule, the famous chemist who discovered the structure of the benzene ring in a dream after having devoted a great deal of conscious thought to its enigmatic structure. Kekule describes the discovery:

> I turned my chair to the fire and dozed. Again the atoms were gamboling before my eyes. This time the smaller groups kept modestly in the background. My mental eye, rendered more acute by repeated visions of this kind, could now distinguish larger structures, of manifold conformation; long rows, sometimes more closely fitted together; all twining and twisting in snakelike motion. But look! What was that? One of the snakes had seized hold of its own tail, and the form whirled mockingly before my eyes. As if by a flash of lightning, I awoke.

The result of the dream was Kekule's brilliant insight that organic compounds such as benzene were closed rings rather than open structures.

In *Experiences in Visual Thinking,* Bob McKim writes of three kinds of visual imagery that are necessary in effective visual thinking. The first, perceptual imagery, is sensory experience of the physical world; it is what one sees and records in the brain. The second is mental imagery, which is constructed in the mind and utilizes information recorded from perceptual imagery. The third type is graphic imagery. This is imagery that is sketched, doodled, drawn, or otherwise put down in a written communicable form, either to aid in your own process of thinking or to aid in communication with others.

Let us first of all briefly consider perceptual imagery, or seeing. By asking you to draw a telephone keyboard in chapter two, I hope I convinced you that you do not record everything you look at, at least at an accessible level (under hypnosis, you might be able to draw the buttons on a telephone properly). People see poorly for several reasons. One reason is an oversaturation of input. Another is lack of motivation. People tend to see better those things that are more important to them, more unusual, or of an easily recorded visual character.

You can learn to see better through conscious effort, especially if you are convinced that seeing better is important to you. One method of rapidly developing your seeing ability is to engage in activities where you must reproduce things you have seen.

> **Exercise:** You can exercise your seeing ability by looking at things and then drawing them. Such an activity requires not only seeing, but imagining and drawing, which will be discussed later. Try this procedure with objects around you, or better yet, objects in your profession that you think it would be helpful to know more about.

A drawing course can improve your seeing ability. If you have to draw trees, you will really start seeing them. I took an art course once in which the teacher took delight in asking us to make quick sketches of friends, family, pets, home, and neighborhood. I found this extremely interesting because I looked at my immediate environment at least two orders of magnitude more closely. One of my colleagues took a photography course in which the instructor taught the students to photograph scenery by taking a jar of beans and the students into a field, throwing a bean into the field for each member of the class, and then telling each student to stand on his bean and spend the day shooting scenic pictures. Such exercises make you see. You can take pictures of the Grand Canyon or other scenic wonders without putting a great deal of effort into detailed seeing. However, taking a beautiful picture while standing on your bean in a field requires that you truly use your powers of visual perception.

Now let us talk about the second type of visualization: mental imagery. These mental images are probably the most important for the conceptualizer. According to McKim, there are two aspects of visual imagery that are important. The first he calls clarity: How sharp and filled with detail are the images? The second he calls control: How well can you manipulate them? Here is an exercise to let you evaluate your visual imaging capability.

Exercise: Imagine the following. After each, mark clear (c), vague (v), or nothing (n) in accordance with how clear, sharp, and detailed the image is in your mind.

1. The face of a friend
2. Your kitchen
3. The grille on the front of your car
4. A camellia blossom
5. A fiddler crab
6. A Boeing 747
7. A running cow

8. The earth from orbit
9. Your first car
10. The president of the United States

The clarity of your mental images depends upon several factors. First of all, this type of exercise depends on seeing. If you have never seen a fiddler crab or a running cow, your mental images were probably not too sharp. It also depends on your seeing ability. This, as I have mentioned, depends on motivation (your camellia was probably clearer if you are a camellia freak), the visual character of the object (US presidents are probably fairly clear because they are characterized so often in the news and in political cartoons), timing (your first car may have grown dim by now), and saturation (you probably see your car grille every day). Finally, it depends upon the image-reproduction mechanism of your brain. There is certainly individual variation in the ability to visually imagine that goes beyond the variability mentioned above. If you ask a roomful of people to visualize a brick or an apple, and then ask individual members of the room questions about their image, you will get a range of answers, the clarity of which extends from images vivid in color, detail, texture, background, and shadows to no particular image at all.

> **Exercise:** Try visualizing a series of objects and see if you can determine a pattern in your own imaging ability. Are you better at visualizing people than objects? Are you better at two-dimensional objects than three-dimensional? Are you better at small things than large things? Where do you see your image? Is it out in front of your eyes or back in your skull somewhere?

Visual imaging ability is complex, since it depends upon not only your ability to form images, but also the supply of pertinent imagery that is stored in the mind. However, it seems safe to say that you can improve your visual imaging capability by devoting effort to it and making it a higher priority in problem-solving. Visual images can be consciously enhanced. When I was a student of John Arnold at Stanford, he was constantly hitting me with "visualize an apple"–type problems. As a result, I became so conditioned that when asked to visualize something, I still concentrate all of the information and energy I can on the task.

Now let us look at your ability to manipulate visual imagery.

Exercise: Imagine the following:

1. A pot of water coming to a boil and boiling over
2. Your Boeing 747 being towed from the terminal, taxiing to the runway, waiting for a couple of other planes, and then taking off
3. Your running cow changing slowly into a galloping race-horse
4. An old person you know well changing back into a teen-ager
5. A speeding car colliding with a giant feather pillow
6. The image of number 5 in reverse

Are you better at manipulating images you have actually seen or in creating new ones? Can you modify images in a fantastic, non-real way? Take some time, and see whether you can extend your understanding of your ability to control your visual imagery. Try manipulating various types of images and inventing new ones in your mind. Many people feel that the ability to control visual images can be developed through practice. In *Experiences in Visual Thinking*, McKim discusses what he calls "directed fantasy" as a way of strengthening imagination. The participants are asked to fantasize in a number of directions that take them through a wider range of imaginative activities. They are forced to exercise their imaginative abilities and confront imaginative blocks that they would ordinarily avoid. By finding that they are able to wander freely through these areas and allow their imagination to range widely without catastrophic results, they become encouraged to feel more familiar with the use of visual imagery in conceptualization.

Now let us discuss the third type of visualization: graphic imagery. In order to take full advantage of visual thinking ability, drawing is a must. Drawing allows the recording, storage, manipulation, and communication of images to augment the pictures you can generate in your imagination. These days, there are many tools and surfaces that allow one to draw. Computer-aided design is popular, but there is still much to be said for the tactile experience of drawing with the hand, with a pencil, pen, charcoal stick, or whatever. I may still be biased from my high school experience, in which I took mechanical drawing and was sneered at by the art students. Yet there is beauty and speed in drawing with the hand, unavailable from the machine. Draw a line along a straightedge and then next to it draw a line by hand. Which one is more interesting?

Drawing can be divided into two categories: that which is done to make money, and that which is done to communicate with oneself or colleagues and friends. Examples of the first include architectural drawings to be shown to clients, or illustrations for a book or magazine, or art to be hung on walls. But as far as creativity is concerned, informal drawing is perhaps more important. Your skills don't need to be museum-worthy to produce idea sketches for yourself and your colleagues.

To learn to draw well enough to make a living from it requires a major investment of time and probably formal courses of instruction. Sketching to aid in conceptualizing or communicating ideas requires far less skill and is an important adjunct to visual thinking. Given a large pad of paper and a pencil, most people will make sketches as they work on sample problem exercises. Strangely enough, the same people often will not go to the trouble of summoning their drawing materials on their own in a problem-solving situation.

I am probably sensitized to these particular problems because I have spent quite a bit of time teaching design in a university setting that attracts an extremely verbal group of students. A great deal of effort has been put into their verbal and mathematical abilities during their formal education, but little into their visual ability. When they come to Stanford, many are visual illiterates. They often are not used to drawing, nor to using visual imagery as a thinking mode. Although their drawing is generally not good, it is usually good enough (especially with a few helpful hints) to use as a thinking aid. Nonetheless, they are extremely reluctant to draw because their drawings compare so badly with drawings made by professionals. In design, we try to encourage crude but informative drawings for the student's own purposes. We also try to encourage improving one's drawing skills, since we find that good drawing skill is a powerful conceptual aid. Try the following exercise and see whether your drawing skills (no matter how marginal) help you in conceptualizing.

Exercise: Buy a cheap notebook of a convenient size (small enough to accompany you, but as big as possible otherwise) and provide yourself with the most satisfying line maker you can find. A good one is a Pentel-type pen, which looks like a ballpoint pen but has a tapered fiber tip that makes an instant dark and smooth line. Make drawings for yourself in this notebook for the next week or so while you are conceptualizing and otherwise involved in solving problems. Your drawings may be doodles, block diagrams, schematics, squiggles, sketches, or what have you. Try to see which of these drawings, if any, help in problem-solving and which do not. Are they of more use in particular portions—for example, at the beginning—of the problem-solving process? Does a lack of drawing skill minimize their effect? Do you use your notebook to refer to your previous work? Does the size of your notebook inhibit you? If so, change to newsprint or butcher paper on the wall or a table and to larger felt pens or color, and try again.

But having said all that, I must admit that there are other advantages to being able to draw well. I have had many experiences in which people who are able to draw well have been able to influence others in a problem-solving situation, for better or worse. This is especially prevalent in design situations where no precedent exists. I remember supervising a student group engaged in the design of a new type of underwater vehicle. One of the students was excellent at making quick renderings. Each time he would put forth a concept, it would seem so real in its rendered form that the group would gleefully adopt it. Then, when he produced another concept the next day, the group would be in temporary consternation until they adopted the new one. I have seen the same thing happen many times in the design of spacecraft, where little visual precedent exists.

I had a student years ago named Peter Dreissigacker, now a friend and one of the founders of Concept2, a very successful company based on the sport of rowing. He was unusually good at sketching and has developed his drawing into a hobby. I have often invited him to come talk to classes. The last time I looked in on one of his lectures, he was describing the company, its products, its location, and so on, but rather than using photographs in his PowerPoint lecture, he was using beautiful drawings he had made. Typically students tend to doze off during PowerPoint presentations because they see so many of them. They were wide awake for Dreissigacker's drawings. A good drawing has amazing power. Fortunately, skill comes from practice.

Drawings, of course, have ability to convey precise information, even if crudely done. One of my oldest and best friends, for instance, is a farmer. When I visit him, I often accompany him on his rounds. Since I am a helpful sort, I try to aid him in his various projects, which often consist of moving large inert objects. Such tasks should be straightforward to someone like me, who is, after all, an engineering professor. However, he gives directions verbally, with the result that I am always bewildered by a version of the situation we encountered in the block-in-the-bag exercise in chapter five. (I have embarked on a long-term project of getting him to draw crude pictures for his people and for me, so I will not stupidly put things in the wrong place.)

> **Exercise:** Use your drawing skills, no matter how marginal, to aid in giving directions to people. Carry a small pad and pencil to do this if necessary. You are probably familiar with drawing crude maps to show people how to get to your house. But have you ever drawn for your children (assuming you have some around) a map of where to pile the leaves they are raking up, or your partner a map of where to put things away in the house, or of how to carve a roast?

Let us now leave visual imagery. If you have the time and inclination to attempt to develop your visual thinking ability, the internet will give you places to start. At the very least, become aware of your abilities and limitations with visual imagery and attempt to use visualization in your thinking process whenever appropriate. It is one of the most basic of all thinking modes and one that is invaluable in problem-solving.

OTHER SENSORY LANGUAGES

We will now go on to explore other sensory languages that are essential in conceptualization and are used even less frequently in general problem-solving than visual thinking. Just as visual imagery corresponds to the sense of sight, other types of imagery result from their corresponding senses.

Here are some exercises for you to test how good you are at different types of sensory imagery.

Exercise: Imagine the following, and once again rate them clear (c), vague (v), or nothing (n).

The laugh of a friend
The sound of thunder
The sound of a horse walking on a road
The sound of a race car
The feel of wet grass
The feel of your wife's/husband's/girlfriend's/
    boyfriend's/pet's hair
The feel of diving into a cold swimming pool
The feel of a runny nose
The smell of bread toasting
The smell of fish
The smell of gasoline
The smell of leaves burning
The taste of a pineapple
The taste of Tabasco sauce
The taste of toothpaste
The muscular sensation of pulling on a rope
The muscular sensation of throwing a rock
The muscular sensation of running
The muscular sensation of squatting

The sensation of being uncomfortably cold
The sensation of having eaten too much
The sensation of extreme happiness
The sensation of a long attack of hiccups

Now try the following for control of separate sensory images:

The sensation of being uncomfortably cold changing to one
of being uncomfortably hot
The laugh of a friend changing into the sound of thunder
The feel of wet grass changing into the feel of your wife's/
husband's/girlfriend's/boyfriend's/pet's hair
The smell of fish changing into the smell of gasoline
The muscular sensation of pulling on a rope changing into
the muscular sensation of rowing a boat

Such exercises have a function equivalent to the earlier exercises on visual imagery. They may help you develop your sensory imagery ability, if used extensively. In any case, they at least let you learn more about your ability to image in various sensory languages.

Sight tends to be the predominant sense from a physiological standpoint. However, just as verbal thinking should not be allowed to elbow visual thinking out of the way, neither should the visual mode be allowed to overpower other sensory modes. Smell, sound, taste, and touch are extremely important to problem solvers for three reasons:

1. Since they are low on the prestige list in our culture, other senses can lead you to innovative and overlooked solutions. Tarzan had a well-developed sense of smell, but I am sure that no one would expect the same from a Nobel Prize winner.

2. They are necessary for the solution of problems in which smell, sound, taste, and touch are involved (for example, the design of a new hors d'oeuvre).
3. They augment visual imagery and each other to vastly increase the clarity of one's total imagery.

Let us briefly discuss the first reason listed above. I often gave my students problems having to do with developing devices to help blind people. I did this because it proved highly motivating and required ingenuity, and because it made them think about various types of sensory inputs. Most of them attacked the problem initially by imagining that they were blind. This is difficult to do, because sight is such an overwhelming input to most people that they find it hard to take the role of a blind person using their imagination alone. They especially find it hard if they generally think only verbally or mathematically.

After letting them work on the problem a while, I blindfolded the students for an hour or two (with a guide) and let them wander about the campus. This gave them, all at once, a chance to accept input from their other senses. They were then much more likely to use this very important data to solve their problems. This simulation of blindness has limited accuracy, because when you are blindfolded for an hour or two your main problems have to do with walking, whereas blind people have long since overcome this. Still, the simulation is effective in bringing the awareness to messages from the other senses.

Exercise: Try this experience yourself. Find someone to keep you out of trouble (not to physically guide you, just to keep you off the freeway, out of open manholes, away from poison oak, etc.), blindfold yourself, and walk around for an hour or so. You will be amazed at the sensory data you accumulate.

The second reason for using all the senses—that they are necessary for the solution of problems in which smell, sound, taste, and touch are involved—should be obvious. Just as an architect is better off with a good ability to image spaces and forms, so a cook is better off being able to image taste and smell.

The third point, that they augment visual imagery and each other, is more subtle. I am sure that most of you are aware that the senses augment each other. The experience of food is a combination of taste, smell, and sight. Vichyssoise is unsuccessful when one has a cold, and so is an omelet is if it is dyed blue. An electrical storm needs sound as well as sight to be really dramatic. Sexual excitement benefits from feel, smell, and taste as well as sight and sound. Similarly, mental images need the full dimensionality of all the senses to be most effective.

Try to keep in mind that there are a very large number of problem-solving languages, some of which you use easily, some you are familiar with, and some you may never encounter. You don't need to be expert at all of them, although creativity benefits from a larger vocabulary. However, to be uncomfortable with unfamiliar ones simply because they are strange is a definite inhibition to creativity.

COGNITIVE DIVERSITY

As well as thinking languages, there is the issue of cognitive or intellectual style: the type of thinking we prefer to do. The following table lists adjectives that might be applied to the word "thinking."

These words also imply problem-solving styles or thinking specialties. The list is by no means complete; it is included to give you an indication of some types of specialties. The first column contains words that describe thinking strategies and methods of attacking problems. The second column consists

Strategic	Personality Related	Disciplinary	Overall Quality	Miscellaneous
Inductive	Optimisitc	Scientific	Quick	Visual
Deductive	Pessimistic	Humanistic	Slow	Wishful
Critical	Paranoid	Mathematical	Sloppy	Tough-
Intuitive	Neurotic	Verbal	Keen	minded
Analytic	Compulsive	Legal	Fuzzy	Literal
Imaginative	Obsessive	Medical	Clear	Expressive
Converging	Schizophrenic	Technological	Right	Exaggerated
Diverging	Twisted	Anthro-	Shallow	Random
Rational	Warped	pological	Deep	Instinctive
Irrational	Distorted	Sociological	Methodical	Insightful
Forward	Pigheaded	Historical	Plodding	Constructive
Backward	Wrong-	Market-	Brilliant	Aesthetic
Focused	headed	oriented	Mercurial	Creative
Narrow	Stubborn	Product-	Muddled	Efficient
Broad	Maudlin	oriented	Productive	Precise
Incisive	Introverted	People-	Powerful	Innovative
Decisive	Extroverted	oriented		Practical
Indecisive	Weird	Financial		
Judgmental	Sick			
Theoretical	Aggressive			
Applied				
Additive				
Eliminative				
Qualitative				
Quantitative				
Objective				
Subjective				

of words that are often used to describe thinking but which are obviously reflections on personality. Upon compiling this list, I was astounded by the number of words that have negative personality connotations. See if you can add some with positive connotations. The third column refers to disciplinary specializations. These are often related to the schooling we have had and the way we make our living. This column has the potential to be extremely long, of course, because we have all developed specializations that help us be proficient in our jobs. The fourth column contains words that refer to the overall quality of thinking. The last is a miscellaneous column.

As you read the words, notice which ones cause you positive or negative emotion. The positive ones are probably consistent with your preferred problem-solving styles. Which styles are consistent with being able to adapt to change and be creative? Which ones are consistent with the status quo? Which ones do you admire the most? Which ones would you like more of? Can you think of words that should be added to the list? Would you like to see some words deleted? Can you think of a better list format? See if you can list your own preferred and non-preferred problem-solving specialties and those of your friends and the members of your household.

Intellectual specialization is valuable to us. Specialties are psychologically healthy. If you are extraordinarily good at something, you are likely to have a much healthier ego. A common example of this is the apparently fearless venturing of highly credentialed people (Nobel Prize winners, ex-presidents of large corporations, professional athletes, politicians, etc.) into areas for which they have little if any formal training or even competence. Specialties are also socially invaluable. It is simply not possible to maintain the complex social institutions we have without specialization. Organizations would obviously not be able to function as they do without people who have become extremely specialized and, therefore, proficient in their fields. Neither could our nations, our cities, our schools, or even our homes.

THE PROBLEMS OF SPECIALIZATION

However, specialization has a downside as far as creativity is concerned. Intellectual specialties are sometimes described as grooves in the mind, caused by repetition and reward. This is an old metaphor probably tracing back to William James and now a part of our vocabulary. Unfortunately, a groove is not too far from a rut. Many of the problems I see are a result of people attempting to inflict their own preferred problem-solving style on others or not appreciating the value of other methods.

A professional example can be seen in many companies in the interaction, or lack thereof, between the problem-solving styles of marketing and new product development. Both of these activities are necessary in a healthy company and, in fact, many companies get into trouble when one function tends to dominate at the wrong time. However, the specializations of the people involved often lead them into different philosophies. To product-development people, progress is improvement of the product itself, whether functional, visual, or economic. Their focus is internal, toward the company's design, development, manufacturing capability, and pertinent technology.

Marketing people, on the other hand, have an outward focus. They are tuned to customer needs, which may not be consistent with technical progress. It is possible in a company to find the engineers attempting to develop a faster, more expensive printer and the marketing people calling for a slower, cheaper printer. Should this situation continue, great pain can result. Similar differences in attitude come from the relative specializations of product design and manufacturing people, managers and workers, hardware and software experts, research and product development people, first-line managers and middle managers, professors and students, teenagers and parents, and husbands and wives.

Broadening one's vocabulary of problem-solving methods is a good way to increase creativity. So is working with people of other problem-solving styles. Diversity in cognitive approaches leads to greater creativity. It does not always lead to greater harmony and consensus, but harmony and consensus aren't always related to creativity. Let us imagine that we could plot the problem-solving styles of individuals in some way, such as that shown in the figure. There are two extreme ways in which such a group of people could operate. One would be at the overlap, making use of problem-solving specialties that are common to all members. This is not an uncommon way of operating, and in certain situations it gives great benefit. An unstructured group of peers will tend to operate in this way.

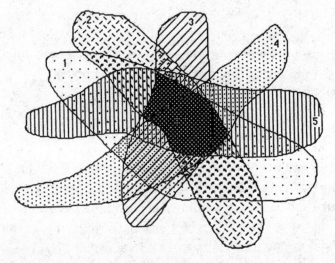

The Problem-Solving Styles of Five Individuals.

If you have ever played a game called Desert Survival (or similar variants called Lunar Survival and Arctic Survival), your group probably operated like this. In this game, you are asked to imagine that you are stranded in a hostile place with a group of fifteen objects. You are to rank the objects in order of usefulness. You first do it as individuals and then as a group. There are experts in these situations, and the group ranking is usually in closer agreement with the expert rankings than the individual rankings are. There are obvious reasons for this. Groups operating in common problem-solving areas are wise, converging, and conservative. They are also smoothly running and quite happy. They are not good at creativity and change, because the success of the group is due to its ability to suppress deviance from conventional wisdom.

The other extreme operating mode would be to use all the individual problem-solving styles. In this case, we have an intellectual capability that far surpasses that of any individual in the group. The group is, if you will, smarter. It is capable of great creativity and change. However, it must be managed carefully, because it will obviously be rife with discomfort, disagreement, and divergence. It is, however, a powerful resource and will not be guilty of groupthink if properly managed.

How can such a group come about? By expanding one's acceptable vocabulary of problem-solving styles, an individual can cultivate the effects of such a group. An existing group of people can be brought closer to this mode by encouragement and proper management. However, an even quicker way is through formation of an ad hoc group, a task force, a study team, or other assemblage of people with different intellectual preferences. Such a group begins with the desired variety of cognitive styles. I will discuss this in more detail in chapters nine and ten, which have to do with group and organizational creativity.

Let us talk about problem-solving specialties still more specifically, in order to reinforce this message. I will discuss three specific sets of problem-solving styles in order to better illustrate what I mean. These three are the typical broad cognitive style differences. There are many others, but if you have an understanding of these, you will be better able to think in terms of cognitive styles and be better equipped to find more productive ways of solving problems in groups.

ANALYSIS-SYNTHESIS

Strictly speaking, the word analysis refers to the separation of the whole into its parts so as to discover the characteristics of these parts and their relationships to each other and to the whole. In this way, it is possible to develop an understanding of the behavior of the whole as a function of its parts. A clear demonstration of this can be seen in mathematics such as calculus, where variables (the parts) are specifically defined and then worked with through equations to find the relationships between them. Analysis is widely used in science, literature, and all other fields. It is high-level human intellectual activity, and phrases such as "let's analyze this" and "analytical thinking" are everywhere.

Synthesis refers to the putting together of parts into a whole. The purpose of synthesis is to come up with a construct to satisfy the goal. An example of pure synthesis, if it exists, would be a painting by a child or the axe of very primitive man. I say "if it exists," because ordinarily even the most basic acts of synthesis are accompanied by some knowledge based on analysis. The child has probably been shown that he should not move the brush toward the bristle end, and the primitive person probably analyzed the act of killing, defense, or construction that led to the concept of an axe.

To use analysis or synthesis alone penalizes us. It is possible to perform analysis as a pure intellectual activity (as in solving calculus equations), but the overall purpose of analysis is to allow better synthesis. In analysis, where unknowns and uncertainty are present, synthesis is necessary to adapt analytical techniques to the problem or, if necessary, to synthesize new analytical techniques. Synthesis also benefits immeasurably from the use of analysis. Complex modern constructions—such as large organizations, aircraft, sewage systems, or Christo's *Running Fence*—simply could not be accomplished without analysis. It is therefore sad when those who identify themselves with one of the two problem-solving approaches become antagonists. The painter and the applied mathematician, the poet and the chemist, the singer and the engineer should all rely on a balance of analysis and synthesis, but they can often be found preaching the virtues of one to the exclusion of the other. This is always a loss, since the combination of the two is essential for creativity and change in complex situations.

CONVERGENCE-DIVERGENCE

Convergent thinking focuses on an answer. Long division is a simple example, as is calculating your income tax. Techniques are used that eliminate uncertainty, simplify complexity, and enhance decision-making ability. Much of education is convergent. Certainly you expect the thinking of experts to be convergent. You would like your doctor to converge on a diagnosis, your architect to converge on a design, your auto mechanic to converge on a solution, and members of your family to converge on a few important problems for you to help them with. Techniques such as trigonometry, sentence parsing, decision analysis, double-entry bookkeeping, TV repair, and recipes for French bread are all convergent.

Divergent thinking refers to the process of generation of ideas, concepts, and approaches. It is an extremely powerful process and is perhaps less familiar because less emphasis is placed on it in our schools and public consciousness. It is possible to radically increase divergent thinking in problem-solving. To the extent that more concepts are generated, decision-making becomes more complicated. However, more alternatives result in a greater probability of a better solution. Certainly more options are likely to permit a more creative solution, since initial concepts tend to be closely related to tradition.

Once again, the competent problem solver or problem-solving group should be able to handle both modes of thinking well and, in fact, in most problem-solving activities there is an overlap. It is inefficient merely to continue to generate ideas with no accompanying convergent thinking, as the pool will grow to a size that will make decision-making nearly impossible. Similarly, it is foolish to converge without spending some effort to ensure that alternatives have at least been examined, if not consciously generated. However, once again we find individuals, groups, and even organizations identifying only with the divergent (blue-sky, creative, idea person) or the convergent (tough-minded, decisive, practical). We find engineering schools obsessed with convergence and art schools obsessed with divergence, even though, as a practitioner in one and at least a dabbler in the other, I do not find the difference in intellectual activities between the machine designer and the sculptor to be that great. As in the previous cases, separation by specialty is a loss, especially in situations requiring creativity and change.

DEDUCTION-INDUCTION

Deduction and induction are another way of slicing the pie. Deduction has to do with reasoning from the general to the specific. It is usually associated with analysis, but this can be misleading. We use it to go from a theory to specific facts or from an equation to an answer. We use it a lot in school and when we are applying a technique. We expect that great detectives, such as Sherlock Holmes, use it, because their overall knowledge is so scientific and complete that they can deduce the criminal.

Induction, on the other hand, is reasoning from the specific to the general. It is the way that scientific theories are created and how we often solve problems. In most of life, adequate theory does not exist. We try to figure out the problem and the answer from observing specific shortcomings. Induction does not have as much mystique as deduction because it does not seem as right-answer oriented. In that sense, it falls in with synthesis and divergent thinking. However, we rely upon it a great deal, especially in creativity and change. Competent problem-solving requires both specializations.

CHAPTER 7

Kinds of Blockbusters

ONE WAY TO INCREASE INDIVIDUAL CREATIVITY IS TO FIRST
make the brain more aware of the advantages of doing so, and
to equip it with techniques that work for you. I will discuss some
of the tried-and-true ways to increase creativity in this chapter,
as well as mention a few books on creativity techniques in my
suggested reading section. But it's important to remember that
learning two hundred methods of increasing creativity is valuable only if you want to write a book on two hundred methods
of creativity, or pass yourself off as a creativity consultant. Better
to learn and use a few, so that the brain learns to not always take
the first answer to a problem it thinks of and run with it.

The use of a rich vocabulary of thinking languages and cognitive diversity, as discussed in chapter six, is one way to overcome
conceptual blocks. However, there are many other methods. We
will look at some such techniques in this chapter. We will explore a few techniques that allow the use of the conscious mind
to overpower conceptual blocks. In a sense, these techniques
force thoughts that would not otherwise occur. The last part
of the chapter is about becoming more relaxed, more intellectually playful, and perhaps less critical during problem-solving.
Chapters eight and nine will contain additional blockbusters.

You may wonder why this book has focused on blocks to creativity, rather than guaranteed methods of winning Nobel and Pulitzer prizes, Oscar and Tony awards, and great wealth and fan clubs. It is because, in my experience, both brains and people respond better to a challenge than a goal. I have come to believe that for those of us who read books like this, if our brain becomes more conscious of these blocks, it will become annoyed by them and attack them. After all, one's brain should think it is terrific (which it is) and be above being tripped up by such things. You might also wonder why we restrict ourselves to individual blocks. That is the raw material in creativity. We will talk a bit more about brains and nervous systems in the next chapter, and then about groups and organizations in chapters eight and nine.

The process of consciously identifying conceptual blocks takes one quite a distance toward overpowering them. Still, there are specific methods of going further. Many of these blocks exist because of our achievement-oriented, competitive, and compulsive nature. However, this very combination of characteristics outfits us optimally for consciously overpowering such blocks. Students who are interested solely in good grades are often not as creative in school as they could be. However, if they are put in a course that is graded on creative output, they become much more creative. Their motivation and mental discipline are sufficient that they quickly figure out ways to become more creative and act accordingly. Let us talk about a few such methods that can be consciously applied to problem-solving.

A QUESTIONING ATTITUDE

One of the most important capabilities in a creative person is a questioning attitude. Everyone has a questioning attitude as a small child, because of the need to assimilate an incredible amount of information in a few years. The knowledge that you acquire between the ages of zero and five, for instance, enormously exceeds what has been consciously taught. A great amount of knowledge is gained through observation and questioning. Unfortunately, as we grow older, many of us lose our questioning attitude. There are two principal reasons. The first is that we are discouraged from inquiry. After the child reaches a certain age, parents and others are often not as patient with questions. This is especially the case if they are busy or do not know the answer, or the question does not seem socially pertinent. (Why can you see through glass? Why are leaves green?) In such cases, the adults tend to discourage the questioner. Our educational institutions can barely convey the knowledge they are held responsible for, such as reading, writing, arithmetic, and cultural lore. There is little time available for answering questions, so questions are effectively limited and discouraged. Many professors begin their lectures with a plea for questions and then include so much material that there is neither the time nor the encouraging attitude necessary to get to them.

The second reason the child's inquisitive nature is socialized out of us, or at least diminished, has to do with the great knowledge game. We learn as we grow older that it is good to be smart. Smartness is often associated with the amount of knowledge we possess. A question is an admission that we do not know or understand something, and therefore leaves us open to suspicion that we are not omniscient. Thus, we see the almost incredible ability of students to sit totally confused in class, at a university that costs thousands of dollars a year to attend, and not ask questions. We find people at cocktail parties listening politely to conversations they do not understand, and people in highly technical fields accepting jargon they cannot follow.

One of my colleagues from my aerospace days used to delight in feeding nonsense jargon and erroneous arguments to people in other specialties. They would seldom question him in sufficient depth to find out that he was faking. I have another friend who—at my request, in order to increase student attention—once successfully delivered a totally fraudulent lecture on aerospace medicine (about which he knew nothing) to one of my classes. When his nonexistent credentials were revealed to the students at the end of the lecture, they immediately voiced the doubts that they had accumulated during the hour. They also registered extreme displeasure toward both the speaker and me for violating their trust and wasting their time. However, during the talk itself, the competence and facts of the speaker were not questioned, probably because of the confidence with which he spoke and his extremely articulate lecturing style.

As I previously said, the questioning attitude is necessary in the broadest sense to motivate conceptualization. If you accept the status quo unquestioningly, you will have no reason to innovate. You will not be able to see needs and problems, and sensitivity to problems is one of the more important qualities of the creative person. Once the problem is sensed, the questioning attitude must be used continually to ensure a creative solution. A creative person should have a healthy skepticism about existing answers, techniques, and approaches.

In a fascinating book called *The Universal Traveler: A Soft-Systems Guide to Creativity, Problem-Solving, and the Process of Reaching Goals,* the authors Don Koberg and Jim Bagnall discuss what they call "constructive discontent." In their words,

> Arrival at the age of 16 is usually all that is required for achieving half of this important attribute of creativity. It is unusual to find a "contented" young person; discontent goes with that time of life. To the young, everything needs improvement. As we age, our discontent wanes; we learn from our society that "fault-finders" disturb the status quo

of the normal, average "others." Squelch tactics are introduced. It becomes "good" not to "make waves" or "rock the boat" and to "let sleeping dogs lie" and "be seen but not heard." It is "good" to be invisible and enjoy your "autonomy." It is "bad" to be a problem-maker. And so everything is upside-down for creativity and its development. Thus, constructive attitudes are necessary for a dynamic condition; discontent is prerequisite to problem solving. Combined, they define a primary quality of the creative problem-solver: a constantly developing Constructive Discontent.

This questioning attitude can be achieved by conscious effort. You merely need to start questioning. An emotional block is involved here, since you are apparently laying your ignorance out in the open. However, it is a block that will rapidly disappear once you discover the low degree of omniscience present in the human race. No one has all of the answers, and the questioner, instead of appearing stupid, will often show his insight and reveal others to be not as bright as they thought. The most learned man can be overrun merely by continually applying the questions "why" and "how." Pick a scientist, for instance, and ask him a naive question about something in his discipline. A few questions will drive him back through the basic knowledge. Most of the questions you used to wonder about in your youth (What is beyond the farthest star? What is life? Why do people die? Where do they go after they die?) are still unanswered.

In fact, the person who often is most admired at scholarly meetings is the penetrating questioner, who asks the apparently simple question that points out the flaws in a complex theorem or other structure of knowledge. Therefore, you have nothing to lose and a great deal to gain by questioning. The only thing you need to remember is that not everyone is as enlightened about knowledge as you now are, and some people will become unhappy if questioned to the degree that their omniscience becomes suspect. ("Why should man be creative?" "Because creativity allows self-actualization." "What good is self-actualization?" "It allows man to be happy." "What is happiness?" "Well-being." "What is well-being?" "Go to hell.")

If you still hesitate to ask questions, here are a few harmless and innocent ones. Ask them of anyone, and you will find that you are not as relatively ignorant as you thought.

1. Why do people sleep?
2. Do mirrors make letters appear backward? If so, why do they not make them appear upside down?
3. A canary is standing on the bottom of a large sealed bottle that is placed on a scale. He takes off and flies around the inside of the bottle. What happens to the reading of the scale? What if he is a fish and the bottle is full of water?
4. What is licorice made out of? Why is it black?
5. Many cosmologists presently agree that the universe was created by a big bang, or explosion, and that all of the stars are traveling outward from the original bang. What preceded the big bang?

Exercise: Questioning is especially important in problem finding and problem definition. You are going to use questioning in this manner. To play the game, you need a cooperative person who is in a profession with which you are not very familiar. This exercise may take a reasonable amount of time, but if the person is a friend of yours or is interested in activities such as this, he should not object. Begin by asking him questions and ask them until you have a specific problem in his profession isolated and defined. Don't be satisfied with a vague, overly general, big-picture problem (medical care for the aged is inadequate). Try for a specific problem statement that is obviously solvable with a small amount of effort (for example, the sight of a Novocain needle scares people).

As you ask your questions, be aware of where your difficulties lie. Are certain types of questions more difficult to ask than others? Can you observe the difficult period that results when you have used up your social questions and have to get down to work? What is your subject's response to different types of questions? Do you find it interesting to find out so rapidly about another profession? Were you able to go from a very general problem statement to a specific one? Did you work with several problem statements on the way to your final one?

WORKING ON THE RIGHT PROBLEM

In chapter two I mentioned the importance of framing problems: beginning with a broader frame makes for more ideas, and potentially more creativity, although at some point the frame must be resized to fit the constraints. But there is also the issue of working on the right problem. We are all familiar with our tendency to work on problems that we know how to solve or that are the most apparent, rather than the core problems on which we should be concentrating. I previously mentioned the often-used adage, "If the only tool you have is a hammer, you tend to treat everything like a nail." I would like to offer some alternate versions: "If you are good with a hammer, you prefer nails." Or, "If you see the nail most clearly, you grab your hammer." The skilled physician knows to look for the cause of the symptoms, rather than merely trying to get rid of the symptoms.

The skilled problem solver knows to look for that core problem that causes all of the other, lesser problems.

Prioritization is not always easy, but it must be done. Earlier, I mentioned Jerry Porras, an emeritus professor at the Stanford Graduate School of Business, whose book *Stream Analysis* offers an interesting approach to finding the core problems in business. I had a chance to see its effectiveness in business situations firsthand and have occasionally suggested it to individuals, with positive results. In one exercise, Porras asks his clients to take a large piece of blank paper, divide the paper into four areas—work, material goods, loved ones, and miscellaneous—and write down all of the problems they can think of. He then asks them to draw arrows between the problems, showing which ones resulted in other problems.

Most people can, in a reasonably short time, cover the piece of paper and ask for another. The crucial step is to draw the arrows between the problems, beginning at the causing problem and ending at the resulting one. Ideally, most of the problems will have both arrows in and arrows out. Looking at the piece of paper often gives the person or group new insights to their problems and how to prioritize them. If a problem causes several other problems, which in turn each do the same, it is a pretty important one to work on. On the other hand, if many arrows point to a single problem, it may be difficult to solve. One should also look at the arrows coming in, to see if something can be done to the problems at the other end to decrease the pressure.

This exercise is also interesting because it produces a graphic representation of what you consider your problems to be—and it can be just as useful for individuals as it is for organizations. My experience is that, as professors age and therefore slow down, they tend to take on more problems and get more behind. I understand my life better if I spread my problems out and try to prioritize, or at least look at, them. Not only do I continue to go into my office to talk to students and alumni, advise a museum or two, give talks to various groups, and spend time with my growing family, but, as an engineer, I also own dozens of antique machines I want to get running and restore (some thirty of them have engines). And I want to finish a couple more books after this one, keep my workspaces shipshape, and stay open to new experiences. I suppose I should simply get rid of most of what my wife calls "Jim's stuff," and which I call "my treasures." Even Porras's exercise is not strong enough to make that happen just yet. But trying to prioritize the problems in my life, and especially the work on my treasures, makes me think about it.

My most recent discovery is that my computer is a major problem and that it consumes too much time. I am therefore focusing on tasks such as completing this book, rather than answering e-mail and text messages, writing posts for my blog, looking at social networks I once joined, playing with YouTube, streaming movies and music, and upgrading software. I am probably seen as less social and helpful than before, but prioritizing sometimes does that.

I also find in prioritizing my life that my choices are not often understood by my friends. If I tell them what they are, they argue with me. For instance, writing this book has caused me to neglect minor wear on our house. This makes my wonderful wife a bit miffed and my friends inquire as to why I don't hire people to do the work. The answer is that I love the house and working on it. My friends reply by giving me the names of terrific painters, plumbers, and electricians. Poor friends! They don't understand the joy of fixing things. Although my priorities make sense to me, others may not choose to organize their problems in the same way.

TIME AND EFFORT FOCUSERS AND SET BREAKERS

Fluency and flexibility of thinking are necessary for creativity. Fortunately, there are exercises that can improve both. List making is one of the simplest, most direct, probably most widely used methods of increasing your conceptual ability. People often compile lists as memory aids, such as shopping lists and to-do lists. However, lists are less frequently used as thinking aids. List making is surprisingly powerful, as it utilizes the compulsive side of most of us in a way that makes us into extremely productive conceptualizers. It does not require—in fact, it would suffer from—changes in behavior, and it flourishes in a competitive environment. Our brains, which normally prefer System 1 thinking, seem to shift rapidly to System 2 if they sense competition for a reward, whether it is tangible or simply pleasure. In order to give you a better feel for list making, let me give you an exercise based on the "brick use" test attributed to J. P. Guilford.

> **Exercise:** Imagine that you are a consultant for a brickyard that makes common red construction bricks and is in financial difficulties. The manager of the brickyard is interested in new uses for his products and has asked you to provide him with some. Spend a few minutes thinking about the problem and then write down some new uses for bricks.

Were you aware of what went on in your mind when you were thinking about the problem? You probably did some type of ad hoc listing of alternatives. However, your conceptualization may have suffered from lack of focus, premature judgment (rejecting ideas that seemed impractical), and labeling (choosing only the stereotyped usages).

Exercise: Now take a blank piece of paper and spend four minutes listing all of the uses you can think of for bricks. Remember to aim for fluency and flexibility of thinking and not to get hooked into premature judgment or labeling. Make as long a list as you can. Go.

When your four minutes were up, did you wish you had a bit more time? That's your brain performing under self-imposed pressure. You may have noticed (especially if you did this exercise with others) that people tend to be very intense when listing ideas, particularly when a time limit is involved. This is perhaps a remnant from test taking in our educational system and the general competitive nature of Homo sapiens. However, whatever the cause, listing focuses your conceptual energy in a rather efficient way and produces a written record of the output—both advantageous features. If the above exercise was successful, your listing effort should have gotten you much further conceptually than your original nondirected "spend a few minutes" effort. Were you fluent and flexible? As a calibration point in fluency, our design students average between ten and twenty uses on this exercise. Some produce between five and ten, others between ten and twenty, and others between twenty and thirty; a few produce under five or over thirty the first time through. The curve is roughly bell shaped. But fluency, of course, is not enough in conceptualizing.

If your list were to consist of entries such as build a wall, build a fireplace, build a patio floor, build a shoe store, build a hardware store, build a clothing store, build a grocery store, and so on, you might be fluent, but your ideas would be of limited use to the brickyard owner, who is probably already familiar with these uses. Flexibility of thought is also needed. You are flexible if your list included usages such as the storing of water, the warming of sheets on cold nights, the leveling of dirt, raw material for sculpture, playground blocks for children, and objects for a new track-and-field event (the brick-put). Such usages show an ability to see beyond the conventional role of bricks.

If you were doing this exercise with others, swap lists around and read them. Remember that some of the ideas should strike you as funny if your flexibility is working well. If your list is lacking in flexibility, you may be suffering from the premature labeling block I discussed in chapter two. Bricks are heavily stereotyped as a construction material.

Many creativity techniques have to do with breaking our mental set—diverting us from accepting the answer that first occurs to us by making us develop and consider other answers—and causing us to speed up our brain and point it in a particular direction. In chapter two, I discussed the listing of attributes as a method to escape the inhibiting effects of premature labeling. The listing of attributes is a powerful way to rapidly get more insight into the possible usefulness of an object, which in turn is an advantage in conceptualizing.

Let us list the attributes of a brick. Some of them are as follows:

> weight
> color
> rectangularity (sharp edges, flat faces)
> porosity
> strength
> roughness
> the capacity to store and conduct heat
> poor capacity to conduct electricity
> hardness

Think of more, if you can, and add to the list. How about economic considerations? Aesthetic aspects? I am sure that you can now see that by taking any attribute, it becomes rather easy to list nonconventional uses for a brick. For example, the attribute weight give us the possibilities of anchor, ballast, doorstop, counterweight, holding down tarpaulins or waste newspapers, and projectiles in wars, riots, and neighborhood rumbles.

Another variation on attribute listing, credited to astronomer Fritz Zwicky, is called morphological analysis. It is an automatic method of linking parameters into new combinations for the later review of the problem solver. For instance, in an example done by John Arnold and taken from *A Source Book for Creative Thinking*, the problem is to provide a new concept in personal transportation. First of all, three parameters of importance are selected (more than three could be selected, but they could not easily be drawn on a piece of paper). Alternate possibilities for the three chosen parameters (for example, power source, type of passenger support, and where the vehicle operates) are then listed on three orthogonal axes, as shown in the figure.

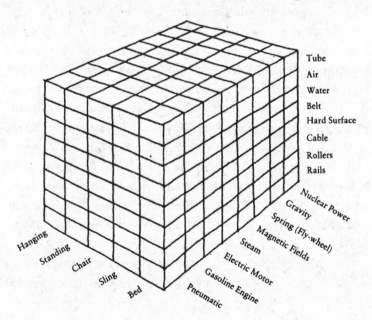

Each box represents a particular combination of our three parameters. For instance, one represents a steam-driven system that runs on rails and has passengers in chairs. This is not so interesting because it is a train and has already been thought of. So has the system that is driven by electricity and slings people from a cable (ski lift) and the gasoline engine–powered one that seats people and travels on a hard surface (car). However, what about the pneumatic-powered one in which people lie down and are transported through a tube, or the gravity-powered one in which people stand and are transported down a belt? If one has access to a computer and can therefore consider large numbers of parameters, this technique can furnish enough combinations to keep the problem solver well out of trouble as he sifts through them looking for something to spark an elegant solution to a problem. The creative purist would tend to scoff at this method as being too mechanistic. However, morphological analysis does, in fact, produce conceptual information.

Let me give you another example of the use of lists as thinking aids. I am going to ask you to make a bug list. People with a healthy fantasy life often play with the concept of inventing something the world needs and retiring on the proceeds. However, relatively few of them accomplish this. There are two factors that explain this lack of follow-through. The first is the difficulty in thinking of something specific that the world needs. The second is that creating something new may require many years of apprehension, financial deprivation, and foundering family life before an invention can be made to pay off. The second factor is the more serious. However, since it is not important unless the first hurdle can be cleared, and since we have no solutions here for it, let us pursue the first.

In order to think of a potentially successful invention, it is necessary to establish a specific need. One way to establish or locate such a need is to interview people. For instance, you could go to the nearest hospital and start asking people on the staff what they desire. Another method is to play the role of a consumer group. Imagine you are a truck driver and see if you can think of something that would help you with your job. A third and perhaps simpler method is to use yourself as the consumer. You must have needs that other people in the world share, and if you could identify such needs you could invent something to satisfy them.

A problem that most people must cope with here is a tendency to generalize. If one of your needs is to eliminate air pollution or violence, you are setting yourself a tall task. A better need would be eliminating dog droppings from your front lawn. The best way of starting on your invention is probably to come up with a list of specific, small-scale needs: a bug list. It is as fluent and flexible and specific and personal a list as possible of things that bug you.

> **Exercise:** Take a paper and pencil and construct such a list. Remember humor. If you run out of bugs before ten minutes, you are either suffering from a perceptual or emotional block or have life unusually under control. If you cannot think of any bugs, I would like to meet you.

A list of bugs from present-day Stanford students follows. After you are done with your list, see if your bugs are as flexible, specific, and personal as theirs. (You may also feel free to draw any conclusions you care to concerning students on your own time.)

If properly done, your bug list should spark ideas in your mind for inventions. The list should ensure that specific areas of need are illuminated and that you have put in a reasonable amount of fluency and flexibility of thought. It should contain far-out bugs as well as common ones. For many of you, it may be the most specific thinking you have ever done about precisely what small details in life bother you.

After my students make such lists, I often ask them to turn their bugs into inventions. Almost invariably, an interesting invention results. This requires first of all that the list be reduced to a few bugs of more-than-average potential. As you identify your bugs, some preliminary thinking of solutions may occur. Needs always seem to have more potential if a clever solution is available. Next, I ask the students to produce several concepts for the solution of each chosen bug. I then ask them to choose a concept and work it out in detail (including physical designs, where pertinent, and implementation plans). You may try this process if you would like. If you succeed and make a lot of money, send me some of it and I will use it for a charitable cause (a contribution to my kids' house payments).

Bug List

TV dinners	plastic flowers	push-button water taps
buying a car	instant breakfast	Pres-to-Logs
relatives	buttons that must be sewn	one sock
paperless toilets	stamps that don't stick	men's fashions
hangnails	chairs that won't slide on the floor	rotten oranges
small, yapping dogs	hair curlers in bed	waste of throwaway cans
banana slugs	hypodermic needles for shots	trying to get change out of pockets
soft ice cream	sweet potatoes	red tape
cleaning the oven	prize shows on TV	smelly exhausts
no urinals in home bathrooms	high tuition	writing letters
bumper stickers that cannot be removed	ditches for pipe that are dug too large	strip mining
dull knives	broken shoelaces	bathtubs
conversion of farm-land to homes	ID cards that don't do the job	cigarettes
balls that have to be pumped up	chlorine in swim-ming pools	pictures that don't hang straight
polishing shoes	ice cubes that are cloudy	reading road map while driving
stripped threads	cold tea	X-rated movies that shouldn't be X-rated

bras	shoe heels that wear out	mowing lawns
weather	locating books in library	newspaper ink that rubs off
miniature poodles	bikes parked in wrong place	parents deciding a kid's career
soap dishes that you can't get the soap out of	lousy books	solicitors— telephone and door-to-door
blunt pencils	burned-out light bulbs	vending machines that take your money with no return
portable computer batteries	pantyhose	thermodynamics
shock absorbers that don't work	dirty aquariums	noisy clocks
shaving	writing books	

Another type of list is the checklist. This is a list that you can apply to the thinking process to make sure that you have not been trapped by blocks. The following checklist was first put forth by Alex Osborn in his book *Applied Imagination*.

Check List for New Ideas

Put to other uses?
New ways to use as is? Other uses if modified?

Adapt?
What else is like this? What other idea does this suggest? Does past offer a parallel? What could I copy? Whom could I emulate?

Modify?
New twist? Change meaning, color, motion, sound, odor, form, shape? Other changes?

Magnify?
What to add? More time? Greater frequency? Stronger? Higher? Longer? Thicker? Extra value? Plus ingredient? Duplicate? Multiply? Exaggerate?

Minify?
What to subtract? Smaller? Condensed? Miniature? Lower? Shorter? Lighter? Omit? Streamline? Split up? Understate?

Substitute?
Who else instead? What else instead? Other ingredient? Other material? Other process? Other power? Other place? Other approach? Other tone of voice?

Rearrange?
Interchange components? Other pattern? Other layout? Other sequence? Transpose cause and effect? Change pace? Change schedule?

Reverse?
Transpose positive and negative? How about opposites? Turn it backward? Turn it upside down? Reverse roles? Change shoes? Turn tables? Turn other cheek?

Combine?
How about a blend, an alloy, an assortment, an ensemble? Combine units? Combine purposes? Combine appeals? Combine ideas?

A perhaps even more thorough checklist is the one below, developed by George Pólya of Stanford for use in solving single-answer mathematical problems. It first appeared in his book *How to Solve It* many years ago. Pólya was a much-loved fixture around Stanford for many years—he lived to be over one hundred and died while giving a talk, the perfect professorial life. This list not only exercises questioning ability, but also your fluency, flexibility, and originality through increased observation and association.

Understanding the Problem

What is the unknown? What are the data? What is the condition? Is it possible to satisfy the condition? Is the condition sufficient to determine the unknown? Or is it insufficient? Or redundant? Or contradictory? Draw a figure. Introduce suitable notation. Separate the various parts of the condition. Can you write them down?

Devising a Plan

Have you seen it before? Or have you seen the same problem in a slightly different form? Do you know a related problem? Do you know a theorem that could be useful? Look at the unknown! Try to think of a familiar problem having the same or a similar unknown.

Here is a problem related to yours and solved before. Could you use it? Could you use its results? Could you use its method? Should you introduce some auxiliary element in order to make its use possible? Could you restate the problem? Could you restate it still differently? Go back to definitions.

If you cannot solve the proposed problem, try to solve first some related problem. Could you imagine a more accessible related problem? A more general problem? A more special problem? An analogous problem? Could you solve a part of the problem? Keep only a part of the condition, drop the other part; how far is the unknown then determined, how can it vary?

Could you derive something useful from the data? Could you think of other data appropriate to determine the unknown? Could you change the unknown or the data, or both, if necessary, so that the new unknown and the new data are nearer to each other? Did you use all the data? Did you use the whole condition? Have you taken into account all essential notions involved in the problem?

Carrying Out the Plan

While carrying out your plan of the solution, check each step. Can you see clearly that the step is correct? Can you prove that it is correct?

Examining the Solution Obtained

Can you check the result? Can you check the argument? Can you derive the result differently? Can you see it at a glance? Can you use the result of the method for some other problem?

List-making techniques can be used by anyone to assemble alternate concepts. They apply to the most rigid thinker as well as the most playful. They not only ensure good definition, but also that the ideas will last, since they are committed to paper.

As we have already mentioned, ideas beget other ideas. If they are listed, they will lie around for days goading the idea seeker into other thoughts.

In a sense, such techniques as design notebooks, idea books, sketchbooks, and problem journals are list-making techniques. A chronological record of a problem's solution is a list of all of the thoughts that have occurred during the solving process. By its very existence, it causes the problem solver to have more and increasingly imaginative concepts, especially if occasionally reviewed by others. I used to ask most of my students to keep design notebooks during their project work. These notebooks were to be complete chronological records of the thinking they did and the information they acquired. I collected the notebooks periodically for grading. I know that many of the students considered them to be an odious task and of questionable value and made most of their entries the night before I collected them. The impact this last-minute "keeping up-to-date" had on their thinking was obvious. Groups that were apparently stuck on a problem would magically come up with new approaches the day that they handed in their notebooks. The intensive list making they went through when padding their notebook to meet my expectations was a powerful stimulus to conceptualization.

There are set breakers other than lists, of course. Anything that breaks the usual context of thinking can function in the same way. George Prince, the cofounder of Synectics, was fond of opening a book, placing his finger on the page without looking, and then trying to incorporate the word his finger hit into his thinking. Roger von Oech, author of *A Whack on the Side of the Head* and *A Kick in the Seat of the Pants,* developed a deck of tarot-like cards, which he calls a Whack Pack. Each of them is inscribed with something to do with your present state of thinking. Many of my friends have physical rituals, ranging from running to golf, that they claim break them out of their mental ruts. There are an increasing number of software programs intended to jog you in new directions in your problem-solving.

Conscious blockbusters can be found in almost any how-to book on creativity. A couple of these are mentioned in the reader's guide. Many of these books utilize some degree of list making. Most of them include some gimmick to encourage playful thinking without the requirement of confronting playfulness head-on. Because of the difference in cognitive styles referred to in chapter six, some techniques are better suited to a particular individual than others. Effort is required to utilize them in a realistic problem-solving situation. The tendency of most teachers and authors (myself included) when trying to show the power of a technique is to include a sample problem that is a setup for demonstrating it. Usually, it is a simple problem that can be instantly solved if the technique is used and only with difficulty if it is not (for example, the monk puzzle). The game becomes more difficult when you leave sample problems.

However, if you acquire sufficient practice with conscious blockbusters, they can be applied to complex, real problems quite successfully. In fact, after sufficient usage, they will become second nature. The specific listing of conceptual blocks is a conscious blockbusting technique. If specific examples are furnished, it is seemingly easy to gain an appreciation for these blocks. However, it is harder to identify them in one's own thinking, both because they are blocks and because one's thinking is usually more complex than the examples. If you put a good deal of conscious effort into looking for blocks, though, you will learn to identify them. You will learn what types of blocks to expect in various situations, aggressively search them out, and gleefully violate them.

USING OTHER PEOPLE'S IDEAS

One good way to break a set is to interact with other people who think differently than you—an easy assignment, since everyone does. This is an especially powerful way of increasing creativity, since we have been brought up glorifying the independent individual creator and are conflicted about getting help with our problems. When reading history books, I am always fascinated with the fact that individuals such as Johannes Gutenberg, James Watt, Cyrus McCormick, and Thomas Edison are given credit for new directions in technology. I suspect this is because of the desire of historians to reach simple conclusions and avoid becoming entangled in technological specifics. If we look at contemporary developments (for example, the computer, digital television, Prozac, the artificial hip joint, the space craft) we have a little more trouble naming an individual who gets the credit, don't we?

I am a believer that most significant human developments have been the work of many, and that if Edison had not been born we still would be enjoying electric lights. If one reads history books in non-Western cultures, there is less of a tendency to give credit to an individual. One of the reasons for the disagreement over intellectual property rights between the United States and China is that the Chinese are not as sure as Americans are that ideas belong to individuals—they joined the international patent system relatively recently. Therefore, such problems as "not invented here" syndrome (placing less value on something because you did not think of it) are not as significant. Think of the stigma placed upon copying. It took US industry a long time to admit the benefits of benchmarking (keeping track of your competitor's products) and reverse engineering (devising solutions from your competitor's products). Americans sat for many years insulting the Japanese for doing such things, while Japanese products improved rapidly. Eventually, for reasons of survival, US industry had to admit that such things are good to do.

As previously mentioned, cognitive diversity is a benefit to creativity. A good test is to ask for ideas from a large number of people, including some who are not your friends. You will be surprised at the variety of responses you get, some of which you will find fascinating because they are so far from solutions you had considered. One of my most successful creativity techniques is to bounce ideas off of a group of people who think so differently than I do that they may be extraterrestrials. (I don't want to ask if they are because they are so helpful that I don't want them to go back to their planet.)

This is not a suggestion that you break the law and end up in jail for patent infringement or kicked out of school for plagiarism. But you certainly can make more use of the cognitive styles and specialties around you. This is one of the reasons for the success of brainstorming. It is both free and pleasurable, since other people like showing off their brilliance in solving your problems, a low-risk activity compared to solving their own. In a corporation, there are specialists who act as free consultants. Some people who do not think twice about asking advice from these specialists feel strange about asking for help from people outside of work. This is dumb. Life is hard enough without using all of the resources available to solve problems, and it is not cheating to use other people's experience.

CROSSING DISCIPLINES

Disciplines were mentioned in the discussion on specialization in the last chapter, but they are worth a bit more attention. As knowledge and intellectual approaches have increased, we have subdivided them into disciplines. We first meet them in school, where we encounter spelling, arithmetic, and music, then English, algebra, languages, and social studies. If we go to college, we find that anthropology, sociology, and psychology are different, and if we stay there long enough we find that cognitive psychology is a very different animal than behavioral. As a professor, I live in a world where thermodynamics experts, engineering mechanics experts, and design experts all live in different intellectual camps—although undergraduates in mechanical engineering know that these disciplines are all part of mechanical engineering, and should be given more of a chance to integrate them in school than is often the case.

Disciplines are accompanied by jargon, methodology, journals, and societies. Their benefit is that they promote depth of understanding, control the quality of work in their purview (sometimes, unfortunately, according to traditional standards), and provide satisfying tribal affiliation for their members. However, more creativity is now taking place between disciplines. I originally became a mechanical engineer because I did not like my electrical engineering classes—a not unusual way to pick a major in college. Now much creativity in mechanical engineering happens by applying electrical engineering (integrated circuits, micro-miniature sensors and actuators, and computers) to mechanical devices. Many breakthroughs in physics are through application of mathematics, in chemistry through application of physics, and in medicine through application of chemistry.

Discomfort in dealing with diverse disciplines, or at least with people who are experts in these disciplines, is a major block to creativity and often based on long-obsolete experiences: bad teachers, dull books, and old approaches. My advice to students is to demand more interaction. From observing students, I get the impression that history becomes much more interesting as one ages. This is not just a problem in engineering. Just because you might have disliked history in high school doesn't mean you won't find it fascinating in college, especially if it is integrated with other social sciences of the same period. The same is true of many other fields.

CROSSING CULTURES AND CHANGING ENVIRONMENTS

As mentioned in chapter four, there are great benefits from becoming knowledgeable about and comfortable with different cultures. Creativity demands both depth and breadth. Travel, living abroad, and mixing with people from different parts of society are broadening experiences. Trying to understand what computer experts are saying if you are not a computer expert is both challenging and educational. If you are an elderly rich white male, attempting to understand the world as seen by a young poor black female can be a great help in increasing creativity. If you are a business person, attempting to understand people who are highly critical of business may help you increase your sales.

Changing environments is also an excellent creativity technique, but it must be done thoughtfully. I have attended many company off-site meetings, usually called retreats, and most of them could accomplish more. Companies will ship their people long distances to beautiful places and then schedule them inside a conference room full of communication equipment. They could just as well stay home. If you are trying to encourage people to bond, you need a common stressful experience, not a conference room. The Marine Corps knows that. If you are an automobile supply company trying to get your engineers to think like Google, maybe you should try to convince Google to host your meeting at one of their locations—and let some of their engineers attend so that they can learn more about the automobile market. Also, if you want people to think creatively, the retreat should not be scheduled down to the minute. Environmental change must be tailored to the desired goal and level of creativity.

RELAXING JUDGMENT

Judgment is clearly necessary in life, but it is often automatic. It's not hard to see why: life becomes simpler if one makes rapid judgments, and a person is rewarded if those judgments are later seen to be right. But premature judgment can be the enemy of creativity. You are undoubtedly familiar with that by the common phenomenon of a better idea that emerges just as soon as you commit to another one.

In his writings, Sigmund Freud discussed the critical role played by the unconscious mind and its inhibition by the ego and superego. So far in this chapter, we have discussed techniques whereby you can consciously force your way through conceptual blocks. Through the use of various forms of listing and by consciously questioning and striving for fluency and flexibility of thought, it is possible to improve considerably your conceptual performance. These techniques work by utilizing the intellectual problem-solving capability of the conscious mind. But in Freud's terms, how do we decrease the inhibiting effect of the ego and superego on the unconscious mind? His unconscious mind is where much creativity takes place.

The ego and superego suppress ideas by judging them to be somehow out of order as they try to work their way up to the conscious level. If this judging can be put aside for a while, many more ideas will live until they can be seen by the conscious mind. The dangers of premature judgment are alluded to in the following statement by Friedrich Schiller (taken from a personal letter to a friend and contained in *The Basic Writings of Sigmund Freud*).

The reason for your complaint [about not being creative] lies, it seems to me, in the constraint which your intellect imposes upon your imagination. Here I will make an observation, and illustrate it by an allegory. Apparently, it is not good—and indeed it hinders the creative work of the mind—if the intellect examines too closely the ideas already pouring in, as it were, at the gates. Regarded in isolation, an idea may be quite insignificant, and venturesome in the extreme, but it may acquire importance from an idea which follows it; perhaps, in a certain collocation with other ideas, which may seem equally absurd, it may be capable of furnishing a very serviceable link. The intellect cannot judge all those ideas unless it can retain them until it has considered them in connection with these other ideas. In the case of a creative mind, it seems to me, the intellect has withdrawn its watchers from the gates, and the ideas rush in pell-mell, and only then does it review and inspect the multitude. You worthy critics, or whatever you may call yourselves, are ashamed or afraid of the momentary and passing madness which is found in all real creators, the longer or shorter duration of which distinguishes the thinking artist from the dreamer. Hence your complaints of unfruitfulness, for you reject too soon and discriminate too severely.

Delaying judgment does not come easily to most people, since we are taught to be severe critics of anything impractical, unrealistic, flippant, flawed, or socially frowned upon. Often we do not want to admit, even to ourselves, the existence of such thoughts in our mind. We certainly do not want to admit to others that we might think of roofing a building with feathers, of reducing air pollution by substituting sedan chairs for automobiles, or perhaps even of legalizing heroin to reduce crime. However, our minds should be able to conjure up these and much wilder ideas if we are to be truly creative thinkers. How, then, do we delay judgment? We can begin by using the conscious mind. Often, if we can consciously make our ego relax a little, the success of the idea generation that follows may cause it to relax even further. We begin a game that is to some extent self-perpetuating. The easiest way to begin this game is to formally (by agreement with oneself or with others) establish a judgment-suspension session. Individually, I may say to myself, "All right, I need some fresh ideas on this problem I am working on and I have a little time to spend, so I will suspend judgment and see what ideas I can think of. It doesn't matter if my thoughts are weird at times, since no one can see what I am up to." I am then free to conceptualize without judging the practicality of the ideas, since I am not imperiling my ego. After all, I officially announced to myself that I would undergo this activity and therefore it is not typical of my usual mental deportment.

Is it possible to somehow relax the control of the ego and superego in general, so that one may make better use of the unconscious mind? The answer is yes, but it is not simple. As mentioned previously, although there are many theories to explain various characteristics of conceptualization, complete understanding of the process does not exist. Many psychologists have attempted to explain the mental processes needed in creative thought and the motivations and characteristics of creative people. A couple of venerable examples follow.

MASLOW

Abraham Maslow was one of the more significant figures in the attempt to understand creativity. He preferred to talk about primary and secondary processes rather than about the unconscious and the conscious. Rather than referring to the primary mental process as the unconscious, he called it the deeper self, in the sense that it is hidden beneath the surface. Maslow also discussed primary and secondary creativity, as mentioned in chapter three. Secondary creativity is that which is evidenced by most people working in a system that requires a great amount of discipline work. It utilizes right-handed thinking and is based upon breakthroughs, or primary creativity, made by others.

To Maslow, primary creativity comes from the deeper or primary self. It is common and universal in children, but in many adults is blocked off to a great extent. In an address called "Creativity in Self-Actualizing People," Maslow discussed a study he did of people who were especially creative and, as he puts it, "self-actualizing." He prefaces his discussion with the admission that very early on he abandoned the notion that health, genius, talent, and productivity went together. Maslow found that a great number of people he studied were highly creative in terms of their own self-actualizing capacity, yet were neither particularly productive nor possessors of great talent or genius. He was particularly struck by those people among his subjects who, though they had no noteworthy talent in any area conventionally associated with creativity, were in their daily lives original, novel, ingenious, and inventive.

From this, Maslow says he learned to apply the word "creativeness" to many activities, processes, and attitudes other than the standard categories to which the quality is typically ascribed, such as literature, art, and theory. Thus evolved Maslow's distinguishing between the "special talent creativeness" that is typically associated with creativity, and what he calls "self-actualizing creativeness," which can be manifest in anything we do, including our most ordinary, mundane activities. In studying the traits of self-actualizing people who bring to their everyday affairs an attitude and manner of creativeness, Maslow located certain commonalities. He found these people to be more spontaneous, expressive, and natural and less controlled and inhibited in their behavior than average. Their behavior seemed less blocked and less self-critical: "This ability to express ideas and impulses without strangulation and without fear of ridicule from others turned out to be an essential aspect of self-actualizing creativeness." Maslow found his subjects to be different from the average person in another way that he felt made creativity more likely: "Self-actualizing people are relatively un-frightened by the unknown, the mysterious, the puzzling, and often are positively attracted by it; i.e., selectively pick it out to puzzle over, to meditate on, and to be absorbed with."

Maslow saw a connection between creativity in one's actions and the inner integration of one's self: "To the extent that creativeness is constructive, synthesizing, unifying, and integrative, to that extent does it depend in part on the inner integration of the person." Maslow traces this to "the relative absence of fear" found in these subjects. They were unafraid of the judgment of others and, especially, of their own emotions, impulses, and thoughts. "It was this approval and acceptance of their deeper selves that made it possible to perceive bravely the real nature of the world and also made their behavior more spontaneous (less controlled, less inhibited, less planned, less 'willed,' and designed). By contrast, average and neurotic people walled off, through fear, much that lay within themselves. They controlled, they inhibited, they repressed, and they suppressed. They disapproved of their deeper selves and expected that others did, too." By doing this, Maslow explains, the person "loses a great deal, too, for these depths are also the source of all his joys, his ability to play, to love, to laugh, and, most important for us, to be creative."

BARRON

Frank Barron, another psychologist who did a great deal of research on creativity, took a slightly different approach. He was unwilling to accept overall psychological health as the criterion for a creative person, because he felt it necessary to formulate criteria that admitted to such creative talents as Ludwig van Beethoven, Jonathan Swift, Vincent van Gogh, Arthur Rimbaud, Charles Baudelaire, Charlotte and Emily Brontë, Heinrich Heine, Richard Wagner, and others who created out of unhappiness. In an article in *Scientific American*, Barron stated:

I would propose the following statements as descriptive of creative artists, and perhaps also of creative scientists:

Creative people are especially observant, and they value accurate observation (telling themselves the truth) more than other people do.

They often express part-truths, but this they do vividly; the part they express is the generally unrecognized; by displacement of accent and apparent disproportion in statement they seek to point to the usually unobserved.

They see things as others do, but also as others do not.

They are thus independent in their cognition, and they also value clearer cognition. They will suffer great personal pain to testify correctly.

They are motivated to this value and to the exercise of this talent (independent, sharp observation) both for reasons of self-preservation and in the interest of human culture and its future.

They are born with greater brain capacity; they have more ability to hold many ideas at once, and to compare more ideas with one another—hence to make a richer synthesis.

In addition to unusual endowment in terms of cognitive ability, they are by constitution more vigorous and have available to them an exceptional fund of psychic and physical energy.

Their universe is thus more complex, and in addition they usually lead more complex lives, seeking tension in the interest of the pleasure they obtain upon its discharge.

They have more contact than most people do with the life of the unconscious, with fantasy, reverie, the world of imagination.

They have exceptionally broad and flexible awareness of themselves. The self is strongest when it can regress (admits primitive fantasies, naive ideas, tabooed impulses into consciousness and behavior), and yet return to a high degree of rationality and self-criticism. The creative person is both more primitive and more cultured, more destructive and more constructive, crazier and saner, than the average person.

OTHER PATHS FOR FREEING THE UNCONSCIOUS

Others have hypothesized different models of the creative person, ranging from the happy, well-balanced, suntanned, confident extrovert to the pain-riddled, warped, moody neurotic. Yet, the theme of unguarded unconscious (or preconscious or primary self or whatever term we use) surfaces again and again. Therefore let us ask the question: What can we do to free the unconscious from its overzealous warden?

Psychoanalysis might be an obvious thought, for it is intended to better integrate a personality by making the unconscious more conscious. It supposedly can ameliorate obsessive-compulsive behavior and therefore unlock the primary self. Many psychologists who have studied creativity agree that the goals of psychoanalysts, if reached, should enhance creativity. The fear that psychoanalysis will somehow ruin the creative powers of a person has been dismissed by most experts. However, for most people, psychoanalysis appears to be somewhat strong medicine for the improvement of creativity. It is expensive, it takes a long time, and its success is not predictable. Psychoanalysis may be attractive if one's behavior is such that life has become acutely unpleasant or unbearable. However, for "normal neurotics," it is perhaps overkill.

Are there other ways to free the unconscious? Probably many. Maslow argues that any technique that increases self-knowledge should in principle increase creativity. In the cultures of the Middle and Far East there have existed for many hundreds of years what Robert Ornstein, in his book *The Psychology of Consciousness,* calls "the traditional esoteric psychologies." These have been concerned with personal, empirical approaches to self-knowledge, rather than with impersonal, scientific approaches. These psychologies have often developed within disciplines such as Buddhism or yoga and have utilized techniques such as meditation that are specifically designed to temporarily minimize linear logical thought and strengthen certain mental processes ascribed to the unconscious. Science is just beginning to understand such mystical experiences and different levels of consciousness. Ornstein believes that these experiences may be instances where the analytical left side of the brain relinquishes its usual control of consciousness and enables the right side to more freely interpret stimuli in a nonlinear, nondeductive way. In his book, Ornstein makes a compelling argument for integrating such psychologies and techniques with the right-handed psychology with which we are familiar. Certainly a higher degree of self-knowledge would result, along with an increased respect for left-handed thinking. However, these techniques take time and effort, and though they are currently becoming increasingly popular in the Western world, many of us are far from being able or willing to use them to improve our conceptual ability.

What paths are easily available to allow us right-handed Westerners to better free the unconscious? Maslow suggests education as one, and I—as an educator rather than a psychiatrist or mystic—must heartily agree. Maslow suspects that although education does little for relieving the repression of instinct and forbidden impulses, it is quite effective in integrating the primary processes and conscious life. Knowledge about psychological processes and problem-solving, and especially about one's self, can loosen the control of one's ego. The principle involved is a simple one: things are not as threatening when they are understood. Fears are lessened if their sources are clear, and most people's egos are smart enough to relax a bit if they are convinced that the results may be positive.

Understanding the workings of your mind perhaps is somewhat like understanding a golf swing. It allows you to work on changing your present actions in a detailed and conscious way. However, in the case of creative thinking, a side benefit is achieved in gaining a greater understanding of the workings of other people's minds as well. Many fears demand a comparison with other people for their maintenance. The fear of asking questions is often predicated on exposing your ignorance to others. The fear goes away when you realize that others are ignorant too. Similarly, you are less afraid of expressing your emotions when you learn that others have similar emotions, whether they have repressed them or not. Brainstorming works because the other people have silly ideas too. You are more willing to struggle with a problem when you realize that few people consistently give birth to answers or solutions in a blinding flash of pure inspiration.

Therefore, I encourage you to read. The sport of thinking about thinking is an interesting one, and the literature to help you in this pastime is extensive. It can only lead to a better ability to use your own mind; a thorough knowledge of psychological theory and creativity research cannot help but increase your creativity. I feel that I have some effect on the creativity of my students merely by making a big deal out of creativity. When elevated to the status of a class subject and thus brought out of the underground, creativity gets the same importance as other academic subjects, and therefore the students feel that they should, in fact, be more creative.

Many books and articles are available concerning the strengthening of one's self-esteem and self-confidence and freeing oneself from unnecessary fears and insecurities. I have drawn from a number of such books. The reader's guide section also outlines a number of starting points, should you desire to journey further, with references to creativity research, psychological theory, and self-therapy. The books on creativity research will give you a better overview of what is known about creative thinking and the characteristics of highly creative people. Psychological theory books will help you understand human behavior and how the mind works. The self-therapy books seek to apply psychological theory in a way that can affect your own behavior.

Reading, of course, is not the only way to gather knowledge about creativity and conceptualization. You may talk to psychologists and psychiatrists who are involved in trying to give people freer access to their unconscious mind. You may observe those around you and attempt to correlate their actions and thought processes to their creative output. You may become more introspective about your own thinking (a must in any case) in an attempt to make it more creatively powerful and efficient.

One of the most important activities is trying to engage in creative thinking. If you use techniques to increase your creativity (such as those discussed in the next chapter) or merely consciously force yourself to be creative (by using lists), a strange thing happens. First of all, you usually find that, if anything, you are more successful in the world, rather than less. You will also find that creative thinking comes easier to you. There are psychological reasons for this. If you use your brain more, your consciousness gets the message that such activities are all right. This message is strongly reinforced if some of the outputs result in successes that the ego can revel in. The more creative thinking is done, the more natural and rewarding it becomes and the more the ego relaxes.

INCUBATION AND SLEEPING ON IT

This is a fitting end to this chapter, since these two approaches to problem-solving require no consciousness at all. Both of them are such favorite approaches for so many people that there must be some truth in them. In the next chapter we will talk a bit about dreaming, since it is obvious that the brain continues working during dreams. But even though we may recall the dream when awakened, we are not conscious during the dream itself. That leads us to wonder: Can it be that the brain can also be working on problems while we are unconscious? It is true that we sometimes awaken with an answer to a problem. Is that because of nocturnal brain activity?

Studies in areas having to do with "unconscious work" vary. But many experiments show that there is such a thing, since it might explain the sudden appearance of a conclusion or a forgotten fact at an unexpected time. Most of us have probably experienced this. For example, has it ever happened that, while giving a talk, you can't remember something until later in the talk, or even that evening, or the next day? I am sometimes fascinated when something I can't remember occurs to me hours later. Where was it stored? What took it so long? This topic has been extensively explored by researchers in the sleep and dream area, but never conclusively resolved. There are several theories as to why incubation does work: data gets stirred up; problem-solving is going on at an unconscious level and presents the solution when it occurs; the prefrontal cortex, which ordinarily helps keep the brain on a logical track, shuts down during sleep, decreasing the realistic barriers in our dreams. There are also theories that incubation doesn't work.

Many guides to creativity suggest a break while working on a problem to let incubation occur. It works for me, but who knows, maybe it has simply become a tradition for my brain to follow. If I am stuck on a problem requiring creativity in the evening, I am fairly confident that at least a new, if not brilliant, solution will be waiting for me in the morning, or maybe even when I wake up during the night. That could be the result of unconscious work, or it could be that in the evening my brain was simply tired, short of sugar or oxygen, dehydrated, or adrift on alcohol.

There are a number of somewhat mysterious brain activities that are either too subtle or too difficult to measure. I am always fascinated when I am driving on a familiar section of road, usually a freeway, and suddenly realize I am twenty miles further than I thought—clearly following twenty miles of unconscious work. This is called highway hypnosis, and it is not recommended. I am often pleased in the morning to realize that I again had the most-recalled of all dreams for the college educated: some version of totally missing a crucial final exam. Why is the body paralyzed during REM sleep, when dreaming is at its most extreme? To prevent you from hurting yourself? And what is daydreaming, and is it related to imagination and curiosity?

My advice on this topic is to keep a record of times when ideas suddenly rise to your consciousness when you have just awakened or when you have been interrupted from your work and are beginning again. If this happens reasonably often, check out some of the research, and thank your brain for letting your consciousness relax while it works on your problem.

CHAPTER 8

Groups

So far, we have considered only indirectly the effects of other people on individual thinking. However, much problem-solving takes place in group settings. We conceptualize with family members, friends, community groups, volunteer committees, and professional colleagues. In such situations, we directly affect other people's conceptual processes and they directly affect ours.

It should not surprise anyone that the conceptual process can suffer when many people are involved. Groupthink is hardly a term of acclaim; it implies blandness and lack of creativity. Most of us have heard the venerable definition of a camel as a horse designed by a committee. But we must also realize that groups and organizations can and do excel in the conceptual process. Groups of people can bring many diverse perceptions and intellectual specialties to bear on a problem. They can provide a supportive emotional environment and the resources necessary to develop initial concepts into believable detail in a reasonable time. In fact, in most of the projects in which I have been professionally involved, groups have been necessary in order to cover the breadth of disciplines and specialties concerned. The short answer to why groups are beneficial to creativity is that they have a bigger brain!

During the past fifty years, much attention has been paid to groups because of the realization that teams rather than individuals have been the most powerful source of innovation. Interest in group dynamics increased in the 1960s when the perceived superiority of the Japanese approach led to study of the differences between Japanese and American working groups. Business schools, companies, and nonprofit institutions responded by increasing their focus on group dynamics and related topics. The resulting research and discussion has led to much clearer insight into the nature of the creative group, in industry and elsewhere. Some of the more important conceptual blocks that apply to groups are:

1. Inadequate knowledge of the creative process and of the use of group creativity techniques
2. Poor understanding of the roles of affiliation and ego needs
3. Poor leadership
4. Inadequate or unbalanced group membership
5. Lack of proper support

THE PROCESS

I have been a leader of or consultant to creative groups often enough that I am frequently asked, "How do you help a group become more creative?" Probably the best incentive you can offer a group is a project that is challenging and important and has the potential to benefit the world. But how to boost the creativity of that group as they work? The approach that works the best for me is to get the members of the group interested in the creative process, the blocks and techniques outlined in the previous eight chapters. The people with whom I work are difficult to trick into being more creative, but they can easily become interested in the problem-solving process. Once interested, they seem to have an internal motivation to demonstrate that they can rise above conceptual blocks. In fact, that is probably the reason that this book is still around. *Who me? Conceptual blocks? I'll show you . . .*

There are group creativity techniques just as there are individual ones. Perhaps the best known such technique is brainstorming, a group problem-solving method invented many years ago and given its name by Alex Osborn, one of the founders of the advertising firm Batten, Barton, Durstine & Osborn. Brainstorming groups generally consist of five to ten people who work on a specific problem.

Four main rules govern their behavior. The first is that no evaluation of any kind is permitted. Osborn's explanation was that a judgmental attitude will cause the people in the group to be more concerned with defending ideas than with generating them. His second rule was that all participants be encouraged to think of the wildest ideas possible. His thinking here was that it is easier to tame down than to think up, and by encouraging wild ideas, internal judgment in the minds of the individual participants can be decreased. Third, Osborn encouraged quantity of ideas, both because quantity helps to control internal evaluation and because he felt that quantity leads to quality. The final rule was that participants must build upon or modify the ideas of others because, in his words, "combinations or modifications of previously suggested ideas often lead to new ideas that are superior to those that sparked them."

Brainstorming has become ubiquitous. It takes many forms in different places, and that is one of the reasons it has had such a long life, with no end in sight. The brainstorming process benefits from having one member of the group act as a recorder, since a list of the ideas as they are developed ensures that the group has continual access to its output and that ideas are not lost. The recording method should ideally be large enough in scale so that ideas are easily readable by everyone in the group. Brainstorming is most effective when the problem to be solved is simple and can be well defined, but it is useful at all levels of problem-solving, from the original attempt to formulate broad concepts to the final detailed definition.

There are a variety of behavioral reasons for brainstorming's success as a problem-solving technique. A study group at Harvard that investigated brainstorming in the 1950s when the process was new and exciting listed the following:

1. Less inhibition and defeatism: rapid-fire ideas presented by the group quickly explode the myth that the individual often casts up that the problem overwhelms him, and that he can't think of a new and different solution
2. Contagion of enthusiasm
3. Development of competitive spirit; everyone wants to top the other's idea

But I think delay of judgment is perhaps the most important factor that makes brainstorming work.

Brainstorming has at times received a bad name because it has been credited with generating ideas that are both shallow and in questionable taste. It has also been heavily spoofed and is sometimes identified with weirdness rather than thoughtfulness. However, the brainstorming process has some solid advantages and, if used appropriately, can be extremely effective. A brainstorming group allows for the pooling of diverse backgrounds. Shallowness of output is often due to inadequate information available to the group and poor subsequent judgment, not to the technique. Brainstorming initially progresses rapidly when it attacks a problem because it is able to utilize common solutions. However, after these are used up, the process becomes more difficult, because the members must come up with new concepts. It is in this later period that the technique has the most value. If the session is allowed to stop when the original rush of enthusiasm dies down, it will not live up to its potential.

It's no accident that the technique of brainstorming was invented by someone from the advertising business. Having worked with such people, I find them quick to recognize an idea that fits their criteria and captures positive interest. After that, implementation of the idea is relatively straightforward. My professional experience, on the other hand, is mostly with complex systems requiring careful interaction between parts—there are few simple answers, and criticism is necessary because of the different specialties on the team. If someone suggests something that violates the second law of thermodynamics, someone should politely mention it. When I lead a brainstorming group of that sort, I must admit that I am a bit soft on the no criticism rule and instead count on humor to keep people involved. Brainstorming goes a lot more slowly in such a case, because the people on the team usually have conflicting interests, but it still is a valid method for boosting creativity.

The most effective way to learn more about brainstorming is to experience it.

Exercise: Find a group of people and set up a brainstorming session on a problem that is easily stated in precise terms. Try to think of a problem that is important to all of you. If you cannot, try one of the following:

1. Invent some sort of social function that would allow you to become friends with a few fascinating people whom you know of, but do not know personally.
2. Invent (in reasonable detail) a better way to divide a large (2,000 sq. ft. or so) room into smaller spaces that

can be used by various groups. This is an ongoing problem in schools. The dividing system should be flexible,
cheap, and aesthetically pleasing.

3. Invent an astounding entrée for a far-out dinner party.

4. Invent a better way for handling road maps in a car, assuming your navigational system has failed.

5. Invent a Christmas greeting card you can mail to your
friends that will impress them for all time and let you
avoid mailing future cards.

There has been some discussion of whether brainstorming
results in more or better ideas than the individuals might produce working separately. Fortunately, there is research assessing
how brainstorming works in practice. Andrew Hargadon, the
Charles J. Soderquist chair in entrepreneurship and a professor
of technology management at the UC Davis Graduate School
of Management, as part of his dissertation work spent a year
observing and contributing to weekly brainstorming sessions in
the consulting design firm IDEO. These sessions have become
a tradition at the company and are conducted with high energy,
much humor, and fierce competition to be the most creative
individual in the group. Hargadon concluded that the sessions
not only generated ideas but added to the unity of the groups,
as well as the creative confidence and morale of the members.
In a paper he wrote in conjunction with Robert Sutton, professor of management science at the Stanford School of Engineering, he listed the following benefits to the company:

These sessions had six important consequences for this
firm, its design engineers, and its clients that are not evident in the brainstorming literature, or are reported but
not labeled as effectiveness outcomes: (1) supporting the
organizational memory of design solutions; (2) providing

skill variety for designers; (3) supporting an attitude of wisdom (acting with knowledge while doubting what one knows); (4) creating a status auction (a competition for status based on technical skill); (5) impressing clients; and (6) providing income for the firm. This study suggests that when brainstorming sessions are viewed in organizational context and the "effectiveness at what" and "effectiveness for whom" questions are asked, efficiency at idea generation may deserve no special status as an effectiveness outcome.

For more of Hargadon's thoughts on creativity and entrepreneurship, try his book *How Breakthroughs Happen: The Surprising Truth about How Companies Innovate.*

SYNECTICS

There are many individuals and companies who offer group creativity approaches that differ from brainstorming, and because of mutual interest and timing, I met and got to know two such people, William J. J. Gordon and George Prince, many years ago. After studying group creativity as employees at the consulting company Arthur D. Little, they quit with a couple of friends in 1960 and put together their own technique and company called Synectics. Their technique was based on a study of many meetings of industrial groups. When I joined the Stanford faculty in 1966, I visited Synectics several times, even though they were in Boston and I was in Palo Alto. I found their approach to be a very interesting contrast: more complex but perhaps also more sophisticated than brainstorming, in that it allowed criticism and a higher level of technical expertise.

Due to changes in my Stanford work and in personnel at Synectics (Gordon died in 2003, and Prince in 2009 at age ninety-one), I lost track of the company. But at the time of this writing it is still apparently going strong, now called Synecticsworld, and appears to be on a similar path to the company I knew.

A Synectics session was, first of all, centered upon a client with a problem. The session was designed to allow the client ample opportunity to provide input to the group. He or she would describe the problem, and then the group would come up with ideas of how to solve it. The leader of the group was a Synectics employee, serving as a facilitator and a recorder. Though the leaders did not contribute directly to the problem solution, they were very good at preventing behavior that was negative or that would impede creativity. The two illustrations are taken from a 1983 article entitled "Synectics: Twenty-Five Years into Creativity and Group Process," by George Prince, and show the types of actions within a group that he felt encouraged and discouraged creativity.

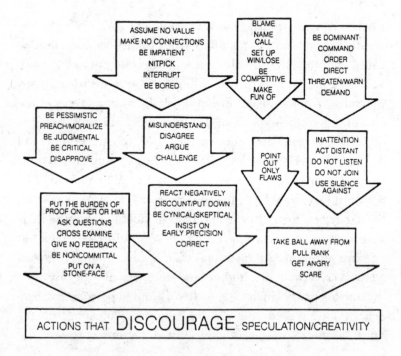

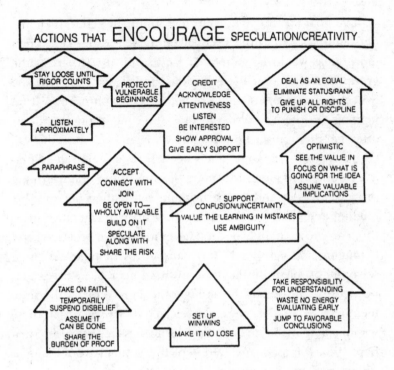

The group would generate a number of ideas, but I do not remember the frenzy and the need to cover all walls with ideas, as is the case in a brainstorming session. The client would then respond to these ideas, selecting a few that seemed the most interesting. He would explain his choices to the group, with the interesting proviso that any negative comments would be preceded by two positive ones.

The positives served to give the group continual indication of the desires of the client. They also reinforced the originator of the idea and helped maintain a psychological atmosphere that was conducive to creativity. The criticism was couched as a reservation rather than an overall "no" and could be made the problem for the next round. In this manner, rather strong criticism could be accommodated without inhibiting conceptualization.

The goal was for the group to continually refine their understanding of what the client liked as well as disliked. Then more ideas would be generated, and so on. I was part of the group in a couple of these sessions, and it was clear that the Synectics group members were getting their satisfaction from helping the client, whereas in brainstorming, group members often get their satisfaction from how imaginative or off-the-wall their ideas are. The tone of a Synectics session was quite different from that of a brainstorming session. In the brainstorming process, ideas fly and the participants satisfy their need for belonging and their ego by seeing how many imaginative ideas they can produce. In Synectics, fewer ideas were produced and belonging and ego needs were satisfied by helping the client solve the problem. In fact, one of the traits a Synectics leader needed to acquire was the ability to deal gracefully with group members whose ideas were not selected. It was clear that these sessions were meant to be led by a Synectics employee, and perhaps the complexity involved kept this strategy from being as widely used and as popular as brainstorming is today.

The second difference was that brainstorming sessions typically lasted an hour, and Synectics sessions were intended to go on until everyone was convinced that there was a high probability that the idea would be implemented—no guarantee, but the client should seem eager to build a prototype as soon as possible. If you are interested in the original thinking behind Synectics, Prince wrote a book entitled *The Practice of Creativity Through Synectics—The Proven Method of Group Problem Solving*.

Techniques such as brainstorming and Synectics are effective in group problem-solving because they deal with affiliation and ego needs in ways that decrease conceptual blocks. However, a group can accomplish the same ends without such formal techniques, providing it understands the factors that inhibit the conceptual process. Such knowledge is especially important in the group leaders, whether formal or informal, since they are in a position either to support or squelch conceptualization. However, conceptualization will flow even more freely if all members share this knowledge.

AFFILIATION AND EGO NEEDS

In order to fulfill its function, a group must often operate like an individual. It must be able to find problems, think up possible solutions, and make decisions. It must also operate with a reasonable level of creativity: too much and it loses its stability, too little and it fails to come up with solutions at all. However, a group or organization differs from an individual in that each concept or action causes a response within each member. It may elate some, depress others, fill some with fear, and seem misguided to the rest. A group or organization is in effect a minisociety that, in its need to operate as if it had a single mind, places great pressure upon its members.

Each member of a group or organization has strong affiliation and ego needs. Affiliation needs urge the individual to act so as to gain the social acclaim of the group: to be liked, respected, and valued. Many psychological experiments have shown the strength of these needs, particularly one well-known experiment performed by Solomon Asch, a professor of psychology at Swarthmore College. In this experiment, people in various groups were asked in turn to estimate which of three lines of obviously different lengths was equal in length to a fourth line. Only one person in each group was a real experimental subject. The others were shills who had been instructed to reach erroneous conclusions. About one-third of the experimental subjects who went through this experience changed their initial correct judgment to agree with that of the shills, even though the difference in line lengths was clearly discernible. Their desire to be part of the group overwhelmed the obvious correct answer.

Another example of the strength of affiliation needs is provided in a passage from Professor Harold Leavitt's classic book *Managerial Psychology*. This passage asks you to assume that you are a member of a professional committee who arrives at a meeting with a strong position on the first item on the agenda. After some discussion, you become aware that the other members of the committee share an opinion that is very different from yours. Initially, the other members of the committee show interest in your position and honestly attempt to understand it. They also attempt to explain the validity of their stand to you, but you are sure of your position. As time goes by, the mood of the meeting begins to change. The other members grow impatient as they are unable to sway you to the majority viewpoint. You become aware that you are starting to be attacked, and your mouth dries and your stomach tightens. They accuse you of being hostile, of sticking to a position even though you cannot come up with new reasons to defend it, and of delaying discussion of more important matters by your reluctance to join the consensus. However, you feel that you must ethically stick to your point.

After an hour and a half of discussion, you are the focus of the group. All the other members are heatedly arguing with you and using everything they can think of to sway you, since this is a committee that likes to operate by consensus and you are keeping them from reaching the type of agreement they pride themselves on. Finally, one of the committee members turns to the chairman and proposes that the committee agree on the majority opinion and move on to other matters. At this point, you realize that you are to be cut out of the group, and in fact you are. The members turn their chairs and face toward the chairman. As the chairman summarizes the reasoning for adopting the majority opinion, you occasionally protest points you consider absurd. However, except for occasional glares, you get no acknowledgment from the committee. You have been disaffiliated.

It is easy for most people to identify with the character in Leavitt's passage. It does not feel good. Most of us have had experiences with being psychologically rejected by a group of people we care about because we do not accept the common judgment. It is no wonder that people will accept long lines at the DMV and majority opinions that they consider wrong.

Affiliation needs underlie many of the conceptual blocks discussed in earlier chapters. People will like you if you think the way they do. But to the extent that you succeed in aligning your thoughts with those of others, you can add to your perceptual and intellectual blocks. Problem-solving groups often become tightly knit and often consist of people who respect each other a great deal. Affiliation needs are particularly strong in such a situation, and severe emotional blocks can result. No one wants to fail in front of respected peers. A problem-solving group plays a strong role in creating its own subculture and environment, and blocks appear if they are not supportive to conceptualization. When a new concept deviates from the group's consensus, the originator may feel tempted to modify or swallow it. Groupthink can result.

However, when channeled positively, affiliation needs can result in high motivation and a high degree of support. A group that understands the conceptual process can motivate individual members to think creatively, support them in doing so, and provide the atmosphere of trust that is vital if members are to conceptualize freely.

Ego needs at times may work at cross-purposes with affiliation needs. They urge an individual to influence others, to lead, to be significant, to be outstanding. Unfortunately, one of the easiest ways to be significant within a group is to be critical, but, as we saw earlier, a critical approach can be highly detrimental to conceptualization.

Equally detrimental, however, are misdirected attempts—especially those of a leader—to influence others. Influence techniques that are the most satisfying to the ego are not always the most supportive to conceptualization. The use of authority, for example, is a classic Western method of influencing others, and it can be very gratifying to the person issuing orders. We have all experienced authority because it is widely used by parents. It has certain advantages: it is quick and requires a minimum of knowledge about those in subordinate positions.

The authoritative style of influence usually results in people being told quite precisely what to do. Unfortunately, this can decrease the motivation to do anything else—a clear inhibition to creativity. Authoritative leaders tend to give their subordinates answers, not problems; in addition, they often inspire rebellion. A climate of mutiny is hardly ideal for maximizing the conceptual output of a person or group. Rather than overthrow the ruler, people can rebel by having no ideas at all. They can mentally drop out and cease to contribute productively and creatively.

By contrast, a collaborative style of influence can be relatively cumbersome, but it encourages conceptualization. Communication tends to be more informal; each member is encouraged and expected to contribute, and each feels a responsibility for the success of the group venture and therefore gains satisfaction of affiliation and ego needs from the problem-solving process.

Which approach do you think would elicit the best conceptual output from you: authority or collaboration? Since you are a thinking person (otherwise you would not be reading this book), you would probably choose collaboration, and you would be right. Unfortunately, since collaborative management techniques do not always satisfy the ego needs of managers as thoroughly as do authoritative techniques, they are often overlooked in an egocentric culture.

LEADERSHIP

A few comments are in order about leadership. The classic authority-based, top-down leadership is not presently in vogue for innovative groups, yet there continue to be examples of revolutionary outputs from groups led in the style of Attila the Hun. What's going on? I sometimes divide groups into the following three categories:

1. Safe, compromising, wise, traditional groups
2. Groups with an extraordinarily creative and dominant leader and supportive members
3. Groups that use integrated, synthesis-oriented collaboration and have a team-oriented leader

The first type of group is both extremely common and essential to the stability of our lives. In such a group, extreme viewpoints are muted, there is little dissension, and conclusions are often by consensus. They are safe and wise because they tend to value the tried and true over the new and unproven. They are not especially creative, but in many problem-solving situations they are exactly what is needed. In these groups, the leader often has power either because of rank or because of expertise acquired in solving similar problems.

The second type of group can be highly creative. It is often found in start-ups or in situations where success depends on a few unusually creative people. If you think of the outstanding people in any field, they often operate in this manner. Many good examples are in tech, such as Steve Jobs and Elon Musk.

But there is a downside to this type of group. It does not take full advantage of the creativity of the people in the group. Motivation to be creative is higher if one has significant ownership in the problem, rather than simply helping someone who calls all the shots and gets all of the glory. Dominant leaders do not necessarily help group members grow and develop to the point where they might find their dominance challenged. A group dependent on one person is also fragile. If that person leaves, the group may find that it is short a successor.

The third type of group has many advantages, as could be expected from all of the buzzwords in its description. It operates as a team in which the members gain satisfaction both from their individual performance and from the accomplishments of the group. Personal and professional growth of the members tends to be higher, and the output tends to reflect a wider variation of disciplines and cognitive styles. Additionally, members of such a group are highly motivated not only to solve the problem but also to implement the solution.

Leadership is needed in a creative group. In the 1970s and '80s there were many experiments with so-called leaderless groups that operated by consensus. One of the results was that an informal leader often evolved, but the role of this person was often confused because the group was supposed to be leaderless. In addition, this leader often did not have much clout outside of the group, and therefore was handicapped in securing support. Leader or not, there were enough flaws in such groups that they are now seldom found. Groups involved in creative problem-solving need a strong sense of direction and good political and economic interaction with the context in which they operate. In addition, groups benefit greatly if someone with good personal skills plays the roles of referee and cheerleader. This is especially true if the group consists of independent people representing different disciplines and problem-solving styles, as is desirable in creative groups.

A good example of the importance of such leadership, or lack of same, can be seen in the type of university in which I have earned my paycheck. Most scholarly creativity takes place in faculty research groups that typically consist of a dominant professor aided and abetted by graduate students and perhaps professional aides. This is the traditional university model that assumes that the most important source of creativity is the individual. But times are changing. Much potentially exciting work involves a number of disciplines. New technology is altering the way in which information is stored and delivered. Student and public expectations are not the same as they used to be. A great deal of creativity is needed to augment the traditional model.

As a longtime professor, I am a staunch believer in the principle that the faculty of a school should make the decisions about academic directions. At my school, the faculty does this. Problems are typically addressed by groups of faculty members who either represent a discipline (research groups, divisions, departments, schools) or who are appointed to a standing or ad hoc committee. However, these faculty members individually raise much of the money for their own activities, are focused on a narrow area of their discipline, are quite allergic to being managed, and can easily move to other jobs, usually at a higher salary and with more perks. They are also leery about the effect of any change on their own activities. Consensus is usually sought for decisions, and the nominal chair often takes a relatively inactive role. The result is relative difficulty in exploring new directions involving interdisciplinary thinking and alternate ways of doing business. More leadership is needed to help all of these groups be a bit more adventurous, but the need is not acknowledged and the resources are generally not available. The result is a great deal of inertia that slows any attempt to pursue exciting new directions. Universities are replete with the first two types of groups mentioned above. The third type is scarce.

GROUP MEMBERSHIP

The makeup of creative groups is particularly important. One of the many books written on groups in the 1990s that has proven to possess staying power is *The Wisdom of Teams,* by Jon Katzenbach and Douglas Smith. In this book, the authors list six basic elements for good teams.

1. Small enough in number
2. Adequate in levels of complementary skills
3. Truly meaningful purpose
4. Specific goal or goals
5. Clear working approach
6. Sense of mutual accountability

I would like to add a seventh: people who know and are comfortable with each other.

A creative group should be big enough to represent the necessary disciplines and skills but small enough so that the members can easily interact and contribute. In my mind, five to ten is ideal. If large numbers of interests and disciplines must be represented, members should be chosen who are broad enough to represent several, and they should be supported by specialists in the various pertinent areas. As has been mentioned, not only must the necessary intellectual skills be represented in the group, but also diversity of problem-solving styles and appropriate people skills. Robert Sutton, a friend of mine and a professor who studies organizations, is fond of saying that a creative group should have intellectual diversity but not affective conflict. In other words, they should disagree, but not fight.

As for people skills, those who are good in creative groups tend to respect and appreciate the thoughts and disciplines of others, have a good sense of their own competence, add to the ideas of others as well as submit their own, and have a sense of humor. Confidence is valuable, because it seems to help people work with new concepts and support others in the group. It is not necessary to be the ultimate brilliant extrovert. I have worked with many people who are extremely effective in creative groups, but who are quiet, unassuming, and even brusque. However, they enthusiastically and selflessly contribute to the cause. Many extremely valuable people in groups are not the top people in their field. However, they know their discipline, their own limitations, and the people who are the leaders. People who are bad news in creative groups tend to drag down the group through negativity, attempts to garner credit and control, and general divisiveness.

The other factors on the list have to do with the values and the experience of the individuals in the group. Hopefully, the group has a truly meaningful purpose, and if it feels it does not, it should certainly question its own existence. Similarly, it should have a specific goal or goals. In the case of creativity, the group should be responsible for ensuring that its goals are stated in a way to be consistent with the amount of creativity desired. A clear working approach and mutual accountability are also up to the group to establish. An edict from the leader concerning either will simply not result in the necessary buy-in from all group members.

It is certainly possible to improve one's effectiveness in a creative group, but it is necessary to encourage feedback from others and to practice the lessons that people have learned. If one looks at fields interested in groups, such as organizational behavior, sociology, anthropology, and psychology, one finds a tremendous amount of material having to do with the way people interact. Because of the complexity involved, there is no simple formula for the perfect creative group or the perfect creative group member. But there is great insight in these fields, and it is well worth perusing.

But before we leave this topic, I must make one comment about my friend Robert Sutton. A wonderful person and teacher, he has had particular success with a series of books, beginning with one entitled *The No Asshole Rule*. There is great wisdom in this series, and Bob also contributed greatly to the term "asshole" becoming a common noun in our society. Even so, "don't hire assholes" may be putting it a little strongly. The latest book in his series is entitled *The Asshole Survival Guide: How to Deal with People Who Treat You Like Dirt,* and, having worked with many people who would fit Bob's description, I can confirm that even assholes can be immensely talented to the point of being invaluable. To those people, I say, "Come join my team, asshole."

Nevertheless, there are team wreckers—people who are so ego driven that they detract from the team by continually seeking to dominate it. There are others who wallow in their superiority because they know something the rest of the team members don't and are reluctant to share their knowledge. They are few in number, and over time may get over themselves. But if not, they must go. I seem to have spent much of my career as a team leader and first-level manager—lieutenant in the air force, group manager at the Jet Propulsion Laboratory, department chair at Stanford, associate dean of the School of Engineering, chair of many ad hoc and interdisciplinary teams—and I seem to like that level of life, being in the action, but not particularly owned by anybody. Good teams can be built, and I have many methods for doing it. Two important ones are getting to know your people and not underestimating the power of alcohol.

PROPER SUPPORT

In their book *Peopleware: Productive Projects and Teams,* Tom DeMarco and Timothy Lister state that they do not know how to build the perfect group, but they know how to wreck one. Among ways to do this are managers who are afraid of risk or of a team that is smarter than they are, bureaucracy, physical separation of members, fragmentation of people's time, and reduction of goals. Another way to wreck a team is phony deadlines. The authors maintain that sophisticated problem solvers have a good idea of how long something will take, and will not seriously buy into a project that allows less. In Tracy Kidder's classic book *The Soul of a New Machine,* the project managers solved this by hiring brand new graduates who didn't know how difficult the job was. But this can only be done in cases where brand new graduates have the necessary skills, and probably only once with a given set of people. The individuals and groups I know probably function better under some time pressure. But if there is not enough time to explore different paths in enough detail so that they can compete with past practice, creativity cannot flourish.

Similarly, money is important. It is important not only because it buys the necessary people and equipment, but also rightly or wrongly it is a measure of the importance of the project. Support for project initiation is particularly critical. As is well known, the initial funding for projects is often bootlegged from other efforts. This is necessary because people in charge of budget allocation want some sort of assurance that projects are feasible before they will fund them. If this bootlegging becomes difficult, creativity suffers. I have been part of two very creative organizations that have been the subject of congressional investigations, one because it did not succeed at an extremely difficult and unprecedented project as fast as some in government thought it should, and the other because it was suspected of misspending government funds. (After much time and pain, they were both found innocent.) In each case, the result was a drastically increased emphasis on accounting and auditing. This, in turn, caused increased difficulty in finding funds to try radical new ideas and, in my opinion, a decrease in creativity. Fortunately, time heals and political vendettas pass and creativity has returned to a high level in both of these organizations.

Access to people is also critical. Not only do teams need members with the proper skills and experience, but they must be able to tap the necessary expertise and thinking outside of the group. High mobility of people is often associated with creativity in an industry. It is one of the reasons used to explain the success of Silicon Valley. The job shifting typical of the younger technical workforce causes rapid dissemination of ideas and skills. Individual companies may not like this, but the region and the industry benefits. Such people are extremely beneficial in creative teams. They often have the combination of experience and intellectual restlessness that is consistent with a high level of creativity.

Support from the group context, whether it be a formal organization or a more informal aggregation of people, is critical. This is a particular favorite of mine, because I seem to have a weakness for serving on groups whose conclusions are destined to die. One example was a group convened by the then governor of California, entitled the Governor's Commission on Toxic Waste. Since an election was in the wind and the incumbent's opponent was making an issue of the environment, it should have been obvious that this group was politically motivated. But California has a real toxic waste problem and this group was full of extremely bright, well-informed, accomplished, and politically powerful people. The group also had great technical support from the University of California system and the members were quite bipartisan as far as political party was concerned. How could it lose? The reason it could (and did), of course, was that upon realizing the severity of the problem, it recommended a number of measures that met opposition from the conservative state government. The government not only failed to support the group but did a good job of suppressing the results. (This is one reason I was glad to see Jerry Brown back again.)

Finally, there is the usually overlooked item of space for teams to do their work. It is typical that the members of teams go from their offices to a conference room, which is often occupied by another group. Even if it isn't, the projector often doesn't work, and even if it does, the window shades don't. This is especially insulting if it happens to be an ad hoc group, and even more so if that group has been told that its work is high priority but the members have many other projects going on that are more central to their main responsibilities. If a group activity involving creativity is to be done rapidly and well, it sometimes helps motivation if the team is given space for the duration of the project, especially if prototypes, hardware, or other items that are difficult to carry around are involved. Ad hoc teams are often told how important it is for them to solve some problem and then forced to solve it in space so unworkable that no one else wants to use it. For a group to accomplish anything worthwhile, it is necessary that the members feel that their work is valued.

CHAPTER 9

Organizations

WE ARE DEPENDENT ON ORGANIZATIONS. MANY OF US WORK in one, and each organization is in turn influenced by other business, governmental, legal, and financial organizations. Volunteer organizations often affect our lives, as do medical and educational ones. The cities we live in are organized, as are the stores and entertainment centers we patronize. In fact, any enterprise involving over twenty people had better be organized if it is to be effective. It would be quite difficult for an informal gathering of ten thousand, one thousand, or even one hundred people to solve a complicated problem quickly and economically. But the characteristics that allow large numbers of people in an organization to cooperate in accomplishing collective goals can and often do inhibit creativity. Like individuals and groups, organizations suffer from conceptual blocks. It is worth looking at a few common ones:

1. Too much or too little control
2. Age and size
3. Tradition and past success
4. Inappropriate reward system and support
5. Lack of challenge
6. Inhibitive culture

CONTROL VERSUS CREATIVITY

Organizations control money, people, facilities, equipment, and other resources necessary to accomplish their goals. This control is necessary to allow large numbers of people to move in the same direction. But control inhibits divergence, spontaneity, experimentation, and therefore creativity. A major organizational problem is to properly balance creativity and control. Too much control and the organization may eventually become obsolete through lack of innovation. Too little and it may fail through lack of focus and efficiency. This balance is a critical problem, and too few organizations worry enough about it.

It is a complex problem because control in an organization is a function of many things, including the output, the organizational function and level, the size, and the age. At present, more product innovation is expected in the computer business than in the plumbing-fixture business. If Apple were to focus merely on producing cheaper versions of its products rather than what its avid followers would regard as new and improved ones, its immense profits would not last very long. Similarly, a company planning to sell radically improved bidets would not succeed in Iowa.

Within a given organization, one also finds different amounts of control. People working on internal audits are expected to be more concerned with control than those doing advanced research. Control also varies with level in an organization. Some time ago, I conducted an unofficial experiment by calling people at different levels of the organizational chart at a large company and asking them whether they would like to hire extremely creative graduates who would pursue their own ideas—even if they would bend the rules to find support and ignore advice to drop their projects. People without management responsibility were enthusiastic. They would tell me how such an irreverent attitude is exactly what is needed to make something happen in a large organization. First-level managers were a bit unsure. They liked the idea of the strongheaded entrepreneur, but were not sure they wanted to manage one. People in middle management were negative. A typical comment was, "We've got too many ideas around here already. The last thing we need is people running in even more directions." People at the top were enthusiastic again. They were clear on the advantage of people who would start new ventures within the organization. Of course, they assumed that the people below them had the details under control.

Let us consider age and size. Successful organizations seem to grow. Why? Large organizations have many advantages. One is their ability to make large impacts upon the world. Large businesses interact with large numbers of customers, make large amounts of money, and can have significant influence upon social institutions, governments, and individuals. Large universities can offer many programs and projects and focus sufficient resources to attain high quality. Large armies can overwhelm smaller ones, and large think tanks and architecture firms can often win contracts that smaller ones cannot.

There is tremendous satisfaction in being involved in large-scale, complex projects that involve a wide array of sophistication and interaction. One has only to spend time with someone involved in the design and construction of a large dam, ship, bridge, transportation system, or missile system to discover this. I was involved in the early days of the US space effort, and you do not want to ask me about it unless you have quite a bit of free time. It was large and I loved it, though I must admit that the Jet Propulsion Lab was a relatively small piece of the larger space program.

Large organizations are also stable. One of the first modern organizational theorists, a German sociologist named Max

Weber, coined the word "bureaucracy." To him, this was a word with very positive connotations. A bureaucracy was a wonderful, stable structure. Large, formal organizations—in which jobs are tightly defined and control is rigorously exerted according to lines of hierarchy—are relatively insensitive to the loss of individuals. This, we must admit, is an advantage we take for granted, albeit one that sounds somewhat inhuman.

Large organizations are also relatively resilient in the face of changes in the market and during economic shifts. They tend to have a wider diversity in products and customers that protect them against changes in demand for a single product or by a single customer group. They have access to large amounts of capital and are able to exert political force when necessary—for example, the famous government loan to Chrysler in 1980.

Large organizations also offer certain advantages to employees. They offer predictable paychecks and a high degree of job stability. Though taken for granted by many people, it is impressive to those who have been without regular paychecks. At one time in my career, when I was involved in hiring, I found that it was surprisingly easy to hire consultants into salaried positions. The freedom and glamour of a freelance existence often does not offset the wonder of a reliable paycheck. Large organizations also allow employees room to move and advance. It is possible to grow in one's career without sacrificing the specific knowledge one has obtained. In a similar fashion, large organizations provide a wide variety of mentors and opportunities to learn. They also offer prestige, especially to managers. People are more impressed by the president of General Motors than the president of the consulting company that consists of me and my wife (and yes, she is president).

Finally, growth itself is an advantage because it gives individuals more opportunity to increase the scale of their own operation and advance. Besides lending excitement and a feeling of success to those involved, growth is also rewarded generally by our growth-oriented culture. Have you been a member of an organization that voluntarily decided not to grow? They are rare, since most organizations can easily persuade themselves that they could perform their work a bit better with a little more help. Even if such a decision is made, no growth is difficult to maintain because of its cost in morale.

Previously, I made some comments about growth at Stanford University from an inside perspective. Let me make a few from a more institutional view. The university has long opted not to radically increase the size of its student body. This was a rational decision, because there are many very good state universities that receive a large stipend from the state government. Schools like Stanford had to be clever in competing with such universities. If it tried to compete with them, it might fail, since lack of subsidy would cause the university to market a similar product at a much higher cost. Stanford's advantage lay in being smaller, swifter, and friendlier to the high-paying students. However, the pressure to grow is hard to resist, and increases in student aid, gifts, and research, and perhaps decreases in state support, have caused Stanford to creep upward in student population, as the faculty, facilities, outside-funded activities, nonteaching staff, numbers of transactions per month, acres of lawn and parking, and myriad activities all expand every year. The campus has become somewhat like an airport, with constant construction, change, and expansion. And there is of course even more talk about increasing the size of the student body through the addition of distant campuses.

Growth has its virtues, such as bringing improved capability and room for individuals to move. But the empire-builder dwelling within most of us is rarely completely satisfied.

THE PATTERN OF GROWTH

If growth and resulting bigness have all of these positive attributes, why are the advantages of smallness now a topic of interest? After all, most large companies were at one time small. They have grown for valid reasons. However, they have not grown without costs, and these costs have to do with our topic of creativity and change.

Structural formality inhibits communication and results in fiefdoms that can become protective of their turf. But free communication and the ability to combine activities in new ways are necessary for creativity. Perceived problems must be questioned, knowledge must be transmitted, and new and fragile concepts must first be brought to a state of reality and then sold to a conservative organization. Additionally, structural formality is usually accompanied by increased authoritarianism. In authoritative systems, individuals attempt to perform well according to their job descriptions. But how many job descriptions contain the phrase "take risks"? Structural formality is also associated with routinizing, decreasing uncertainty, and increasing predictability. These may be healthy directions for business as usual, but not for creativity.

Large organizations necessarily devote a major amount of energy to control in order to be able to deal with the uncertainties inherent in complexity. It is not too difficult in any large organization to find people whose job is to prevent mistakes. Preventing mistakes involves reducing risk, which is also at odds with creativity. Because of this necessary control, the type of manager it attracts, and the more global responsibility of large organizations, big companies are conservative. An organization such as General Motors has far more difficulty betting on a new product, service, or direction than a small start-up.

Large organizations can also be depersonalizing, and here one runs directly into the motivational problem in creativity. Large numbers of people may be operating under extrinsic motivation, and rewards therefore become critical. Individuals and groups must be recognized for creative and innovative output. However, in large organizations standardized reward systems often dominate, and the individual innovator is lost. It is not uncommon for successful founders of companies to bemoan what they see as a loss of creativity in their now-large enterprises. It is instructive for them to compare the financial and psychological reward systems in effect during the start-up phase with those in effect during the mature phase.

Finally, large organizations can be too slow. The layers of procedure and control often are not consistent with the unpredictability of creativity. Resources are needed to allow creative developments. This is especially true in large organizations because concepts must be taken to a stage of development that will make them acceptable to a conservative decision-making structure. Prototypes must be made available when and where they are needed. Lack of time, money, people, and facilities to pursue new concepts can paralyze creativity in any large organization.

In 1998, Larry E. Greiner, now a professor emeritus of management and organization at the University of Southern California, wrote an article that appeared in the *Harvard Business Review* entitled "Evolution and Revolution as Organizations Grow," detailing a process that is probably familiar to anyone who has been involved in any sort of organization. In the article, he described phases of growth in an organization and illuminated common crises. These crises occurred at the ends of stable phases and could be abrupt or lengthy. They might or might not cause displacements in management and overall employment. They were all caused by growth.

The first phase was the start-up. During this period, the fledgling organization has a few to dozens of people, probably a unique product or service, very high motivation, pride of ownership and excitement among the employees, and informal and free communication. In the electronic business, this represents the revered company in a garage. Greiner calls this the creative phase because such an enterprise is capable of a high degree of day-to-day creativity. Constraints are few and precedent is lacking. The people involved are proud of the fact that they are blazing new paths and must be clever to survive. If a problem arises, they solve it, because they have no choice.

The first crisis, leadership, occurs when the organization becomes large enough (perhaps on the order of one hundred people) that it can no longer operate efficiently through completely informal organizational methods. It has hired many employees who do not have a sense of ownership, it is tying up too much of its resources in inventory, jobs are overlapping and difficult to describe to new employees, enough people are around that criticism meets most moves, and it is being heavily influenced by the IRS and various attorneys. At this stage, the founders of the company, even though they can read the handwriting on the wall, seem not to be reacting rapidly enough. In certain dire cases, they may not even want to acknowledge the situation at all. It is not unusual for management to resist increased formalization to the point where higher powers have to influence them or at least augment them with other individuals who are more formal in their organizational philosophy. If the organization is to continue to be successful, it will adapt. It will adopt a greater degree of control and formality.

Organizational charts, job descriptions, clear hierarchies, and systems for inventory control, production control, and accounting will appear. This is not to say that all organizations must take on the philosophies of the nineteenth-century British Royal

Marines. Management may remain approachable and informal in style and should preserve as much of the motivation of the start-up as possible, but the organization must somehow simplify life for the members of what is becoming a mob. Some organizations have such a dislike of the trappings of traditional large companies that they choose to exert control through nontraditional means, such as corporate belief systems and pseudo-familial authority structures. However, with growth, more control becomes necessary. Control and communication systems become formalized in order to ensure that effort is not consumed in redundancy and contradictory decisions. The people-oriented chief may continue to leave the door open to all employees. However, a lower percentage of people walk through it.

The organization now does very well indeed with its new control-oriented habits and continues its growth. It may continue to think of itself as small, even as it grows and acquires competition. However, eventually it runs into trouble again. It becomes increasingly cumbersome. As size increases, the advantages of a strict linear hierarchy tend to be overcome by the complexity of communication and control procedures. People at the working level must simply wait too long for permission to act from the top. A point is reached where delegation is necessary. Decisions must be made lower in the organization, and such organizational entities as profit centers, product-based groups, and geographically decentralized operating units must be established. Once again, Greiner predicts a crisis. Managers who prefer direct control may not be eager for a change and may have to be pushed from above. However, if the organization is to remain healthy, a change will occur and the organization will enter the delegation phase.

There are other stages and other crises on the curve. Another crisis occurs at the point when the divisions of the organization have become so strong that upper management realizes that their units could become independent. The organization will then usually respond by taking advantage of possible synthesis. Companies will become concerned with coordination, company image, product balance, centralized policy, logos, product identity, and so on. The next crisis occurs when the organization has become so large that it is floundering in red tape, litigation, political forces, and general complexity. Those interested in more details should read the article. For our purposes here, we must only decide whether we think that there is truth in the article (I obviously think that it is of almost biblical stature), and, if so, what it has to do with creativity and change.

As the folklore suggests, creativity and responsiveness to change are more natural in small organizations than large formal ones. In the start-up, probably no one is even thinking specifically about creativity and change. The organization just does it without self-consciousness as it solves problems. However, as the organization grows, it becomes necessary for it to adjust and self-consciously provide the environment for the desired creativity. In business, it is not uncommon for a start-up to be dominated by people who are oriented toward the development of a product or service. As the organization grows, emphasis necessarily shifts toward manufacturing the product more efficiently and selling it, because, as competition enters, selling becomes more difficult and costs become a significant concern.

At this point, the development of follow-up products and services often receives short shrift, and it becomes necessary to provide consciously for these activities. As organizational rewards shift toward those who control and cut costs, it is necessary to ensure that rewards for the development of new products and services do not stop. In other words, as resources move from product development to marketing to manufacturing, it is necessary to make sure that product development isn't forgotten. At a later phase, as delegation occurs, it becomes necessary to worry about whether time, effort, and rewards are made available to encourage creativity and response to change at the proper locations in the now more complex organization. It also becomes necessary to ensure that the proper people are involved and that all the locations have the small and flexible nature that best encourages creativity and response to change. This often requires creating garage-type shops in the midst of a bureaucracy.

Examples of this can be seen in many highly creative companies. Lockheed Skunk Works and Bell Labs became famous for their creative output and contributions to their companies. Later, HP Labs and Xerox PARC engaged in similar activities. Today, the best example is Alphabet's various divisions. These units must have the proper environment in which to function—such as support from upper management, adequate budget, and proper location—be staffed with the right people, and be managed in the right way. They must also be well integrated into the main organization in order to be successful. Many company R&D centers have been relatively ineffectual because they have become divorced from company realities. One of the reasons for the success of Skunk Works, above and beyond its technical capability, was that Kelly Johnson, its long-time director, had been a vice president of the company, knew the culture and politics, and was buddies with the other top managers.

But as you may have recognized, this story is still incomplete, since organizations eventually die. There are many reasons for this, and organizations don't like to think about it, but if you look at history, it happens. We'll call that the final crisis.

TRADITION AND PAST SUCCESS

One of the most difficult challenges to continued creativity within an organization is past success. Some of you probably remember the shock in the 1960s and '70s as the United States was jarred from its postwar complacency by Japanese industry. The United States had emerged from the war as the supreme industrial power in the world. Competitors such as Germany and Japan had been virtually destroyed while American gross national product had tripled. The United States became so confident of its innate industrial superiority that it could hardly believe it when basic US industries such as shipbuilding and raw-steel production lost their ability to compete—followed by competition in optical equipment, consumer electronics, and even to some extent automobiles and machine tools. It took many years of looking for scapegoats, like low labor costs and unfair trade practices, before US industry finally admitted that it was lagging in innovation. America had become so successful that it simply could not believe that anyone could beat it. Part of the problem with US industry was that its strength in product design had caused it to ignore creativity in production. US companies often had developed products first—tape recorders, computers—but were simply beaten in the factory.

Another example of complacency, this time in the 1970s and '80s, was the neglect of creativity in marketing by many technology-based companies. They were so successful at devising miraculous products that they forgot that people had to want them. Realization came when some companies achieved outstanding success through learning more about their customers and employing sophisticated marketing techniques. I remember Intel's successful and obviously expensive advertising program, when they realized that they could no longer sell their (at the time) esoteric products to computer manufacturers solely by stressing cost and performance. Another example was the reemphasis on invention in the advertisements of Hewlett-Packard, a company that had always been highly innovative but perhaps allowed the public to forget that fact amidst the flurry of attention paid to start-ups.

Finally, there were companies that failed to keep up. A much-discussed example is Kodak, which in a sense owned the photography world for a time, but missed the digital revolution. Borders, Sears, Motorola, Yahoo, Dell, Sony, and Blockbuster are others that have suffered. Once a company falls behind, it is very difficult to assume the lead again, among other reasons because it loses the reputation attached to being the best. In fact, there have been a flurry of books on companies that did not hold on to their lead in technology, many in the digital world. Looking beyond the digital, there is also Richard Foster's book *Innovation: The Attacker's Advantage,* which discusses tire cord. The original material, cotton, was displaced by rayon, which was much stronger and did not rot. DuPont and a company named American Viscose were the major producers of this rayon cord. DuPont, however, switched to its proprietary nylon, and American Viscose lost out. The next development was polyester, and DuPont was involved in this development, as were Celanese and some other companies. Eventually, Celanese became the largest producer of polyester cord. Foster hypothesizes that this is because DuPont had a vested interest in nylon. In any case, DuPont lost their lead by staying with an old technology, just as the cotton cord manufacturers and American Viscose had.

REWARD SYSTEM AND SUPPORT

All of us, no matter how accomplished and independent, are affected by rewards, so it is not surprising that reward systems play a large role in organizational creativity. I have been a consultant to a large number of companies whose upper managers seemed to want to increase innovation. Upon talking to the people lower down in the organizational chart, I have often come to the conclusion that one does better in the company if one simply carries out orders and avoids rocking the boat. My friend Bob Sutton, whose field is organizational behavior, is fond of saying that non-innovative companies reward success, punish failure, and accept inaction. Innovative companies reward both success and failure (assuming it follows a valiant attempt) and punish inaction.

Psychologists often divide rewards into intrinsic (internal) and extrinsic (external). Both are important to creativity. The importance of intrinsic reward becomes obvious when one considers the many people who have caused change despite adversity. Think of Mahatma Gandhi, Martin Luther King Jr., Nelson Mandela, and Jesus. Consider the artists who are discovered after their death. Work by Teresa Amabile, a psychologist now on the faculty at the Harvard Business School, shows that in many cases intrinsic reward is primary. In her excellent (though technical) book *The Social Psychology of Creativity,* she summarizes experiments that she has conducted with children and adults on creative tasks such as collage, storytelling, poetry, and cartoon captioning. She found that her subjects were most creative when motivated intrinsically. Extrinsic motivation factors (evaluation, peer observation, and rewards based on the quality of the output) decreased creativity.

In one typical experiment, collages were constructed by ninety-five students enrolled in an introductory psychology course at Stanford University. They were not artists and had no significant previous experience in collage work. The collage was to convey the feeling of "silliness." The results were evaluated by fifteen artists, who were shown to agree quite closely on their ratings.

The subjects were randomly divided into eight groups. Three of the groups were told that the only thing of interest was their mood and that their design itself was unimportant—therefore, there was no expectation of evaluation and no external motivation. The subjects in the first group were given no further focus, those in the second were asked to concentrate upon "technical goodness," and those in the third to concentrate upon creativity.

The subjects in the other five groups were told that their designs would be evaluated by a panel of artists and that the quality of their collage would be part of the experimental data— thereby establishing an evaluation expectation and external motivation. Once again, those in the first group were given no further focus and those in the second were told that the judges would base their evaluation on "technical goodness." Those in the third group were told that they would be evaluated on how good their collages were technically, but were also given six detailed technical elements that the judges would consider. The subjects in the fourth group were told that the judges would base their evaluation on how creative the designs were, and those in the fifth group not only were told they would be evaluated on creativity, but were given seven specific criteria that the judges would consider.

There was a major difference in the two groups that were given no focus. The subjects that were not expecting evaluation (intrinsic motivation) averaged much higher in creativity. The same is true of the three groups with the technical focus. Evaluation expectation also degraded the creativity of the subjects who were simply asked to focus on creativity. However, interestingly enough, those in the eighth group (to be evaluated on creativity and given seven specific criteria that the judges would consider) were judged to be the most creative of all.

As I have said, I believe strongly in the benefits of widespread knowledge of the problem-solving process in groups and organizations. It seems to me that in this case, Amabile might have been cheering for groups that had no specific rules. She explains the unusual creativity of those who were given the specific creativity instructions as follows:

> For two reasons, this high creativity of the specific creativity instructions group must be interpreted cautiously. On a practical level, it is unlikely that creativity in everyday performance could be enhanced by telling people exactly what constitutes a creative performance. The reason we value creative work so highly is that we cannot know beforehand just how to achieve a novel and appropriate response. On a theoretical level, the conceptual definition of creativity clearly disallows the consideration of the specific instructions task as "creative." According to that definition, the task must be heuristic (no right answer or known technique to obtain the answer) in order for the product of task engagement to be considered creative. In this study, specific instructions on how to make a collage that would be judged as "creative" rendered the task algorithmic. Thus, according to the conceptual definition, it is simply inappropriate to assign the label "creative" to the performance of the specific instructions group.

I agree with her interpretation in the case of highly original concepts in individual work. But how about more pragmatic situations where many people are involved and the results must be sold to the world, the typical state of groups and organizations? In such situations, it seems reasonable to me that people with a more specific understanding of creativity and its characteristics would produce outputs that would be judged to be more creative. Most of us are not Leonardo da Vinci, Wolfgang Amadeus Mozart, or Albert Einstein, and we perform better in a game if we know the rules.

Research such as this underlines the critical influence of evaluation and judgment in creativity. I spent some time as an art student, have taught many courses in design, and am impressed with teachers who can handle evaluation well. The challenge is to give students enough freedom and encouragement that they will explore, but also enough evaluation and feedback so that they will learn. Once again, the right balance of creativity and control is necessary.

Since creativity seems to respond to intrinsic reward, organizations seeking more innovation should take special effort to match people to tasks that they will be motivated to do through interest and personal satisfaction. This argues for mobility in organizations, so that people can move as they learn more about the tasks they prefer. Innovative organizations support such moves as a long-term strengthening strategy. Managers who block such moves for selfish reasons are blocking increased creativity.

Can organizations rely totally upon intrinsic rewards to ensure creativity? There are several reasons why they cannot. One problem is that such an approach is counter to some traditional values in organizations. They think in terms of assigning people to work that needs to be done, not necessarily work that best matches their interests. The Protestant ethic also suggests to us that perhaps work should be of a nature that requires external reward. As my father used to say, "If work was fun, somebody would do it for free." Another shortcoming is that, even given activities that are so pleasurable that motivation is intrinsic, most of us do not have doors that are entirely clear of wolves. The people I know, for better or worse, are old friends with external motivation in life. I myself am a good example.

In general, I consider myself extremely fortunate in that I am involved in activities that bring great satisfaction to me. However, the activities that bring me pleasure are more complex than collage making. I have not yet found a way to escape the short-term drudgery that accompanies my long-term satisfaction. I am therefore continually fighting against my schedule and the clock to finish activities that are not as much fun as my hobbies: woodwork, metalwork, rescuing old machinery, reading trashy books (sometimes even good ones), trying to help starving museums, and daydreaming. Along the way, I am affected by rewards and often evaluated, by others and by myself. Am I weak? Should I tell the world to bug off, find a rich patron, and settle down to the things I most love to do? I don't think so. I am afraid that I would lose in the long run. I am afraid that I am normal. The things that give me long-term satisfaction often require short-term agony. My values seem to vote against rich patrons. I live in a world of heavy extrinsic motivation. In such a world, rewards are effective, and evaluation, inadequate resources, and peer opinion are part of life.

The design of an effective external rewards program for creativity within an organization requires a good bit of sensitivity. As an example, the process should be recognized as well as the product. It is often the case that highly creative developments do not succeed for a reason other than the quality of the work put into the project. Apple's first laptop failed, despite the fact that it was consistent with well-done market research and technically successful. All indications from the marketing studies were that people wanted the smallest possible computer that would offer all of the characteristics of the desktop: many hours of battery life, full-size keyboard, lots of drives and accessories. The result failed because using the technology of the time resulted in a large and heavy device. At the time, no one realized that people would settle for minimal battery life, a smaller keyboard, and other shortcomings in order to get a very small package. Apple found that out with its first PowerBook. The original laptop design team was very creative even though the product failed, and the company learned a lot from the attempt. Hopefully the team members were rewarded for their creativity, but in many companies such recognition would be unusual.

MONETARY REWARDS

It is necessary to fit the reward to the individual. A reward of $250 might be wonderful to a creative farmworker but insulting to a creative vice president. Publication in a company technical journal might mean more to someone intending an academic career than someone who considers technical journals to have little value in the "real world." There are also many forms of reward, all having advantages and disadvantages. Money is a traditional one, but it is controversial. Some people feel it detracts from intrinsic motivation. A classical psychological experiment asked subjects to do a boring repetitive task at different rates of pay. Those receiving higher pay thought the task to be more boring, the apparent reason being that they would not have been paid so much had the task been pleasant. Monetary rewards cost money, so it is cheaper for an organization not to bestow lavish prizes on creative employees. And, if given too frequently, such as the performance bonus, extra compensation can be assumed to be part of normal pay and therefore lose its effect. Monetary rewards can also complicate life for managers.

I once gave a talk to a company seeking to increase creativity. I later heard from one of its managers that they had returned home from the retreat and tried an experiment. A particular software design team of eight people was beginning work on a project that the managers assumed would take a year. They asked the team to estimate the earliest date the project could be completed if all went well and if people worked as hard as they could. The answer came back as eight months. This was a project that would result in a large profit if it was finished earlier, so the company offered the team a cash reward of $80,000 ($10,000 per person) if they completed the project in eight months. So far, so good, right? But they were one week late. What would you have done as manager of the team? This is one of those situations where there is no good answer. The company gave each member of the group $100. I imagine this makes you groan. However, any solution to the problem would result in some groaning.

These arguments are all valid. The counterargument is that monetary rewards offset the risks involved in creativity and change. There is an increasing amount of experimentation taking place across industries. For example, the commission is reemerging in sales. In the past, there was a swing toward providing salaries, not only because it appeared more professional, but also because it helped sales forces involved in selling products that were extremely difficult to move. However, recently companies have rediscovered the motivating force of the commission. If you sold one hundred widgets last year and made $50,000, but next year I pay you $25,000 and $250 per widget, how many will you sell? The answer is probably more than one hundred. In order to sell more than one hundred, you just may become more creative and change your ways.

It is not unusual to offer cash rewards to hourly employees for creative suggestions. In fact, these awards are often a direct function of profit or savings (for example, 10 percent of the net savings over the next year). In the past, it has been unusual to see such awards being given to salaried people, although there has been an increase in monetary rewards for creative achievements of the type that would be expected of them anyway.

Indirect uses of monetary rewards can also promote creativity and change. Through these systems, new activities lead to rapid advancement in a traditional hierarchy. In one large company that long had such a system, an employee or group of employees could present a product concept to a corporate evaluation board. If the executives found that it had good market potential and was compatible with their business, they would capitalize the development of the concept. If capable, the employee or group supervisor could remain head of the project, which if successful could become a division of the company, with resulting fast organization climbs for the inventor(s). This policy was installed because the company had long had a philosophy that at least 25 percent of their sales should be based on products that did not exist five years previously. The system worked magnificently with the only downside being an overabundance of divisions and a rather complex organizational chart. Such a reward system, of course, gives the winner much more than money. The psychological reward associated with promotion and peer esteem are also gained.

PSYCHOLOGICAL REWARDS

Monetary rewards obviously have high psychological significance. In fact, the psychological component may predominate. Successful founders of companies enjoy their wealth. However, I believe that they enjoy it as a symbol of their creative ability as much as for what it can buy. When it comes to rewarding creativity, the prizes can be mainly psychological and escape some of the controversy of monetary awards. Such rewards can be very effective without needing to consider capital flow and salary equity. There are fears about all rewards—they should not be necessary, they will destroy the team, etc.—but I have rarely observed harm caused by well-thought-out psychological rewards. It is true that in certain cases colleagues will feel more deserving than the recipient. However, there seems to be enough pragmatism or cynicism in all of us to weather that storm and, on the positive side, we realize that the organization cares—it just gave the reward to the wrong person. Similarly, in most healthy situations, people are quite pleased when one or a few among them come into possession of something nice. I have seen only a few situations where rewards were overdone, especially psychological ones. It is theoretically possible, but most of us are so biased in the other direction that it is not a real worry.

One of the benefits of psychological rewards is that external motivation can be internalized. The person who is consistently rewarded for a good chase, independent of the kill, will come to consider herself a better chaser and, in turn, gain more pleasure from it whether a kill is made or not. The employee who profits from a win in a situation involving creativity and change will be more likely to seek similar situations in the future and be more comfortable in them. People who are well rewarded for creative acts can become self-styled idea people, obsessed by the need for originality.

Successful psychological rewards for creativity should be applied directly to those doing outstanding work with the maximum possible fanfare. After all, part of their purpose is to emphasize the value that the organization places upon creativity. Individual recognition causes people to be more productive in a creative situation than if they are anonymous in the group. Social psychologists agree with humanistic psychologists that creativity and change are supported by situations in which one can simultaneously be accepted by a group and personally rewarded for the desired activities.

Psychological awards can take many forms. There are the obvious ones like presentations at banquets involving trophies and certificates. Although people, especially highly educated ones, deny the importance of these ceremonies and become embarrassed, they seem to value them. I have been awarded many such things, and I take them home and hide them when my friends visit, but I like them a lot! Publicity is also effective:

write-ups, newspaper and magazine coverage, TV spots, displays recognizing employee contributions, and such. Managerial compliments are perhaps the cheapest form of psychological feedback for good work and very effective. They are unfortunately rare in certain sectors. Many managers and supervisors simply have difficulty giving compliments. This is partly because in most organizations intellectual interactions take precedence over emotion, and partly because either shyness or personal values can get in the way. I am fond of asking groups of managers for a show of hands from those who have decreased their effectiveness by giving out too much praise to those who report to them. I get few hands.

Humor is a useful ingredient in rewards for creativity. Bob McKim, when he was teaching at Stanford, had a particular problem convincing his students to take risks in one of his senior creativity courses. He therefore inaugurated a prize for the most spectacular failure. Although it had no monetary value, the prize was considered as prestigious as a high grade. Small amounts of money can also result in high positive psychological impact if cleverly spent. I worked with a person once whose contributions were well above the call of duty. Some colleagues and I had noticed that he was a lover of single malt Scotch. When hosting a party, he would disappear occasionally into the kitchen to dip into his bottle rather than the more mundane brand at the bar. It was obvious that his favorite was a luxury. At one point, we had a little party, told him of our gratitude, and gave him a whole case of his favorite single malt. To say he was pleased is an understatement. I think most of us have a secret lust for something that we could probably afford, but that we can't justify buying for ourselves. To have this lust fulfilled as a reward for good work is doubly satisfying.

Professional visibility is an important award. It is a clever organization that recognizes its employees for extraordinary achievement not only within the organization but also in the employee's wider field. There is a perceived risk from increased outside visibility because of the increased possibility of competitors hiring the people away. However, the risk is more than offset by the reward to the employee. Such visibility is standard procedure in universities, since it is the basis for intellectual communication and advertising. It involves the presentation of papers, publication, and the use of the media. It is easy to offer and pays great dividends. Particularly creative R&D groups are masters of this form of reward, which only occasionally can cause problems. I worked at one time for a company that would send members of its technical staff to any meeting that accepted a paper. One person in my division submitted a paper to a conference in Europe, which was duly accepted. Only then did he inform the company that he had a pathological fear of airplanes. Since the policy was so wonderfully open, he was able to travel to his conference by train and ship. He had a wonderful time, but was gone for much longer than the company would have liked. As a result, there were more provisions added to the policy.

SUPPORT

A few words about support for creativity in organizations are in order, because inadequate support is a major conceptual block. As mentioned previously, creativity requires resources in the form of people, time, and money. Resources are necessary to accomplish anything worthwhile, even in business as usual. When we talk about change and creativity, we are talking about the allocation of resources in an atmosphere of increased risk and decreased efficiency. As I said in the introduction, I have seen few free lunches through creativity and no major changes accomplished without costs. In fact, the greater the desired creativity and change, the proportionately larger the required resource investment. This is sometimes a sticking point, because creativity is a word that is often used by people who want more for less.

A small company is successful enough to receive competition from a big one. As the big one tightens the screws, the small company at first assumes that the big company is too traditional and sluggish to harm it and tries to continue on its successful path. At some point, things become bad enough—as recognized by shrinking profits—that the company embarks on a frantic effort of increasing creativity. However, by that time, resources are scarce. The result is often the demise of the small company. Many examples of this could be seen in the computer business, where small, clever groups of people thought that the Hewlett-Packards of the world just could not move fast enough.

Ambivalence in budgeting may occur because of the long-term nature of creativity and change as opposed to the short-term events of quarterly profits or monthly bills. Even if a problem can be solved by creativity, an organization may not be able to solve it instantly. It may have to invest real resources in the short term in order to improve the situation in the future. As the saying goes, R&D comes out of profits—usually this quarter's profits.

For example, when a new computer system is purchased, the desired effect of the customer, of course, is that efficiency will instantly increase and costs will drop. No way! First of all, employees unfamiliar with the system are pushed into experimentation. They must spend considerable time and effort learning to use the system. Not only must they learn to use it, but they must also become good enough at it so that their performance exceeds that under the old procedures. The customer knows this and will demand evidence of its superiority, up to a demonstration.

Resources must be adequate to cover the experimental nature of a creative venture—the probable wrong turns and unexpected complications. Something new must be taken to a high degree of satisfying the customer if it is to compete with something old, because the world is programmed for business as usual. The same is true for influential people within the organization. A business cannot expect a concept on paper to compete with an established product with a sales record. It is difficult to sell the military new concepts in the face of the successes in the last war. In order to be bought, concepts must be brought to something close to reality. This requires one-of-a-kind developments that are expensive, time-consuming, and uncertain.

In order to cover contingencies, resources allocated to new directions cannot be simply based on predicted problems, since unpredicted problems are sure to arrive. The only reasonable way to budget for these events is to use past experience in similar new developments. However, even then the uncertainties are such that often the budget is inadequate both in money and time. This can be seen in the defense business. Because of the advantage of technological superiority and the complexity of modern warfare, the military is extraordinarily good at asking for products that are unprecedented. Because of the way contracts are awarded, technical optimism, and past successes, companies will bid aggressively for the work. Schedules then slip and costs overrun, and we are all familiar with the media coverage that results. The creativity and change involved in this work are great. The ability to predict resource needs and schedule is less. Is it incompetence and dishonesty that results in so many examples of budgets being exceeded and schedules being missed, or is some of it perhaps due to a lack of appreciation for the unknowns involved? I heard the CEO of a large provider of sophisticated weapons to the Department of Defense give a talk shortly after the company had taken a fierce drubbing for exceeding its budget and missing its schedule. He commented that never in history had any agency been as good at asking for the impossible as the Department of Defense, and never in history were there so many suckers like his company ready to submit a low bid for the privilege of providing it.

CULTURE

In their book *Winning through Innovation,* Michael Tushman and Charles O'Reilly laud the importance of the proper organizational culture to innovation. They describe the culture of five unusually creative and very different companies: a South African natural resource company, a European pharmaceutical company, a US financial services firm, an international R&D management firm, and a Japanese beer company. I loved the book, because I agreed with everything in it. There were no surprises in the descriptions of the five company cultures for those of us who study creativity, and organizations who have cultures such as these should not only feel fortunate but also worry a lot about maintaining their special environment.

Many organizations that wish to be more creative are far from these models. How do they change their cultures to be more consistent with their goals? Tushman and O'Reilly prescribe several tools to shape the culture of an organization. One is rigorous selection. Organizations that wish to change should ensure that the process that brings in new people changes. I have had a great deal of experience with company representatives hiring college graduates, and their criteria do not always match the desires of the top management of the company. Company management may be devoutly seeking new directions and more innovation, but the recruiters may be looking for docile gofers. This is particularly likely in large companies where the rank and file may not especially desire the necessary change: "I know that buggies are becoming obsolete, but I can find more uses for buggy whips if I can just hire enough good buggy whip people to help me." To change a culture, it is necessary to bring in people compatible with the new directions who are strong enough to withstand the influence of the old.

Another tool Tushman and O'Reilly mention is socialization—efforts to ensure that new employees, and old ones, are exposed to the core values of the desired culture. A good example of a very successful socialization process is the basic training of the US Marine Corps. They also suggest shaping organizational cultures through participation and commitment. If we are actively involved in something, we become committed to its importance. Again, one of my favorite psychological theories is that of cognitive dissonance. It says that we do not like dissonance in our minds, so we resolve conflicts, but in a way that makes us seem like we have the right answer. It is interesting to watch college-bound high-school seniors anguish over which college to apply to. After two weeks on the campus of the one they finally chose, they can hardly believe they considered any other. If we are putting our all into creative work, it would be hard to think that we are wasting our time. Much better to think that it is the most important type of work around.

The use of rewards and recognition is yet another tool they recommend. I talked about both of these in the previous section. My university is heavily devoted to research and believes that through this research professors can keep classroom material both current and exciting. However, in order to remain strong in research, it is necessary to hire faculty members who love to do research, supervise PhD students, and raise large amounts of money. Over the past years, the university's culture has become strongly biased toward these activities, and a few years ago it began an effort to strengthen the undergraduate program. The university is successfully using both rewards and recognition to do this, although it is definitely not considering doing this at the expense of the research program. If it were, it would have a much harder time. It is easier to add something to a culture than to subtract.

Finally, Tushman and O'Reilly prescribe the use of symbolic management acts. This is a particularly powerful tool and has great influence on an organization. At one time in Hewlett-Packard's history, when quality improvement was in the wind, the company set an extraordinarily ambitious goal. They succeeded partly because John Young, the CEO, made it his number one goal and made sure that everyone knew it. Don Petersen similarly highlighted important goals when he was president of Ford Motor Company. Bob Galvin, a president of Motorola when it was in its glory, was personally extremely interested in creativity. His interest was so widely known and so often expressed by him that it had a very positive effect on the already high creativity level in the company. Certainly that was true of Steve Jobs, and is true of Elon Musk, Ed Catmull, and the Silicon Valley company presidents who garner so much press for their new products. Such symbolic acts should take place at all levels of management. I have had personal experience reporting to a strong manager who did not agree with necessary changes that were happening in the company culture. I can report that it left me and some of my friends who also reported to him in somewhat of a tight spot.

As a final comment, changing an organizational culture is a creative act and requires confronting conceptual blocks. As we have seen, these blocks inhibit creativity, but they also simplify life. It is exciting to overcome them, but like any change, effort is required and uncertainty may result. If I am a manager and the people who report to me are competent, and therefore have alternate possible ways to spend their time, they are not going to change simply because I tell them to. Changing a culture requires sensitivity to the individuals and groups in that culture and the ability to convince them that their lives will be better for the change. I have been involved in many attempts to change organizational cultures and it is difficult indeed. However, thinking about the specific and common conceptual blocks in this book has helped me in the process. Hopefully it will help you.

CHAPTER 10

Raising Creative Children and Creativity in the Future

IT IS IMPORTANT TO REALIZE THAT NOT ONLY ARE WE ALL creative, but most of us are more creative than we think. When people tell me that they are simply not creative, I respond by telling them that if they were not creative, they would not have existed to this point, and that they certainly have what they need to be creative: a brain and nervous system, a body to support them, other people to talk to, and books. The key challenge for most of us is to allow our brain to become more creative by making better use of our consciousness. Then we can ask more of our brain and get increasing pleasure from the result. For many of us, we can find an additional challenge in sharing this creativity with others, by raising children who are creative and will turn into creative adults.

I believe that maintaining and strengthening our creativity is partly a matter of making sure that the brain has challenges and believes in its ability to accomplish rewarding things through creativity. Over time, such behavior will become natural for the brain, and it will grow to like the feelings involved with solving problems involving creativity. There is much ado now about neural plasticity and how much the brain learns through structural and functional changes. Rather than becoming involved in that topic, let's just say the brain learns to be more creative just as it has learned to multiply numbers, drive a car, make your job easier, and say thank you when someone gives you something. The brain learns through usage, effort, practice, and positive feedback. Its resulting synaptic changes can lead to increases in what Twyla Tharp, an outstanding choreographer, calls "the creative habit" in an excellent book she wrote of the same name.

THE ORIGINS OF OUR CREATIVITY

Let's think a bit more depth about this equipment we have for creativity, and what methods we have to improve it. First of all, most of the work in building the equipment has already been done for us through evolution. Viewed from our perspective, it has been and is working very well indeed. Still, Homo sapiens are relatively new critters on earth (about two hundred thousand years and running), so the returns are not in yet. We have reached the point where we have the capability to destroy our species, and if we do, termites (having been around for about 250 million years) will amuse themselves with our fate.

Compared with other forms of life, we are unique in isolating problems and conceptualizing and implementing solutions. Think about how creative we have become in our mere one-fifth-of-a-million years. We have established languages, upgraded from rocks and sticks to far more advanced tools, domesticated plants and animals, and developed beliefs to explain what had been the unexplainable. In the past couple of thousand years, our accomplishments include mathematics, writing, changing the nature of earth through construction, increasing the length and quality of our lives, and inventing science, gunpowder, air travel, digital communication, nuclear weapons, and more. Some of these are good, some potentially bad, and you and I weren't even around most of these years to help. But beyond humanity's collective creativity, there are a few additional important factors that we have not discussed yet: inheritance, birth order, culture, parenting, and education.

INHERITANCE AND CREATIVITY

How much of our creativity is due to our genes? I can safely say quite a bit, though calculating exactly how much is less clear, because many other factors influence our behavior. But to the extent that there are creativity genes, you inherit them from your father and mother, so you can't have less potential than they do.

Genes are made of DNA and there are on the order of twenty thousand of them packaged in our chromosomes. Progress is being made in learning more about how our genes influence our creativity. As an example of a possible link to creativity, lots of attention is being paid to the dopamine D4 receptor gene, which is associated with novelty. There is also a great deal of attention being paid to genealogy, thanks to the availability of private DNA reading services such as Ancestry.com and 23andMe. Although these services have sparked quite a bit of interest— as have advances in genetic testing and medical care, and the high visibility of DNA tests in TV police procedurals—there is a lot we just don't know about genealogy. It is quite common to find people thinking and talking about what programming they might have inherited from their parents and their parents' parents. It will be worthwhile to keep your eye on changes in genealogy over the next few years, because there is much change going on in the underlying theories and there are significant disagreements about its influence.

Although the overall mechanism of how traits are transmitted through inheritance was discovered by Gregor Mendel, who published a paper on his work with pea plants in 1866, it took the discovery of the structure of DNA by some extreme System 2 thinkers—James P. Watson, Francis Crick, Rosalind Franklin, and others—to really open the gates. Look at what has happened since. We now have the ability to acquire a simple reading of our own genome for a cost we can afford, even though the first sequencing (the Human Genome Project) took place only in 2003 and cost on the order of $3 billion. An informative and entertaining book on the topic is *She Has Her Mother's Laugh: The Powers, Perversions, and Potential of Heredity* by Carl Zimmer.

In the case of creativity, the role of inheritance is under debate, especially among cognitive scientists, biologists, and others who study them—most of whom probably lean toward inheritance—and parents, who like to think that their children can be defined by their upbringing, as long as they turn out okay. A book defending the idea that our brain must have a good amount of hardwiring at birth to survive and rapidly learn difficult things such as a language is *The Blank Slate: The Modern Denial of Human Nature,* by Steven Pinker. It is safe to say that our behavior is a result of both inheritance and our upbringing, and to the extent that there are creativity genes, you have them.

I am very sensitive to this because I spent so many years advising very bright and intellectually adventurous Stanford students. Over that time, I met a surprising number of parents who seemed to think they knew better about what their adult children wanted in life than their children did. My response: Give me a break! These students are people who are old enough to vote, to join the army, and to bear children. How can a parent think that they have a better idea of what they should be in life? Students *should* be searching. Some parents seem not to understand genealogy and instead think their kids should be duplicates of them. I deal with these arguments by pointing out that both nature and nurture are important. If pushed to choose which is more important, I will firmly glare at people and tell them it is about fifty-fifty. If that doesn't work, I plead being late for a meeting. For students, working on what they love and being what they want to be is a better platform for creativity than being a copy of one of their parents.

BIRTH ORDER

Like your genome, you had no choice in where you were in birth order, but there is an ongoing argument over how much this influences your behavior. I have heard theories that claim that the oldest child carries the family flag—with first children becoming astronauts and professional quarterbacks—while youngest children diverge from conventional behavior and become artists and actors. That theory holds that the middle children end up somewhere in between, going in directions that involve working with conflict.

I initially didn't believe such stories, but I became more of a believer when I read a heroic book entitled *Born to Rebel: Birth Order, Family Dynamics, and Creative Lives,* written by Frank Sulloway. He is a visiting scholar at the Institute of Personality and Social Research at UC Berkeley and has been awarded a MacArthur fellowship, a Guggenheim fellowship for humanities, and the Pfizer Award. When I say this book is heroic, I mean just that. He has studied a very large number of people, from kings to commoners, from Darwin to the present, and reached conclusions on the effect of birth order on people from all walks of life and cultures. I can't begin to summarize the book here, but if you are interested in birth order and the effect it has on people, it makes a compelling case. I open it occasionally just to be amazed that anyone would do the research to write a book like it, and to find a few statistics that I didn't know.

I wish this book had existed when my own kids were growing up, because it would have been fun to tell the statistics to the kids in a way that challenged them, making sure that they realized that statistics do not apply to a sample of one. You might have been affected if you were the firstborn of several kids and told at the age of four or five that statistically you were likely to be congenial, conservative in your thinking, agreeable, and scrupulous, *but you didn't need to be*. Or, if you were in the middle of the pack, you might have been interested in hearing that you were competing with your siblings for what you could get from your parents. Definitely, if you were the last-born kid, you should be told that your place in the ranking is associated with increased intellectual adventurousness, creativity, and radicalism.

CULTURES, ENVIRONMENT, AND CREATIVITY

There have been many studies on creativity in various cultures—individualist versus collectivist, rainforest versus desert—showing that creativity can be influenced by culture. Amish farmers that are born and live in settlements end up farming and living in traditional ways. If you are a young, would-be technical entrepreneur living in San Francisco these days, it is almost socially required that you be creative, or at least convince others that you are. Studies based on historical behaviors show that wheat farmers in China still tend to be more individualistic than rice farmers, and perhaps more independently minded and creative. US automobile companies some time ago realized the advantages of hiring women in their design studios, because women are often the deciding vote in the purchase of a new car. This shifted the culture of the design studios and nature of the creative output, as it was meant to do. This could not have happened in places like Saudi Arabia, where it was illegal for women to drive and not expected for them to make major decisions on automobile design. The problem perhaps peaks if one lives in a tradition-based culture that disapproves of what one wants to produce, be it food, art, clothing, or just ideas. If you talk with many young US residents from foreign countries, they are here because they find more support, or at least not total disapproval, of their goals. This openness is not universal in Western countries, however—if you are a Muslim woman living in France with a great idea on how make a better burka, you should seriously consider building your factory elsewhere.

It can be sobering to look at studies of creativity among people who grow up in low socioeconomic environments. These studies reveal that brains tuned to day-to-day survival are less focused on long-term thinking and imagining. Such studies usually focus on why the stress of poverty produces brains that make bad decisions, but the results have been extended to inhibitions on adventurousness and creativity. Risk aversion and low self-esteem can also diminish creativity. This would seem to be a solvable problem, and it would be worthwhile for our society to take it on. If any people could benefit from creativity, it would be those growing up and living in such environments. But the best tool for addressing these issues is probably the schools, and, as we know, in extreme-poverty areas the schools are often swamped with other goals.

Environment affects people's creativity in all sorts of ways. At the time of this writing, new Silicon Valley buildings are exploring designs that will informally cause employees doing creative work to interact, in order to increase the flow of ideas. But it is difficult to design an environment that enhances the creativity of a large number of people because of intellectual diversity. Some want quiet, some music. Some want an open office, some closed. Some want bright light, some dim. Some want to be messy, some are highly organized, Some want an office partner, some do not. This plagues architects of large commercial spaces. All I can say here is that people should be given as much choice as possible to individually design their environment—and the problem is much more easily solved in a home.

PARENTING

Now we come to a big one. Childhood, upbringing, and learning are critical in development of our creativity. Providing the proper environment is a challenge for parents, grandparents, and everyone else involved in the child's development. One hears a great amount of heated discussion about authoritarian parenting versus permissive parenting. These are usually extremes, and—as is the case in most situations with extreme sides—the right answer is in between.

For a successful life, we need such things as social skills (a great help in gaining friends and helping to implement one's creative ideas), the habit of following rules (usually associated with cultures that successfully foster creativity), and respect for the beliefs of the tribe and the knowledge and skills of others. Such things tend to come through nurture—initially through teaching from parents, other adults, older siblings, and friends at an early age. As previously mentioned, our prefrontal cortex is not hooked up until we are in our twenties, and so as we grow older we have our own friends, schoolteachers, books and magazines, and older students to help us along, as well as parents. Many times we do not want to do what it takes to acquire such skills and knowledge. Authoritarian parenting can be effective in helping us acquire them in those cases. But authoritarian parenting may also suppress such things as independent thinking, challenges to hierarchy, and creativity.

On the other hand, permissive parenting may lead to a large amount of unique output that does not fit in society and will not be accepted by enough people to sustain it. If the parents lovingly praise all off-the-wall original outputs from a child, she may not learn the difference between the good and the bad. A barely recognizable drawing of a cat by a four-year-old deserves recognition for imagination, but does not mean she is a future Picasso. Perhaps a suggestion to improve the drawing of cats is in order. A random series of notes on the piano may be a good exercise of imagination, but creating a new polonaise should involve a piano teacher or two.

A balance of parenting styles is best: authority to teach the knowledge and habits children need, and permissiveness to allow them to experiment and make mistakes. Ideally parents are capable of both authoritarian and permissive styles and know when to use them. (Loving smile, "Of course you can try to make some cookies"; fierce frown, "Just clean everything up afterward.") But it is often difficult to do.

My primary beliefs about creativity and parenting are based heavily on my own and my friends' kid-raising experiences, on watching our kids grow up, on reading books on the subject and talking with friends who are psychologists, and from working as a teacher at a university for most of my life. Based on these experiences, I have resolved that I will never tell a parent how to raise a creative child. There are many reasons for this. First of all, I consider it none of my business. Second, I have enough responsibility; I don't want any more. Third, there are all flavors of creativity. The painter, the ice skater, and the airplane designer all share the desire to do something fresh that leads to good feelings and rewards but are judged by very different criteria, which in turn vary between judges.

We have an outstanding string quartet on campus that loves Joseph Haydn and plays his music in concerts. They know all about him and usually give a talk about his life as part of their performances. But they don't write the music. Two of my sons are very good jazz musicians, and one of them is also in an indie band that often performs in Europe. They play frequently in various clubs and other environments, but their level of skill and reputation as musicians is not as high as that of the string quartet. They have ample time to improvise, and do when they are playing jazz. The indie band composes all of its music. Which group is more creative, the string quartet, the jazz group, or the indie group? That depends on the judge and the importance given to experiment while playing—and also how much you like their music. In a sense, they all are creative, just in different dimensions. There are also many levels of creativity, and the individual should be allowed to choose among them.

Though, as I said, I would never lay down an ironclad set of rules about parenting a creative kid, I have developed a set of beliefs about encouraging creativity that I will share:

1. Kids should have the time, incentive, and support to experiment and be rewarded for their efforts, whether they end in success or failure. But this should be realistic—the fact that your kid could grasp a brush early does not mean he or she is going to be another Rembrandt. Encourage, but don't delude. The desirable goal is a person that not only thinks creatively, but uses that ability to produce good stuff, rather than junk.

2. Kids should have mentors to gently keep raising the bar and helping them. The skill required here is to raise it each time so that the individual is between being bored and being overwhelmed. These mentors need not be necessarily part of the family to broaden the kid's education and experiences in life.

3. Kids should understand that there is not always a single right answer to everything, especially complex problems, and why.

4. Kids should not be led to believe that any adults are omniscient, especially politicians, school teachers, and, yes, even parents.

Simple, yes? In practice, not always.

As far as belief number one, this free time can be rather difficult to arrange in modern America, with its TVs, computers, smartphones, organized activities, and high kid densities. But kids should be given opportunities and assistance in building things, solving problems, thinking of alternate ways to accomplish things, drawing cartoons, playing with Legos, and all of the other things that both entertain the kid and exercise creativity. Honest feedback and rewards should be lavish.

As far as belief number two, I am biased because I have had many mentors, starting at a very young age, who showed me that there were many things to do in life, and how to do them. They also had different values and goals. I am sure my parents would not have given me these insights, because they probably were hoping that I would stay home and run our small farm. Without my mentors, I might have ended up an embittered farmer forced to sell his farm because his crop could not compete with imports.

Belief number three demands that the kid should be exposed to complicated situations where there are no right answers, either through conversations or by following complicated societal issues that interest the kid, such as homelessness, endless military conflicts, environmental issues, gun control, computer security, and beyond.

Belief number four requires parents to allow the kid to see that they don't know everything and to encourage the kid to ask them questions they, or other people, don't know the answer to. Looking through YouTube or Khan Academy together to find out things parents don't know is a good way to explore this, as are videos of bridges that fall down or airplanes that crash, and nobody knows the reason why. Occasionally viewing debates in which the two sides are matched and entertaining can be educational as well as making the point. Quietly demonstrating that a loudmouth uncle really doesn't know what he is talking about is also effective.

All of the above are fun ways parents can demonstrate to their kid that there is infinite room for creativity. The downside is that you will encourage the already overwhelming number of unanswerable questions of the "Why can you see through glass?" variety that the kid asks you. But that's good for all of you.

Before I leave the topic of creativity and growing up, I want to mention adolescence, which is very critical and gets a whole chapter in Robert Sapolsky's book *Behave*. During adolescence, the brain learns from peers and experience even more than from adults and teachers. Problems with adolescent behavior are due to an immature prefrontal cortex, rather than a flaw with the entire cortex. Adolescence is sometimes called the last chance to see who you are, and it is blamed for the classic behavior that worries adults: experimenting with rules, the body, luck, manners, clothing, alcohol, and what have you. I have been watching my oldest grandson go through this, and it is amazing. When complete, it usually results in a grown-up. Strangely enough, the prefrontal cortex then becomes the conservative governor of behavior. But before that point, boys generally like guns, motorcycles, tattoos, girls, not looking you in the eye, and no handshakes, and they perhaps show a worrisome amount of extroversion or introversion. Girls run in packs, wear clothes you don't approve of, think you are totally out of date, like to talk endlessly on their smartphones, and so forth. So as far as creativity is concerned, perhaps the right thing to do is to cross your fingers and let your adolescent kid rip, while remembering that they still love you, even though they sometimes don't act like it. It is the period in which we get to experiment with what we want to be, hopefully with parental support rather than resistance.

SCHOOL AND CREATIVITY

My schooling, which was probably typical of the time, was very much devoted toward reading, writing, and arithmetic, until high school, when it diverged into other areas. There were occasional venues for problem-solving along the way: building bridges from blocks in kindergarten, medieval cities and other historical dioramas in grades one through six, and woodshop for boys, home economics for girls, and various other shop and art courses in high school. These outlets were all tightly constrained. Along the way, there was little discussion about creativity and few opportunities to experiment with it in school. In fact, I can't remember the word used in that period of my life, except in a couple of art courses I took in high school. People would say, "Ray Cooley is really clever," or "Jean Adams sure can paint," but never that they were creative. Courses were usually based on a book that covered the basic concepts that I guess were selected by the school board, and then supplemented by essays and discussions in class between a few students who sat in the front row and were disliked for being brownnoses. *Silas Marner* in the tenth grade? Give me a break!

Times have changed a great deal. Most schools are increasingly giving students assignments that require creativity, and I have given what seems like countless talks to teachers and principals. High schools are doing much better at exposing students to creativity, but student time is much more limited now because the schools are trying to cover many more topics at a deeper level, resulting in more homework, more reading, and more concern about college admissions. Instead of following my "spare time to experiment" principle, schools seem to be becoming even more structured, and high schools are picking up course content that used to be in college through AP courses. My reaction is, What's the hurry? If schools through high school gave students more of a taste of what people in various fields did, including creativity, they might help students eventually choose a better-suited direction in life.

But the schools and kids are caught in a difficult position. There is great pressure from parents and students to offer AP courses and prepare students to score highly on tests like the SAT that make them more liable to be admitted to the school of their choice. I watch my grandchildren as they are not only pushing for high grades and test scores, but also engaged in many extracurricular activities such as athletics (now unceasing), music, consuming culture and experiencing the world through the computer, the smartphone, and the TV, and just being teenagers. All of this leaves them with little time to experiment. Still, if they develop a liking for creativity, confidence in themselves to be creative, and creative skills early in their lives, I feel confident that they will continue to employ them through life.

Promoting creativity and breadth in college has been a crusade of mine, both as a student and as a professor, and I think I have had an impact along the way through classes, talks, writing, alumni, membership in committees, and administrative support for such activities at Stanford and beyond. I was an undergraduate at Caltech, a school I used to describe as an intellectual boot camp, and which I now realize started me on my life's crusade. I loved the place and the people, but the professors tended to be heroes in their academic specialty and were devoted to research. As undergraduates, we were overwhelmed with learning the basics, which usually came in books dealing only with the field of the professor—who, with a few exceptions, liked analysis (that is, taking things apart and examining them) better than synthesis (putting new things together). Fortunately, I was working summers as an engineer at the same time I was taking courses, and I noticed there was little similarity between my applied sciences courses and my job, which was more focused on creativity.

As student body president, I used to lobby for an increase in the amount of creative work for undergraduates, but I consistently lost. Universities of high standing such as Caltech have professors who feel their specialty is essential, and since they control the curriculum, they try to cram each of their specialties into the requirements and label them fundamentals, which is what we students then slaved to learn. The kind of engineering I like requires breadth and creativity. If I had stayed another year or two as a graduate student, I would have been up to my ears in creativity. But had it not been for my engineering job, I probably would have transferred to a "lesser" university that was more application oriented, as many of my friends who became outstanding engineers did. Happily, Caltech has integrated much more work requiring creativity into their curriculum since I was a student there.

After I graduated, I alternated between the air force, graduate school in engineering, and industry. I found the same thing—lots of creativity in the work outside of school, learning what was already known in school—with the exception of a year I spent as an art student at UCLA. I loved the year at art school, which was all about creativity. Through a series of coincidences, while there, I ran across one of my mentor professors at Caltech, who had quit to take a high-level job in design at General Motors. He wanted to hire someone comfortable in both engineering and art, and I was running out of money. One more coincidence was that he was funding John Arnold, who would become perhaps my most influential mentor. Arnold hired me on GM money to join his crusade toward a more creative approach to design teaching in the Stanford School of Engineering and allowed me to pursue a PhD at the same time.

The crusade was not easy, but looking back, it worked. After I got my degree, I then spent a wonderful five years as a senior engineer and group leader at the Jet Propulsion Laboratory— lucky timing, as space exploration was just beginning. Then I joined the Stanford faculty and became one of we few, we happy few, we band of brothers and sisters who teach courses based on realistic problems and include emphasis on multidisciplinary problem-solving.

THE FUTURE

From what I can tell, the cognitive scientists are doing an outstanding job of understanding the mechanisms of the brain with regard to how it works, how it explains behavior, how various chemicals influence it, where it is limited, and even what it contributes to various aspects of creativity. But creativity has some characteristics that seem to stretch this insight.

When you are thinking creatively, you have two main sources of information: what is written, spoken, or otherwise available to you from outside, and what is already in your brain. If your problem is complex (interdisciplinary, state of the art, or new to you), it is necessary to mix new information with what is already in your memory. The material in your memory has been coded and then stored in one of the memory locations in your brain. It is not complete in all respects, but adequate for most usage. Imaginative thinking involves recalling consciousness, which is not yet fully understood, and mixing it with information inside and outside of your brain—pulled inside by curiosity, also not understood—in an unprecedented way. Wow!

The gap between the pragmatic creativity people and the priests of cognitive science is large. I intend to follow cognitive science as far as I can in its attempts to explain creativity, and perhaps I can better interpret it for the pragmatists. I want to find explanations of the necessary elements of creativity—such as curiosity, imagination, consciousness, and what guides the brain when it is in unprecedented territory—that are satisfying to people who are not cognitive scientists. I think I have my head around some of this, but I haven't yet been able to put it together. I like a comment that Antonio Damasio, a well-known and respected cognitive scientist, made toward the end of his book *Self Comes to Mind: Constructing the Conscious Brain*. As the title hints, the book is an attempt to explain consciousness, including self—a task that many have tried, but no one has yet succeeded to the extent that we noncognitive scientists can understand. He writes, "The idea that we have a firm grasp of what the brain is and what it does is pure folly, but we always know more than we did the year before, and much, much, more than one decade ago." This is progress well worth following.

To hypothesize about the future of creativity, I must start in the past. If we trace human history back to Lucy, famous for leaving the oldest (3.2 million years) remains of a member of our branch of the hominin family, we find that the size of the brain cavity, and therefore the brain, has tripled since then. Much of this growth has been in the last million years. Interestingly, the human brain has not grown, and has possibly shrunk, in the last twenty thousand years. If you are interested, there are lots of arguments as to what this means, because we can measure the probable size of ancient brains, but can't know the details of how they worked.

However, suppose the size of our brain cavities means that we have not been getting any smarter in the last twenty thousand years. Now think of what we have accomplished in that time period. The Neolithic revolution, in which we went from roving small groups living by hunting and gathering, to larger groups growing crops and domesticating animals, to cities, to the enlightenment, to industrial revolution, to now. Could farmers in the Neolithic age imagine modern tomato harvesters and crop dusting? Unlikely. Could knights in shining armor imagine nuclear warheads? Certainly not. Perhaps even more important, could a population of five million, twenty thousand years ago, imagine today's population of 7.6 billion? The United Nations Department of Economic and Social Affairs predicts the world population will expand to 8.5 billion by 2030, 9.7 billion by 2050, and, assuming the present decreasing fertility rate, to 11.2 billion by the year 2100. For argument's sake, assume that population growth was steady before the Neolithic revolution (it was not): we were growing at a rate of about two people a year. Since the years of the plague, we have been growing exponentially. Using the estimates above, between now and the end of this century we will grow at a rate of forty million a year. And our brains will stay the same size.

Now let me add changes in technology. Horses were not domesticated until six thousand years ago. Bronze was invented in 3,600 BC. Early farmers must have used stick and stone tools and their hands, arms, and legs. Modern tractors have GPS, cabin temperature controls, and outstanding sound systems. During the Neolithic period, we had bows, stone arrowheads, and clubs to fight our wars. Now we have drones carrying Hellfire missiles. We would communicate with other settlements with runners. Now we have the internet. How about medicine? How about cities? How about transportation, clothing, housing, and so on? The point is that incredible changes have happened to Homo sapiens since the Neolithic revolution, and the pace of that change in my relatively brief lifetime seems to be increasing—and still our brains have not gotten larger.

There are many more changes that we are causing whether we want to or not, ranging from the environment to human values. Are we growing smarter? There is no agreed upon way of knowing. Is the brain getting more efficient? Same answer. But even in my own lifetime, life has become more complex. That has probably been one reason for the apparent increase in interest in creativity. I think that this interest and the population explosion help explain the huge number of creative products currently on the market. A few years ago, the interest in creativity was heavily oriented toward personal convenience, health, entertainment, becoming wealthier, weapons, and other such areas. I now notice that there seems to be worldwide dissatisfaction with and within such large groups as nations and religions. Where is the creativity needed to mediate within and between them?

Certainly the problems are there. What's with the Catholic Church? Do Christians and Muslims just like to fight? Most of the ones I know don't. Why do people become weird about people of different skin color? Why do so-called advisory groups to leaders of nations often seem so short in experience in their areas, to say nothing of the leaders themselves? How come think tanks seem politically biased?

There are two very deep problems here. The first is that our brains have not grown much. We cling to a set of obsolete beliefs and problem-solving approaches that we have learned and developed to help simplify the complexity of life. One symptom of that is the increasingly intense dislike between people who want to improve life by going backward in time, and those who are convinced that change is inevitable and an opportunity.

The other problem goes back to the slow pace of evolution, especially in complex beings such as humans. As individuals, we may be lacking the ability to change as fast as we would like. Perhaps our brains are better suited to life in a supportive tribe of a few hundred people who don't have a lot of contact with other tribes—something like a medieval lord with castle, noblemen, and serfs, or even like a social networking group. I hope not, since such behavior shuts out the rest of the world. I happen to love the world, frictions and all. I don't want to live in an isolated nation or tribe and be pressured about what I believe.

I have come to think of us as Homo demi sapiens: half wise humans. I think we are terrifically smart compared to other animals, plants, and bacteria, even though they can do things we can't and we are dependent on them. But I don't think we are as wise as we think we are. We seem to be behaving in a way that worked when we lived in tribes of one hundred people but may no longer work today. Below are some examples of such behavior. There are many more. In fact I have started to write a book on it. Make a list yourself. They are blocks!

We Focus on the Short Term, at Most Our Lifetimes

Good twenty thousand years ago: Food and shelter for today and tomorrow

Bad now: Carbon emissions, nuclear weapons proliferation, infrastructure collapse

We Like Powerful Individual Leaders

Good then: Leadership, united tribe, simpler existence, chance for social promotion

Bad now: Adolf Hitler, Bashar al-Assad, Pol Pot, Robert Mugabe, Muammar Gaddafi, Vladimir Putin, Idi Amin, Abdel Fattah el-Sisi

We Are Selfish and Competitive

Good then: More food for the family in times of scarcity, motivation to work hard

Bad now: Obsession with wealth and belongings, trade wars, ridiculous economic disparities

We Want Others to Think Like We Do

Good then: Cohesive tribes, close friendships

Bad now: Christians versus Muslims, capitalists versus socialists, liberals versus conservatives

We Resist Change

Good then: Strong traditions and building of expertise

Bad now: Opposition to vaccinating children, lack of progress on getting rid of nukes, resistance to metric system in the United States

We Depend on Faiths (Religion, Science, Political Party) to Solve Our Problems

Good then: The Shaman gave us an answer—no more worries

Bad now: Good answers require experience, thinking, and experimenting

We Want Simple Answers, Even to Complicated Problems

Good then: We can rapidly implement the answer

Bad now: There are no simple answers to the most important problems

We Ignore Expertise if We Do Not Like What It Says

Good then: We may discover a better answer

Bad now: Climate change, control of nuclear warheads, population explosion

I could go on at great length about these issues and others like them—but I would like you to spend the time thinking about them and other similar ones, even if you don't agree with me.

I am optimistic about the future of Homo sapiens. But it's time we humans quit the short-term squabbling and move toward achieving our potential. I don't think we can avoid it if we want to maintain, or especially increase, the quality of our lives. TO DO THIS WE HAVE TO PUT OUR CREATIVITY INTO OVERDRIVE AND FOCUS ON THE BIG PROBLEMS.

Thank you for reading this book. If you would like more, I have listed some of my favorite books, beyond those mentioned in the text, in the reader's guide. I am not including papers or professional journals, because there are many references in the books I do mention, and such academic texts tend to be a bit tedious unless you are in the profession.

Acknowledgments

This book has had a long life and is well traveled. Its birth was "The Bob and Jim Show," put on in the early 1970s for Stanford alumni by Bob McKim—a friend, colleague, and the founder of the product design program in the Stanford School of Engineering (which played a large part in attracting me to join the Stanford faculty)—and me. By rights Bob should have coauthored this book with me, but he was busy writing his own book at the time. We were both motivated and encouraged to study creativity by John Arnold, whose beliefs and tools are still very much alive in the Design Group of the Mechanical Engineering Department at Stanford University, although Arnold died in 1963.

The book was brought to reality by a number of charming and high-energy employees of the Stanford alumni program, led by Della van Heyst and Sheila Cahill, who had started a series of books entitled the Portable Stanford, intended to keep the alumni up-to-date on what was happening on campus. The original edition was edited and designed by Cynthia Gunn, and—the Alumni Association staff being the entrepreneurial people that they were—it began its travels early.

The first edition was published by the Stanford Alumni Association in 1974, then by W. H. Freeman and Company (distributed by Scribner). The second edition was published by W. W. Norton in 1980, and the third by Addison-Wesley in 1986. The fourth edition was published in the midst of a bit of confusion, for me at least, because the Perseus Books Group bought Addison-Wesley and Basic Books and decided to take a book I wrote, entitled *The Care and Feeding of Ideas*, out of print and asked me to place some of the material that was more pertinent to business into *Conceptual*

Blockbusting. The resulting *Conceptual Blockbusting* was briefly published under the Perseus name, and then moved to Basic Books. I disagreed because I had written the two books as a set (having ideas and implementing ideas), but Perseus was more powerful than I, and as a result editions four and five of *Conceptual Blockbusting* are larger than edition three, and I occasionally get negative comments from people who buy copies of *The Care and Feeding of Ideas* that are still floating around (Amazon, Goodreads, Penguin) and find the same material in both books.

In each of these editions, I have received super support from editors, designers, marketing people, and other professionals associated with publishing, but I am not going to name them all, because if they are reading this, they know I appreciate their work, and they too are associated with a book with legs. For this edition, I thank Lara Heimert for talking me into writing it, Leah Stecher, Brandon Proia, Eric Henney, and Elizabeth Dana for editing my words, and Brynn Warriner for making sure the book was produced in good form. Good work, all of you.

And finally, I am very grateful to three people who helped me a great deal in writing the book. First, Robert Sapolsky, John A. and Cynthia Fry Gunn professor of biology and of neurology and neurosurgery at Stanford, and teacher and writer extraordinaire. I had read his book *Why Zebras Don't Get Ulcers*, and loved it, but it was his later book *Behave* that dragged me out of retirement to immerse myself in cognitive science, an intellectual activity that I find fascinating. His lecturing is of a level that caused me to attend three two-hour lectures per week and read many difficult books during the spring quarter of last year, when my retired friends seemed to be playing. He was generous enough to meet with me many times over coffee and lunch and answer my questions, and then to read through my manuscript to let me know if I was saying stupid things in the realm of cognitive science. And yes, the Cynthia Fry Gunn in his title was the first editor and designer of *Conceptual Blockbusting*.

The second is Matt Ohline, a former student and office partner, holder of degrees in both engineering and English from Stanford, CTO and cofounder of NeoGuide Systems, Inc., CEO and cofounder of Treus Medical, Inc., and now director of the automation, equipment, and test group at Intuitive Surgical and consulting associate professor at Stanford. He is also a restorer of vintage cars—applied creativity personified. He gave my manuscript a thorough reading and gave me a large number of excellent suggestions based on his use of edition four in his various activities, which I incorporated in this edition.

And then there is Marian, my goddess-like wife. She too is retired, after a career that included building and managing the continuing education program in the Stanford Alumni Association and then retiring and starting a firm designing custom education activities for companies. Now she has retired again and is frantically trying to keep track of a large garden, an amazing number of Stanford's courses, lectures, and recitals, a large group of friends, an old house, a host of grandchildren, and me. She is also trying to write a book or two of her own. But she patiently read my writing, pointed out what she saw as the good and bad, checked the grammar, and cheered me up when I became grumpy because I was typing on my computer rather than working on my various outdoor hobbies. Thank you, Marian. Without you, my writing projects would never get finished. I think I may love you.

References

Chapter 1

Kahneman, Daniel. *Thinking, Fast and Slow.* New York: Farrar, Straus and Giroux, 2011.

Koestler, Arthur. *The Act of Creation.* London: Hutchinson & Co., 1964.

Lewis, Michael. *The Undoing Project: A Friendship That Changed Our Minds.* New York: W. W. Norton, 2017.

Chapter 2

De Bono, Edward. *New Think.* New York: Avon Books, 1985.

Ghiselin, Brewster, ed. *The Creative Process: Reflections on Invention in the Arts and Sciences.* Oakland: University of California Press, 1985.

O'Neill, John J. *Prodigal Genius: The Life of Nikola Tesla.* New York: Cosimo, 2006.

Chapter 3

Anderson, Harold H. *Creativity and Its Cultivation.* New York: Harper, 1959.

Ariely, Dan. *The (Honest) Truth about Dishonesty: How We Lie to Everyone—Especially Ourselves.* New York: HarperCollins, 2013.

Ariely, Dan. *Predictably Irrational: The Hidden Forces That Shape Our Decisions.* New York: HarperCollins, 2009.

Ariely, Dan. *The Upside of Irrationality: The Unexpected Benefits of Defying Logic at Work and at Home.* New York: HarperCollins, 2010.

Csikszentmihalyi, Mihaly. *Flow: The Psychology of Optimal Experience.* New York: Harper Perennial, 2008.

De Mille, Richard. *Put Your Mother on the Ceiling: Children's Imagination Games.* New York: Penguin Books, 1973.

Drucker, Peter. *Innovation and Entrepreneurship.* London: Routledge, 2015.

Goleman, Daniel. *Emotional Intelligence: Why It Can Matter More Than IQ.* New York: Bantam, 2005.

Kubie, Lawrence S. *Neurotic Distortion of the Creative Process.* New York: Noonday Press, 1975.

Sapolsky, Robert M. *Behave: The Biology of Humans at Our Best and Worst.* New York: Penguin Press, 2017.

Sapolsky, Robert M. *Why Zebras Don't Get Ulcers.* New York: Holt, 2004.

Chapter 4

Alexander, Christopher. *Notes on the Synthesis of Form.* Cambridge, MA: Harvard University Press, 1964.

Bruner, Jerome. *On Knowing: Essays for the Left Hand.* Cambridge, MA: Belknap Press, 1979.

Kneller, George Frederick. *The Art and Science of Creativity.* New York: Holt, Rinehart and Winston, 1967.

Maslow, Abraham H. "Emotional Blocks to Creativity," in *A Source Book for Creative Thinking,* ed. Sidney J. Parnes and Harold F. Harding. New York: Charles Scribner's Sons, 1962.

Watson, James D. *The Double Helix: A Personal Account of the Discovery of the Structure of DNA.* New York: Scribner, 1998.

Chapter 5

Gordon, William J. J. *Synectics: The Development of Creative Capacity.* New York: Harper & Row, 1961.

Stoll, Clifford. *Silicon Snake Oil: Second Thoughts on the Information Highway.* New York: Doubleday, 1995.

Chapter 6

Arnheim, Rudolf. "Visual Thinking," in *Education of Vision,* ed. Gyorgy Kepes. New York: George Braziller, 1965.

Arnheim, Rudolf. *Visual Thinking.* Oakland: University of California Press, 2004.

McKim, Robert H. *Experiences in Visual Thinking.* Boston: Cengage Learning, 1980.

Sapir, Edward. *Language: An Introduction to the Study of Speech.* Cambridge: Cambridge University Press, 2014.

Vygotsky, Lev S. *Thought and Language.* Translated by Eugenia Hanfmann and Gertrude Vakar. Cambridge, MA: MIT Press, 1962.

Chapter 7

Koberg, Don, and Jim Bagnall. *The Universal Traveler: A Soft-Systems Guide to Creativity, Problem-Solving, and the Process of Reaching Goals.* Menlo Park, CA: Crisp Publications, 2003.

Ornstein, Robert E. *The Psychology of Consciousness.* New York: Penguin, 1996.

Osborn, Alex F. *Applied Imagination: Principles and Procedures in Creative Problem-Solving.* New York: Scribner, 1963.

Polya, G. *How to Solve It: A New Aspect of Mathematical Method.* Princeton, NJ: Princeton University Press, 2014.

Porras, Jerry I. *Stream Analysis: A Powerful Way to Diagnose and Manage Organizational Change.* Reading, MA: Addison-Wesley, 1987.

Von Oech, Roger. *A Whack on the Side of the Head: How You Can Be More Creative.* New York: Grand Central Publishing, 2008.

Chapter 8

DeMarco, Tom, and Timothy Lister. *Peopleware: Productive Projects and Teams.* Upper Saddle River, NJ: Addison-Wesley, 2013.

Hargadon, Andrew. *How Breakthroughs Happen: The Surprising Truth about How Companies Innovate.* Cambridge, MA: Harvard Business Review Press, 2003.

Katzenbach, Jon R., and Douglas K. Smith. *The Wisdom of Teams: Creating the High-Performance Organization.* Cambridge, MA: Harvard Business Review Press, 1999.

Kidder, Tracy. *The Soul of a New Machine.* New York: Back Bay Books, 2000.

Leavitt, Harold J., and Homa Bahrami. *Managerial Psychology: Managing Behavior in Organizations.* Chicago: University of Chicago Press, 1989.

Prince, George. *The Practice of Creativity Through Synectics—The Proven Method of Group Problem Solving.* New York: Collier, 1972.

Chapter 9

Amabile, Teresa. *The Social Psychology of Creativity.* New York: Springer, 1983.

Foster, Richard N. *Innovation: The Attacker's Advantage.* New York: Simon & Schuster, 1986.

Tushman, Michael L., and Charles A. O'Reilly III. *Winning through Innovation: A Practical Guide to Leading Organizational Change and Renewal.* Cambridge, MA: Harvard Business Review Press, 2002.

Chapter 10

Damasio, Antonio. *Self Comes to Mind: Constructing the Conscious Brain.* New York: Pantheon, 2010.

Finke, Ronald A., Thomas B. Ward, and Steven M. Smith. *Creative Cognition: Theory, Research, and Applications.* Cambridge, MA: MIT Press, 1992.

Pinker, Steven. *The Blank Slate: The Modern Denial of Human Nature.* New York: Penguin Books, 2003.

Sulloway, Frank J. *Born to Rebel: Birth Order, Family Dynamics, and Creative Lives.* New York: Vintage, 1997.

Tharp, Twyla. *The Creative Habit: Learn It and Use It for Life.* New York: Simon & Schuster, 2003.

Zimmer, Carl. *She Has Her Mother's Laugh: The Powers, Perversions, and Potential of Heredity.* New York: Dutton, 2018.

Reader's Guide

Times have changed since I wrote the reader's guide for the fourth edition of this book. There are many more books on creativity and innovation in bookstores, and libraries are awash with material. As far as I know, there is no complete and scientifically verified explanation of creative thinking in this mountain of literature. But there is much insight on how to improve one's creative ability. One finds a large number of hypotheses, from the simplistic to the complex, shedding light on the creative act. And there are innumerable techniques for increasing individual, group, and organizational creativity, most of which work for someone and few which work for everyone. Finally there are thoughtful (and non-thoughtful) treatises on what creativity means for all of us.

In this guide, I list some of the books I particularly like that are not mentioned in the text of this edition of *Conceptual Blockbusting,* but be forewarned that my opinion is anything but the final word. I have often gotten myself into trouble by assigning readings to a class and telling them to skip certain portions because they are of less value. Invariably, one of the students will read these portions—presumably to see why they are of less importance—and tell me that they are actually the most valuable parts of the reading. Therefore, take my comments with a grain of salt and spend your effort reading what seems to be most useful to you.

General Overviews of Creativity

A couple of books treating creativity in general have been published recently, and may be worthy of a closer look from some readers. *Creativity and*

Beyond: Cultures, Values, and Change is an ambitious and relatively recent book on creativity by Robert Paul Weiner (New York: SUNY Press, 2000). The author has a broad background in the humanities and treats the topic of creativity from viewpoints ranging from the historical to the contemporary. This book is of particular interest to those seriously interested in history of the topic of creativity.

A number of books treat creativity by focusing on individuals considered to be unusually creative. One excellent book is *The Mathematician's Mind*, by Jacques Hadamard (Princeton, NJ: Princeton University Press, 1996). It is a study of creativity among outstanding mathematicians and scientists and an attempt by the author, himself a well-known mathematician, to explain mathematical and scientific invention.

Many more books by and about highly creative people allow the reader to muse upon the creative process. One good story is *Genius: The Life and Science of Richard Feynman*, by James Gleick (New York: Pantheon, 1992). Feynman, a physicist, drew a large amount of attention not only because of his brilliance in his field but because of his colorful character.

Another is *The Runaway Species: How Human Creativity Remakes the World*, by Anthony Brandt and David Eagleman (New York: Catapult, 2017). Brandt is a composer and professor at the Rice University Shepherd School of Music, and Eagleman is an adjunct professor in the department of psychiatry and behavioral science at Stanford University, a Guggenheim fellow, and the director of the Center for Science and Law, an international nonprofit. Finally, there is *The Origins of Creativity*, by Edward O. Wilson (New York: Liveright, 2017), a Pulitzer Prize winner, researcher, and person everyone should listen to.

For an outstanding treatment of the subject of genius, read *Origins of Genius: Darwinian Perspectives on Creativity*, by Dean Keith Simonton (New York: Oxford University Press, 1999). This book covers a large amount of research on highly creative people and the author's own thinking on the roots of genius and the nature of creativity. It is beautifully written and extremely thought-provoking. This is a very interesting topic to me, because our culture tends to portray genius as a form of madness—like the Mozart portrayed in the movie *Amadeus*. I know quite a few people who may merit the genius label, but they seem to me to be disturbingly normal.

Thinking

Many books on the general topic of thinking either directly or indirectly treat creativity. Over the years, there have been many books and individuals questioning the simplistic measure of the IQ test and proposing different measures of intelligence. They tend to make one think about thinking. One of the pioneers in this area was J. P. Guilford. Two of his books, *Intelligence, Creativity, and Their Educational Implications* (San Diego, CA: Robert R. Knapp, 1968) and *Creative Talents, Their Nature, Uses, and Development* (Buffalo, NY: Bearly Ltd., 1986), are out of print but can be found and give a good indication of his thinking. A widely read book on so-called multiple intelligences is *Frames of Mind: The Theory of Multiple Intelligences,* by Howard Gardner (New York: Basic Books, 2011). This book and Gardner's work have had considerable impact in educational circles, as they emphasize the loss of opportunity from looking too narrowly at the meaning of intelligence.

Since memory is so central to problem-solving, a couple of books on memory are in order. You might be interested in *Don't Forget! Easy Exercises for a Better Memory,* by Danielle C. Lapp (New York: Da Capo Press, 1995) and *Memory: From Mind to Molecules,* by Larry R. Squire and Eric R. Kandel (New York: Holt, 2000). The first is a general discussion of memory, including exercises. The second discusses the mechanics of memory as understood by those working in the neurosciences. The first is a much easier read than the second, but for those of a scientific bent of mind, *Memory* is a good book for an update on how neuroscientists view the subject.

At the time of this writing, a general attack on logic and reason appears to be underway. One good read is *The Enigma of Reason,* by Hugo Mercier and Dan Sperber (Cambridge, MA: Harvard University Press, 2017). This is a book claiming that reason is not a set of grand truths, but a method to be used when arguing a case, as when we reason our way out of a traffic ticket. *Denying to the Grave: Why We Ignore the Facts That Will Save Us,* by Sara E. Gorman and Jack M. Gorman (New York: Oxford University Press, 2017), explores why people turn against such proven health measures as baby inoculations.

Another useful book about thinking is *The Information: A History, a Theory, a Flood,* by James Gleick (New York: Vintage, 2012). It is Gleick's overview of what changes in information have done to human culture.

Finally, there is *Smarter Than You Think: How Technology Is Changing Our Minds for the Better,* by Clive Thomson (New York: Penguin Books, 2013), contributing writer for the *New York Times Magazine* and columnist for *Wired.* And there is *The Knowledge Illusion: Why We Never Think Alone,* by Steven Sloman and Philip Fernbach (New York: Riverhead Books, 2017). Sloman is a professor of cognitive, linguistic, and psychological sciences at Brown University and editor in chief of the journal *Cognition,* and Fernbach is a cognitive scientist and professor of marketing at the University of Colorado's Leeds School of Business.

Psychological Theory

Since much creativity theory is directly drawn from psychology, the psychological literature is of great interest. If you have never taken an introductory psychology course, you should read a good general book on the subject in order to learn the words, the concepts, the names, and the fundamental theories. Lists of the best ones are on the internet, or you can ask a psychology professor or student to whom you have access.

Two books by contemporary psychologists that are well worth reading are *Creativity in Context,* by Teresa M. Amabile (Boulder, CO: Westview Press, 1996), and *Creativity: The Psychology of Discovery and Invention,* by Mihaly Csikszentmihalyi (New York: HarperCollins, 1996). In my opinion, Amabile is one of the best researchers in the area of creativity, and she is particularly concerned with reward. Her book makes a case for the importance of intrinsic motivation. The Csikszentmihalyi book includes interviews with large numbers of highly creative people and hypothesizes a characteristic he calls "flow" as being central to creativity.

The topic of flow is often debated, and I question it, because most of the more creative things I have been involved in (planetary spacecraft, experimental automobiles, manufacturing requirements) have been constrained either by schedule, budget, and performance requirements or by strong existing values and the more pragmatic but essential aspects of engineering (product quality, aesthetics, the "two culture problem"). The flow has often seemed to be in a different direction than I would have chosen. But I have loved the process all the same.

If you would like to delve into the theories of Freud and Jung, I suggest *On Creativity and the Unconscious,* by Sigmund Freud (New York:

Harper & Row, 1958), and *Man and His Symbols,* edited by Carl Jung (New York: Doubleday, 1970). The first is a collection of writings by Freud that are concerned with cultural and humanist matters. Many of the selections in the book deal with the particular problems of creative people and reflect upon psychoanalysis, and are therefore are only marginally pertinent to conceptualization. However, part of the book does treat conceptualization specifically, and the book is an interesting insight into some of the lesser-known interests of Freud. *Man and His Symbols* is a translation of Jungian psychology into language accessible to the lay reader. It was put together by Jung and several collaborators during the last years of Jung's life.

In recent years, there has been a major change in psychology in general, due to increased insight into the nature of behavior, and the resulting widespread use of medications prescribed by physicians. Also, an increasing number of psychologists are entering fields such as business, economics, and other more applied areas, while at the same time growing closer to neuroscience.

The Mind and Brain

As you can see from reading the book, I am particularly interested in this area, as it not only is interesting in its own right but has great potential for insights to creativity. Reading about the science of the brain is a wake-up call for the reader's own mind. A good book on genealogy and the brain is Adam Rutherford's *Brief History of Everyone Who Ever Lived: The Human Story Retold through Our Genes* (New York: The Experiment, 2017). Rutherford is a broadcaster and science writer. Steven Pinker, who is mentioned in the text, is a very productive writer and researcher and the Johnstone Family professor of psychology at Harvard, specializing in cognition, language, and social relations. He has been listed as one of the world's most influential thinkers by *Time, Foreign Policy,* and other magazines. A now somewhat classic book of his is *How the Mind Works* (New York: W. W. Norton, 2009).

Key to my understanding of the mind and brain is the work of Robert Sapolsky, whose books have been mentioned throughout the text. He is a very good writer. I will break my plan to not include papers and articles in this section and say: if he if he wrote it, read it.

Creativity in Business

Much of the attention paid to creativity during the past twenty years has been caused by the high interest in innovation on the part of business. This interest has resulted in a significant market, since business people have a large appetite for knowledge that can improve their lot (and, of course, companies often pay for the books). This knowledge alone, of course, does not guarantee business success.

The reader interested in creativity in business might begin by reading *The Knowing-Doing Gap: How Smart Companies Turn Knowledge into Action*, by Jeffrey Pfeffer and Robert I. Sutton (Cambridge, MA: Harvard Business Review Press, 2000), which attempts to explain why so many managers in business fail to apply what they know. Two other books that should appeal to those seeking to increase innovation in organizations are *The Innovator's Dilemma: The Revolutionary Book That Will Change the Way You Do Business*, by Clayton M. Christensen (New York: HarperBusiness, 2011), and *Weird Ideas That Work: How to Build a Creative Company*, by Robert I. Sutton (New York: Free Press, 2001). The first focuses on large successful companies that are damaged by what the author terms "disruptive" technologies. The second is focused on innovation in general, but is particularly interesting because it is structured around a number of concepts that are counter to traditional business methods.

In this book, I have talked about the inhibition of creativity that can result from the actions of overly dominant individuals. However, influence and power are part and parcel of life, and creative people need to be able to exert the necessary influence to see their ideas become reality. A better understanding of influence and power arms one in case it is being used to block one's efforts. In this regard, I recommend two excellent books. The first is *Influence: The Psychology of Persuasion*, by Robert B. Cialdini (New York: HarperBusiness, 2006), a wonderful read that describes a number of commonly used and highly effective approaches to influencing other people. It will not only educate and entertain you, but make you realize how you are being manipulated by skillful people. The other is *Managing with Power: Politics and Influence in Organizations*, by Jeffrey Pfeffer (Cambridge, MA: Harvard Business Review Press, 1993). In it, Pfeffer talks about aspects of organizational power: what it is, how to gain it, how to use it, and how to lose it.

These days there are many biographies and other books available on founders and saviors of large and successful companies. There is *Creativity, Inc.: Overcoming the Unseen Forces That Stand in the Way of True Inspiration,* by Ed Catmull (New York: Random House, 2014). Catmull is the former president of Pixar and Walt Disney Animation Studios. There is also *American Icon: Alan Mulally and the Fight to Save Ford Motor Company,* by Bryce G. Hoffman (New York: Crown Business, 2012); *Elon Musk: Tesla, SpaceX, and the Quest for a Fantastic Future,* by Ashlee Vance (New York: Ecco, 2015); and *Steve Jobs,* by Walter Isaacson (New York: Simon & Schuster, 2011). Isaacson also wrote a book entitled *The Innovators: How a Group of Hackers, Geniuses, and Geeks Created the Digital Revolution* (New York: Simon & Schuster, 2014). Such books give great insight to the heroes at work and the challenges of building large and influential companies. They are usually entertaining reads, but readers may find little advice on how to be like these creative people, even if they should want to be.

There are many approaches to the problem of managing creativity in business. One interesting and practical book is *Creative People Must Be Stopped: 6 Ways to Kill Innovation (Without Even Trying),* by David A. Owens (San Francisco: Jossey-Bass, 2012). Owens is a professor in Vanderbilt's Graduate School of Management who specializes in management, innovation, and product design. Another book that reads well is *Contagious: Why Things Catch On,* by Jonah Berger (New York: Simon & Schuster, 2013). Berger is the James G. Campbell assistant professor at the Wharton School of the University of Pennsylvania and is a prolific writer. His work has been widely popularized in a large number of magazines and newspapers.

A book that ups the bar a bit is *Iconoclast: A Neuroscientist Reveals How to Think Differently,* by Gregory Berns (Cambridge, MA: Harvard Business Review Press, 2010.) Berns is the distinguished chair of neuroeconomics at Emory University, as well as a professor in the departments of psychiatry and economics at Emory's Goizueta Business School and a founding member of the Society for Neuroeconomics. I give him a high grade for courage, because his appendix, entitled "The Iconoclast's Pharmacopoeia," is a guide to drugs (some illegal) that may aid creativity.

Finally, let me mention two books written by founders of IDEO, a worldwide design and consulting firm headquartered in San Francisco. The first is *The Art of Innovation: Lessons in Creativity from IDEO, America's*

Leading Design Firm, by Tom Kelley (New York: Currency, 2001). The other is *Creative Confidence, Unleashing the Creative Potential within Us All,* by Tom Kelley and David Kelley (New York: Currency, 2013). IDEO has close connections with Stanford through the Hasso Plattner Institute of Design (the d.school) and has put great effort into applying various theories and approaches to creativity to the design process.

How-To Books

There is a large demand for books containing techniques and tools oriented toward increasing creativity. The results can be overwhelming. When I first became interested in creativity, there were fewer, and in my initial excitement I set forth to learn as many of these tools and techniques as I could. Unfortunately, I discovered that the mind does not have a pull-down menu, allowing one to periodically select the optimal technique from one's palette. I find I am better off with a small number of tools that best augment the natural fumbling of my mind. That is why I attempted to categorize them in this book. I recommend that you be discriminating in your search. Many are attractive because they are fun, interesting, and challenging, but make sure they are useful to you, unless you merely want to be entertained.

Two books typical of the genre are *Thinkertoys: A Handbook of Creative-Thinking Techniques,* by Michael Michalko (Berkeley, CA: Ten Speed Press, 2006), and *101 Creative Problem Solving Techniques: The Handbook of New Ideas for Business,* by James M. Higgins (Winter Park, FL: New Management Publishing Company, 2005). Although both are oriented toward business, they contain a large number of tricks and approaches that could be used in a number of situations. *Lateral Thinking: A Textbook of Creativity,* by Edward de Bono (New York: Harper Perennial, 1990) is a long-lasting book from a prolific writer on the subject of creativity. In fact, this book was first published in the 1970s and still remains popular.

Some of these books emphasize routines to alter one's problem-solving style. I mentioned mind mapping, and Tony Buzan's latest is *Mind Map Mastery: The Complete Guide to Learning and Using the Most Powerful Thinking Tool in the Universe* (London: Watkins, 2018). Another that I would like to mention has a somewhat original approach. It is *What I Wish I Knew When I Was 20: A Crash Course on Making Your Place in the World,* by Tina Seelig

(New York: HarperOne, 2009), a professor in the department of management science and engineering at Stanford University and faculty director of the Stanford Technology Ventures Program. She is an outstanding teacher and approaches the topic of creativity through a mixture of her classroom activities and her many contacts with successful entrepreneurs.

As I said, if I were to try to find a how-to book at this point in my life, I would browse the internet and libraries to find out what was out there, look at reader reactions, find some that I thought might fit me, see if I had any friends that used such things, whittle it down to one or two books, find a few techniques that seemed the most inviting and exciting, and try them for a while.

Index

MARIAN ADAMS

James L. Adams is professor emeritus at Stanford University, where he has chaired several programs, taught courses on design and creativity, and participated in many executive programs. Trained as an engineer and artist, he has conducted corporate workshops around the world. He lives in Palo Alto, California.